28 Oct 2012
By **Carol 'avid little bookworm'**
TOP 1000 REVIEWER
"The brain is capable of allowing you to forget and deny that something has happened" are the words of Dr. Browne-Thomas after Janet Holt's most traumatic counselling session and are pivotal to this whole story. The book had me hooked from the first page; I just couldn't put it down.

13 Nov 2012
By **Jood** VINE™ VOICE
I was fascinated by this story from the beginning. There were times when I held my breath whilst reading, but I honestly could not put this book down. Told in a very matter-of-fact but hugely readable way.

31 Oct 2012
By **Philip Spires "Author of two African novels set in Kenya"**
The Stranger In My Life is an autobiography. Its style is matter of fact, its language transparent and often deceptively simple. But the content is stranger than fiction, revealing a person who became a stranger to herself, her very existence denied. There is an immediacy that brings the past to life, though never literally, and it is a past that still might not have fully revealed itself.

21 Oct 2012
Cheryl M-M (United Kingdom)
(TOP 500 REVIEWER)
This isn't just an autobiography. It is a cleansing of the soul. It is well written and even paced. It also manages to create a build up of tension leading up to the grand plot finale. I thought that was exceedingly well done. I wonder what is worse, discovering the horrors behind the door or realising that perhaps nobody will believe you when you do tell them. That conundrum is exactly why the brain creates the vaults to begin with. It must take a lot of guts to expose yourself and your secrets in this manner.

The Stranger In My Life

by

Janet Holt and Helen Parker

Dedication

For Mavis and Walter Holt.

After 34 years I finally discovered the truth. Now all I have to do is learn to live with it.

Janet Holt, 13th April 2010

AUTHOR'S NOTE

Janet Holt

Carting hay with Hero in 1974

My name is Janet Holt. I have farmed at Ball Beard Farm in the Peak District, Derbyshire for almost 40 years, 34 of them alone. My life has been full of incident and amusing stories and for the past few years my friends have been pestering me to write it all down and put it in a book.

There was the day in September 1966 when the havoc I created with a pre-war potato harvester and two nervous Shire horses had them laughing so much they asked if they could buy tickets to watch next time. Or the day when one of my bullocks escaped and went galloping down Glossop high street with me, the police and local newspaper reporters running behind like something out of the Keystone Cops.

So, with retirement looming I decided to sit down and make an attempt to write the book my friends said they wanted to read. I'm not quite sure where the urge came from; it wasn't as if my stories had suddenly grown funnier or I had more time on my hands, in fact it was quite the opposite. I was farming an 80-strong herd of beef cattle all on my own and selling produce direct to customers so free time was definitely at a premium. Nevertheless over a period of 12 months I spent every spare moment I had working on my manuscript until I reached the year 2009 – and then I read it back and realised that the amusing incidents were actually few and far between.

Now, my understanding of a biography is that you include everything. There's no point leaving out the unfortunate bits just because they show you in a bad light so my twenty-year affair with a married man and my two-year prison sentence had to go in alongside the stories of building up my farm business and my previous 'day job' as a legal executive in New Mills, Derbyshire. But in spite of my intention to include everything, there were still some very large gaps in my life story, gaps that I found impossible to fill even though I desperately wanted to fill them.

In March 1976 I lost four days of my life. From 14 March to 18 March I had a complete memory loss and then, on 19 March 1976, my business partner at Ball Beard Farm, Fred Handford disappeared. From that day to this no-one has seen or heard from him and since then I have suffered the most debilitating, horrific and terrifying nightmares, three, sometimes four times a week; nightmares that leave me totally disorientated and sobbing in my bed; nightmares that have affected my life in the most disturbing ways and have made me question my sanity on more than one occasion. I have only ever told one person about these nightmares – until now.

As I say, I don't think it's a good idea to censor your life story and that's why I've written the truth - as I remember it - but it wasn't until my best friend, Mary suggested I see a psychologist that the *full* truth actually emerged. This is that story; it includes my sessions with Dr Belinda Browne-Thomas, a Hyde-based psychologist and the details of how I'm coping with the fall-out –

and yes, I *have* included some of the funny stories, just to keep my friends happy…

NB In writing about my life I have referred to the towns and villages of the Peak District by the correct names but I have changed the names of most of the people - apart from Fred Handford and my parents, Walter and Mavis Holt. Some of the characters are an amalgamation of people I've known over the years but that is the only fiction in this book; everything else is true.

Janet Holt, November 2010

CONTENTS

Prologue

March 1976

The red door is glowing; the black latch taunting me to open it. I strain every muscle in my body, listening to the creak of sinews in my arms and in my shoulders as I stretch further than I know is physically possible. And then the floor gives way and I'm falling: I grab at the darkness, but I can't stop, oh God, I can't stop! My feet turn to lead. I plummet down as the door moves underneath me, the red peeling paint as livid as a burst of lava, ready to burn my whole body and turn me to ash. I open my mouth to scream but nothing comes out. I suck in air and panic as it clogs my lungs. A whirlpool of hay tumbles in, whipping me up in a fury of energy; up, up and away from the door. But I have to go through it; I have to escape. I push hard – ropes of hay tighten around my wrists, refusing to let go. Bile rises in my throat. The red wood begins to melt, flames licking the paint and leaping up towards me, scorching my skin, making me scream in pain. Tears are flowing down my face and dropping at my feet. Which way should I go? How will I escape? I twist and turn as shapes begin to form, coming at me out of the smoke-filled gloom, dark patches of shadow coming together to form images; hideous gargoyles,

12

gurning and grinning their message at me: **You can't escape, there is no escape.** *The words hiss their deathly chorus. I know they're right as I realise in a moment of vicious clarity - I am going to die.*

Chapter One

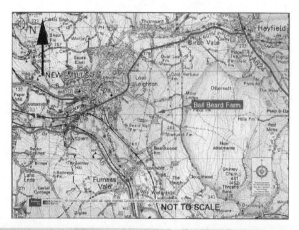

Ball Beard Farm, New Mills, Derbyshire

15 March 2010

I look closely at my reflection; blue eyes, grey hair and a
face lined with the evidence of 40 years spent farming in all
weathers at Ball Beard Farm in Derbyshire. I suck my cheeks in to
see if that makes any difference but I look more like a deflated
balloon than a 59-year-old woman. Even my best friend, Mary has
to admit I have a 'lived in look' but I don't take offence; if your

best friend can't tell you the truth then who can?

I turn, open the cupboard door above my head and stare at the notice; the one I've been reading aloud to myself nearly every day for the past 34 years.

Get out of bed

Feed the dogs

Get washed

Get dressed

Make a cup of tea, eat a slice of toast.

Last night's nightmare had been a particularly bad one and I had to run to the toilet to be sick – not easy when you're living in a mobile home with five dogs. At least I made it to the cubicle. Last time I wasn't so lucky.

I pull my dressing gown tighter, fighting a losing battle with the cold and then tug a comb through my hair. An image of a mass of blonde curls suddenly leaps into my mind: a welcome flashback to happier times you might say, but it doesn't linger long; those sorts of memories never do.

"Righto, Jelly, looks like an early walk," I say, tipping some fresh dog biscuits into a bowl. I bend down to place the bowl on the floor between the cooker and the table and watch Jelly as she tucks in. She eats quickly; she knows she's only got two minutes before I open the door and my other four dogs will race in, battling for their share.

I glance back at the list. I don't have to be in Hyde until this afternoon and with any luck my stomach will have settled by then. I pick up the slip of paper from the table and read it one more time: *Dr Belinda Browne-Thomas, Chartered Counselling Psychologist.* I'm not nervous but I'm sceptical. Mary might think it's a good idea to get to the bottom of the nightmares I've been having for over 30 years but I'm not so sure. She asked me last night in the pub why I hadn't told her about them earlier and I didn't know what to say. *"I thought you'd think I was off me 'ead,"* was all I could come up with. I drew a circle against my temple with my index finger. "I know I'm barmy, but I wouldn't want you to think I was insane." Mary didn't laugh.

"But we've been friends for 30 years, Janet, I don't understand. Why are you telling me this now?"

I looked down at my glass of wine and shrugged. "Don't know, really. I've had enough chances, I suppose, it's just never seemed like the right time."

"What do you mean; *it's never seemed like the right time*? What about all those times when we were walking our dogs, or when we were stood freezing to death at farmers markets, or when we were packing so much beef for your customers I threatened to go vegetarian? You've had more chances to tell me about your nightmares than - than I've had hot dinners." Mary looked at me as if she was looking at me for the first time. "And what about our sweet-eating sessions? Was it never the right time when we were shovelling all those pink shrimps into our mouths?"

"I'm sorry, Mary, but I just couldn't get the words out."

Mary took a deep breath followed by another, and then she

16

laid a hand on my shoulder, leaning forward until her head was almost touching mine. She couldn't stay mad at me for long; that was one of the things I loved about her.

"I'm sorry, I didn't mean to nag. Hey, come on now, we'll get to the bottom of these nightmares, don't you worry." She leant in closer, suddenly suspicious. "Blimey Janet, are you laughing?"

"I couldn't get the words out 'cos my mouth was full of sweets," I spluttered. "And it's me that should be sorry, Mary. You've kept me sane all these years; if you can call this sane." I crossed my eyes and forced my tongue into the side of my cheek. "Who else would 'ave me as a friend?"

"I've often wondered that myself." The corners of her mouth twitched. "Perhaps it's all the walking we do? All those hours up on Round Wood; me telling you about my life as a stressed-out primary school teacher and you telling me about your experiences as a hard working farmer, qualified legal executive, expert dry-stone waller, horse breeder, scarlet woman…" She stopped. "Oh blimey, Janet, I didn't mean…I'm sorry."

I stared into my glass of wine while we both went quiet for a bit; me because I didn't want to sound bitter and Mary because she knew she'd stirred up some nasty memories.

"Come on, he wasn't all bad. I mean, I know he was married but he didn't mind helping us at harvest time. He was pretty useful as I remember."

I said nothing.

"I suppose I should have guessed - but I was only 21. I

didn't know much about people having affairs back then: I was so naïve."

"No reason why you should. As far as you were concerned he was my boss and nothing more."

Mary considered this for a moment. "You were always joking with him. I missed all the signs."

"I do tell a lot of jokes, don't I?"

"It's a bad habit you've got. I've told you about it before, Janet. No-one knows when you're being serious."

"Well, believe it or not, I've got something serious to tell you now."

Mary's voice dropped to a whisper. "Don't Janet; the last time you said you wanted to tell me something serious you …"

"I know, I know, but I promise you, this time it's not that bad."

"You're not going to prison again, then?"

"No, I'm selling Ball Beard Farm."

"You're *what*?"

"I'm selling up. It's time to make a fresh start. I've put the farm on the market and there's a buyer interested. I've asked that I have first refusal if he should sell it on again so I won't be letting go completely and I've arranged to do some dry stone walling on the land once the sale has gone through - but I've made up my mind and I'm going.'"

Mary put her glass down slowly. "Where are you going exactly?"

"I'm not sure. I'll maybe set off with my dogs and the caravan for a holiday in the middle of June and see where the fancy takes me."

"Is it the nightmares?"

I sat quite still for a moment or two, debating whether to tell Mary more of what was going on in my head or whether to make light of it. Why not tell Mary that along with the nightmares I'd also lost four days of my life when I could neither remember what I did nor where I'd been, that although I appeared to have functioned normally, going about my business as usual, I couldn't recall what had happened for four whole days and now, 34 years later, I still couldn't remember.

"I'm selling up because - because I need a break," I said, forcing a smile. "It's a while since I've been anywhere and I fancy a trip to the west coast of Scotland."

Mary raised an eyebrow. "Hmmm, you've not had a holiday in the 30 years I've known you."

"I had a lovely 10 days in Switzerland a while back."

"When?"

"I think it was 1965, when I was 15," I said, po-faced. "I thought it was about time I had another."

Mary wasn't convinced, and I don't blame her. She smelled a rat and frankly, who wouldn't, but she bided her time, trying to get to the bottom of what she thought I was trying to tell her.

"Well, no-one can say you don't deserve it. You've had a rough time. If only you'd married a handsome young farmer and had three strapping sons like I told you to…"

I looked away.

"Blimey, I've done it again, I didn't mean…"

"Don't worry."

"I saw him last week. He doesn't look any different; still wearing those stiff tweed suits and polished leather brogues. How old is he now?"

"Seventy," I snapped, not that I'd been keeping track or anything. "He hasn't worked since the court case. He's still married."

"I never knew what you saw in him," said Mary softly. "I'd heard that he wasn't a particularly good boss; always ogling the young secretaries – and not so young secretaries too, come to think of it." She saw my expression harden. "Sorry, I just thought it might help if we annihilated Miles Ingleby's character over a pie and a pint."

"There's no need, Mary, I hate him and I'll always hate him. He fooled me for almost 20 years and I'll never forgive him for that. Thanks to him I'll always feel like an idiot where men are concerned, not that I've had much experience of men, hardly any in fact." I sighed.

I could tell Mary was deciding whether to put this particular discussion on the back burner. She was 10 years younger than me but at times she treated me like a difficult teenager – which was ironic since I was never a difficult teenager; I seem to have become much more difficult as I've got older.

20

Chapter Two

1952, aged 2, dressed as Bo Peep

1962

My Dad, Walter Holt, never, ever raised his voice to me but he had a way of showing his disapproval that I think I might have inherited. He would start to speak very, very slowly, saying his words more clearly so I had no choice but to listen. Well, I'd listen - but that didn't necessarily mean I'd agree with him.

"Janet, for the last time; you cannot have a pony of your

own. You're 12, not 16. Your brother's girlfriend has already told you that you can ride Dizzy whenever you want to."

"But it's not the same and Pete doesn't like it when I hang around with him and Ellen."

"Well, he is 11 years older than you; he's bound to say that," said Mum who never, as far as I could remember ever disagreed with Dad. "My advice is to keep quiet and he won't notice you're there."

"That'll be a first," said Dad with a laugh. "Since when has our Janet kept quiet? You might be small, my girl, but you make up for it in the noise department. There's plenty of time for horses, concentrate on your school work for now."

I almost stamped my foot. "But Dad, I'm no good at that and besides, I want to be a farmer when I grow up."

Dad's expression changed. He took off his glasses and put them carefully in his lap - and then his voice slowed down even more.

"Now then, Janet; what's brought all this on? Do you have any idea how hard life is as a farmer? Your grandparents worked their fingers to the bone on their land and for what? I'll tell you what, shall I? No pension and no home of their own. Farming is a hard, unforgiving life so you'll put all those young notions to the back of your mind, pass your exams and then you'll apply for a job with prospects."

Mum nodded in agreement as she rolled out pastry on the kitchen table. She was making tater pie but nothing, not even the

26

prospect of my favourite meal could distract me.

"But Dad, Ernie Castleford's getting rid of 'is ponies. He says I can 'ave Lucky if I want her; you know, the lovely little bay with the white scar on her nose. All I've got to do is pay him £25. "
I dared myself to take a step closer, my hands clasped tightly in a knot in front of me as I waited for him to say yes.

Dad put his glasses back on his nose where they belonged and then he picked up his copy of the High Peak Reporter. I lifted a hand up to my face, pushing my blonde curls out of my eyes and waiting as patiently as I could.

"You know I'll look after Lucky better than anyone. I'll feed her and I'll muck her out and I'll visit her every day before school and after school and I'll ride her and I'll…"

Dad turned to the back of the newspaper to check the cricket scores then cleared his throat before folding it again and placing it carefully on the coffee table in front of him. "I've said no, and I mean no."

I glanced up at Mum but she was still rolling out the pastry, backwards and forwards, backwards and forwards, saying nothing. I glared at Dad but I knew I was defeated – for now – so I turned and flounced out of the kitchen, fighting back tears as I ran out the back door and up the path at the side of the house. I ran non-stop until I was out of breath, down the lane and up the fields towards Round Wood, gasping to a halt half way up the steep hill. I knew I wasn't allowed to go this far without Mum and Dad's permission but today, I really didn't care.

The hill was steeper than I remembered and the sun was hot, shining down from a sky as blue as my bedroom walls. I was crying a bit now so I bent forwards so no-one could see, not even the skylarks going about their business, circling and hovering in the space above my head. I slogged on as they sang until I was standing at the top of Round Wood, looking down on the whole world.

From up here the town of New Mills looked like one of Mum's crocheted blankets with the rivers Goyt and Sett stitching the two sides together with their watery, jagged seams. I could see the factory that made my favourite sweets, Love Hearts and Refreshers, and I wondered for the millionth time how a building that ugly could produce such lovely things but then I remembered Mum's words, even though I didn't really want to: '*Appearances can be deceptive, Janet*'.

I turned gloomily away thinking of Mum and Dad at home without me; Dad would still be reading his paper and Mum would be placing her delicate pastry leaves on top of the tater pie. Then she'd be setting the table for tea before putting the kettle on for a cuppa while the pie cooked in the oven. I turned again and looked miserably towards Stockport - a place the Holt family rarely visited - and then further away to the grey blur of Manchester, way off in the distance: it might as well have been on another planet. The only sound was the trill of the skylarks, getting ready to make their plunging descent and then, a few feet away, the chomp of two Shire horses, pulling grass into their mouths. Last week had been

28

my 12th birthday and I'd really thought that Dad would let me have a pony of my own. I sat down on the grass with a thump. How wrong could I be?

I watched the two Shires as they ate, each of them standing higher than 16 hands, giants of the farmyard with feet like dinner plates. I'd heard they belonged to Fred Handford, the farmer who owned Ball Beard Farm, but I didn't know for sure. I'd seen Mr Handford driving his horse and cart around town, sometimes with a girl about my age up there with him. She'd looked down at me once with such a scowl on her face and I'd wondered why: I'd have been smiling if I was her. It made me wonder how different my life would have been if Dad had been a farmer, like Granddad, but then I realised that would never have happened. Mum told me that Dad had a *'steady job with the council'*; he wore suits and carried a briefcase to work. I thought of Fred Handford with his ancient woollen trousers held up with string and a battered flat cap on top of his head and I laughed at how different a dad could be.

One of the horses came towards me, stretching out his beautiful grey head to see if there was anything on offer, nostrils widening like two black eyes. I stood up and stroked him, feeling his hot breath on my hand, and then I stepped boldly up to the bay mare, only to have her lunge at me with her stained, yellow teeth. "Whoa there girl! It's okay, I've been warned." I wasn't frightened of horses; you just had to be careful when you went near them for the first time.

"D'you know," I said, talking to them now as if they

were my best friends, "I'm goin' to own this land one day; I'm going to be a farmer and I'm going to keep horses of my own here at Round Wood and then I'm going to come up with my dogs and look down on the whole of New Mills. Just you wait and see." I scanned the top of the hill and realised with a smile that there was not one tree to be seen on Round Wood - not one - and for the first time in my life I wondered why on earth that should be. Then I turned around, back towards Low Leighton Road and Mum's tater pie. I didn't want to be late for my tea.

It wasn't long before I persuaded Dad to change his mind about buying Lucky. I know he didn't approve of everything I did in my life but I think he understood what was important to me and, at the age of 12, that was horses, my family – and, of course, Mum's cooking.

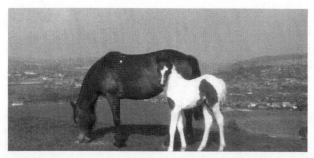

My first pony, Lucky and her foal up on Round Wood

Chapter Three

The farmhouse before renovation

1964

"Has Lucky thrown you off again?" asked Mum, shooing me into a chair at the kitchen table. "Come 'ere, love, let me take your boots off for you."

Mum wiped her hands on her apron, soapy from the Monday wash and gripped hard at the heel of my rubber riding boot, leaning against the sink and tugging at it until it let go of my foot. Then she placed the boot carefully on the mat next to the back door.

"I've scrubbed the floor this morning, so be careful," she warned. "You go on upstairs now and I'll run you a bath."

I didn't move, I just sighed as I pushed the hair out of my eyes. I was exhausted from trying to coax Lucky over those three fences in the field; I wanted to join the hunt this autumn so badly but things weren't going to plan. My friend Ann was already clearing them with ease and it wouldn't be right if Ann rode with the hunt and I didn't.

"Janet, what's wrong?" Mum put a hand on my shoulder then pointed to a batch of scones fresh out of the oven which she thought might help the situation.

"Ernie Castleford's selling his field," I said gloomily, ignoring the scones. "Which means I'll have to look for new grazing for Lucky and there's nothing for miles around and I know Dad doesn't want to drive me over to Disley or Chinley every day now he's got the new car and…"

"Hey, now then, love, nothing's so broken it can't be fixed."

"Oh Mum, you always say that but I can't see how I'm going to fix this."

Mum sat down next to me and took hold of my hand as if I was four years old, not 14. "We'll ask your Dad's advice when he gets home. I'm sure he'll have a suggestion."

Dad's suggestion was a good one. He'd heard on the New Mills' grapevine – where everyone knew everyone else's business – that Fred Handford of Ball Beard Farm might have some grazing available and Ball Beard Farm was only a couple of minutes further on from Ernie's; up Laneside Road, first turning on the right, past the last row of houses on the edge of town.

Dad agreed to drive me up the hill on Saturday afternoon

but he drew the line at turning into the farmyard since he told me the potholes would do 'irreparable' damage to his shiny new Ford Prefect – whatever that meant.

"You want me to go in there all on my own?" I asked, looking warily at the dilapidated farmhouse; even in the sun it looked dark and forbidding. Last year, when we'd been to see Ernie Castleford about grazing for Lucky, Dad had done all the talking and had even warned Ernie's two sons that if he ever heard them swearing in front of his daughter he'd be up there like a shot. Things were obviously a bit different now that I was a little older.

"Yes, Janet, Lucky's your responsibility. Be polite; introduce yourself and tell Mr Handford what you need. I'll wait here."

I was pleased that Dad thought I was old enough to sort out my own affairs but I was a bit put off at having to negotiate the filthy sea of mud between the car and the farmhouse first. I hopped and skipped across the cracked flagstones then knocked on the door, dislodging flakes of red paint with each rap of my knuckles. There was no answer so I knocked again. The door was ajar so I stepped boldly inside.

"Mr Handford?"

The reply came so quick I wondered if he'd been watching me all along. "Aye, in't living room."

I turned to the right. In the gloom I could just make out the faint outline of a man, five foot nine or ten inches tall, silhouetted in the doorway. My eyes adjusted to the light until, bit by bit, his features revealed themselves too; a sharp pointed nose, high cheekbones and a wiry frame all topped off with a flat cap, lying on his head like a collapsed Yorkshire pudding. I glanced past him, into the dark and dingy space beyond and shivered, the only source of light coming from a row of small, filthy windows overlooking the farmyard. I'd never seen the like; it was as if Fred Handford had decided to take up residence in a hovel. Cobwebs hung down from a low ceiling, swaying next to metal hooks where pails, bits of sacking and strange looking farm implements dangled down like cuts of meat. Wisps of smoke mingled in the gloom, suspended in the foetid air. I stared at the hooks; convinced my eyes were playing tricks on me. Was it really what I thought it was? I blinked. Yes, there really was a pig hanging down from the ceiling; its head and feet were missing, but it was definitely a pig. I stood quite still, forgetting to breathe. It wasn't the sort of room where you dared to laugh; it wasn't the sort of room where you wasted your words.

"What can I do for 'y?" His voice sounded like a grumble. My throat was completely dry. I looked down at the floor, away from his pin-sharp gaze, staring at the mud-spattered stone flags which made up the farmhouse floor but then I thought of Dad's words and managed to dredge up the courage to reply. "I've got a pony and I wondered if you've any grazing I could rent?" Fred Handford looked me up and down. I could guess what he was thinking: what's this scrap of a girl with a mess of blond hair doing in my farmhouse. He frowned before he spoke.

"Aye, I can sort you out some grazing, lass. There's two of my Shires up on Round Wood, you can put yours in wi' em. The rent's five bob a week, payable in advance."

He sounded gruff but the fact that he had what I wanted gave me courage. I nodded my thanks and then I looked past him to what could quite possibly have been a witch, sitting motionless in a rocking chair behind him. I stared, my imagination running riot.

"Cup of tea?" asked Fred.

I nodded again, too scared to say no, then I dragged my gaze away to another carcass, this time a dead hen, feathers on, eyes open, staring back at me from a hook next to the pig. The black-clad witch didn't move.

Fred poured as I looked about some more. The walls were lime washed, just like our washhouse at home and a fire was burning in the enormous black range. The fireplace dominated the room, gaping wide like a giant's mouth.

My eyes followed Fred warily as he moved to sit at the table – nothing more than a rough slab of wood, littered with newspapers and a rag-tag assortment of crockery and cutlery. He indicated to me to join him so I inched closer and as I did the witch stirred.

"This is mother; she's a bit deaf," said Fred loudly. I nodded then glanced away, looking over Fred's shoulder towards the door and caught sight of what I assumed was a shotgun, leaning against the wall next to a horse's collar and other assorted harness and, finally, I began to relax. Anything to do with horses made me feel at home.

Two tabby cats perched on the corner of the table, one purring loudly as it washed its paws, the other with its eyes fixed firmly on Fred. He handed me a cracked cup and told me to help myself to the sugar on the table.

"Plate of stew, lass?"

I shook my head. Fred turned to the range and ladled out a single serving before sitting down again and spooning the steaming hot stew into his mouth. One of the cats inched warily towards him. "'Ere," said Fred gruffly. He picked a piece of meat off his plate with his fingers and flicked it accurately at the moggy, hitting it on the nose. The cat jumped on it, picked it up then ran down with it to the floor.

Fred spooned more stew into a saucer and pushed it across the table, watching silently as the other cat started to eat. I tried to imagine the same scenario in my Mum's neat and tidy kitchen at home and found that I couldn't, it was impossible.

"My Dad's outside," I said, eventually.

Fred looked up at me with eyes narrowed to grey slits. "I should come out an' greet 'im, then."

I wasn't sure if he was asking me a question or stating his intent but I stood up anyway then followed him out of the farmhouse, throwing one last frightened glance at the witch before emerging into the light. We walked side by side, towards Dad, who was waiting patiently, sitting in his Ford Prefect, reading his paper.

"This is Mr Handford and this is my Dad, Walter Holt," I said. We both bent low towards the car's open window and as we did I caught the pungent whiff of stale body odour. I wrinkled my nose, my eyes watering in shock as I realised that it wasn't just Fred's home that could do with a good wash and brush up.

"Pleased to meet y'," said Fred, his face stern. Then he repeated the offer of grazing at Round Wood as if I wouldn't have the wherewithal to tell Dad myself.

"That sounds reasonable enough to me," said Dad, shaking Fred's hand in a man-to-man sort of way. "Janet will arrange to move Lucky up here as soon as possible, if that's acceptable to you, Mr Handford."

"Aye, and it's Fred," said Fred, giving what I thought might have been a slight incline of his head. I was a bit surprised at the gesture; I think I'd already decided that Fred wasn't the submissive type.

And that was how I first met Fred Handford. Looking back, I wonder sometimes how different things would have been if I hadn't had to go looking for grazing for Lucky or if Dad hadn't heard the rumours that Fred had grazing to spare or, indeed, if I hadn't come to love the farm so much. But I don't suppose it serves any purpose thinking about things that are already set in stone. As so many people say: hindsight is a wonderful thing. But in my opinion hindsight can just as easily make you regret things.

But back to 1964 and a time when I knew no better. The day I moved Lucky into Fred Handford's field was the happiest day of my life. Ten minutes after finishing my breakfast I could be putting on Lucky's saddle and trotting off across the fields since the walk from Low Leighton up to Round Wood took no time at all – and, at the age of 14 nothing in my life was more important than that.

1946 Fred Handford ploughing at Ball Beard Farm

Chapter Four

1965 and nothing's changed: Fred Handford mowing with Bonny and Dick

1966

By the time I turned 16 Dad had become resigned to my love of the outdoor life although he was still wary of letting my hobby become my career. Fortunately, Fred had no such qualms: he encouraged my offers of help and before he knew it, I'd become quite an asset. I whiled away the summer, waiting for my 'O' level results, riding Lucky and helping out at Ball Beard Farm whenever I could.

There was something about Ball Beard Farm that appealed to me on every level; it had 40 acres of wide open spaces, fresh air, animals and that all important magic ingredient – horses, although the horses at the farm weren't the riding kind like Lucky, but the type of horse that worked hard for its living. Other farms in the Peak District had moved on since the Second World War and had accepted mechanisation as a way of life but Ball Beard remained firmly in the past: tractors would never be contemplated and Fred clung on to his beloved Shires as if his life depended on it. This meant long hours and a huge amount of hard, manual labour but, for me – and I presume for Fred too – there were daily compensations in using these magnificent animals for the provision of real horse power.

Fred taught me the tricks of his trade: I leant how to hitch the Shires up to all the machinery, he taught me how to plough, ridge potatoes, cart muck, mow and turn hay and, thanks to his quiet, steady patience, I became quite a skilled milker. Meanwhile, the 'witch' became more and more incapacitated with each week that went by until it became clear to me that Fred was caring for his mother as well as himself.

I never pried into Fred's personal life but it was obvious that he rarely saw the rest of his family and he never spoke of his daughter Katrina or his ex-wife, Nan. Mum would invite him for tea now and again and he always scrubbed up well and was on his best behaviour but we didn't ask too many questions. Fred was very private. The only time he was chatty was when we spoke about the farm and even then he was hardly what you'd call eloquent. Looking back now I wish I'd asked him more about Ernie Castleford's pre-war potato digger, his description of how it operated wasn't quite detailed enough for my liking and very nearly created havoc at Ball Beard Farm one weekend in early autumn.

Ernie had offered us the loan of the digger so that this year, for the first time ever, Fred didn't have to dig his potatoes by hand. Ernie delivered the ancient contraption early one morning and Fred decided in his wisdom that I was more than up to the job although I don't know where he got that idea from; I was still only four feet ten.

Anyway, we stood there weighing up its rusty appearance, me looking doubtful, Fred a bit more chatty than usual.

"Bonny and Star know what they're doin'," Fred said, tugging his cap lower over his eyes. "Hitch them up like I said; it's similar to the Bamford mowing machine I showed y' last week, 'cept the wheels are higher and much closer together, designed to run either side of the ridges of potatoes. Hop up on't seat and keep hold o' the reins, lass, and the horses and the scoops on the front should do the job for y'."

I looked at Bonny the bay mare, her ears pressed back on her neck as usual and I have to be honest, I didn't believe a word of what Fred had just said to me. Bonny hadn't changed since the first time we'd met on Round Wood four years ago, she was still wary of everyone except her owner. I turned my attention to Star

41

instead, Bonny's foal, who was young, inexperienced but eager to please. Fred wasn't daft; he noticed my hesitation.

"It'll be fine, lass, you run up the ridges – same as ploughin' – and this wheel turns around, the little forks scoop through the soil, throwin' the potatoes out to the left, ready for picking up. Set yourself up at the beginning of the row, put it in gear and off you go. Two things to remember: Ernie warned it's very low geared – which means it's made to work at a slow walking pace, and take care turning at the end of the field; the wheels are close together so it's easy to tip the whole thing up. Anyhow, I'll hang around for 10 minutes and make sure everything's okay then I'll leave y' to it."

Fred turned to look at a section of walling that needed attention while I prepared to drive to the edge of the first row. The horses stood in between the ridges, Star champing at the bit, impatient to get going while I gripped the reins, my legs barely reaching the floor of the digger. I glanced up to see if I could catch Fred's attention for one last nod of approval but he was already on to the next task so I steeled myself to get on with it just as I spotted a girl my own age walk into the field and make directly for him. She spoke and I saw Fred turn. I strained to hear what she was saying but her voice was so low I couldn't make out the words. Her arms were pressed against her side, as rigid as an Irish clog dancer and then, suddenly, I heard her shout "No!" and point with an accusing finger at the farmhouse. At the sound of her voice ringing out across the field Bonny jumped forward and pulled so hard I had to use all my strength to hold her back.

"You dunna understand," Fred shouted and then both of the horses jerked forward as if Fred was shouting at them. Was it Fred's daughter? I strained harder to hear what they were saying but could only grasp the occasional word. If it was Katrina then she certainly didn't have the sort of relationship I had with my own father: I would never, in a million years, dare to challenge Dad in this way and I didn't recognise the man Fred had become at the far side of the field; he was like a cornered animal, his back to the dry stone wall.

"What do you expect?" said Katrina - for it must have been her. "You have no idea..."

"Nor you, lass," shouted Fred.

"Why must it all be Ball Beard Farm?"

"Because it must."

Bonny shifted impatiently from foot to foot. Star felt the mare's anxiety and pulled harder on the bit.

"What about Mother?" Katrina's words rang out across the field like a shotgun. Star bucked violently and I felt the reins slip further from my grasp. "Don't you dare..." I strained every muscle but both horses leapt forward, Star plunging into her collar, feeling the sound of Fred and Katrina's voices as sharply as she heard them. I was almost yanked from my seat. As I fought with the reins, Bonny sped up to a trot, shocked out of her usual patient walk by Star's antics, who appeared to have been possessed by the spirit of a wild thing, legs pistoning up and down, head high in the

43

air, fighting with me and lashing out viciously at the chains attaching her to the digger. Fred and Katrina's words were lost in the turmoil, accusations flying as fast as the wheel of forks, which was now spinning frantically across the ground. The potato machine hurtled to the end of the field then made a sudden, sharp turn. One more like that and we would tip over, just as Ernie had warned we would. I fought to free my hands from the reins to pull the gear lever but I didn't have the strength.

Katrina continued to shout at Fred and Fred carried on shouting back but I couldn't quite make out what they were saying. All I was aware of was the potatoes, scooped out of the soil and hurled through the air like missiles. I saw Fred turn away, shoulders hunched, before he realised this other drama taking place right in front of him and he immediately switched his attention from Katrina to me. I caught his look of horror as he saw me turn, pick up speed and then carry on down the field, full pelt now, the digger unable to do its job properly. He ran down the ridge, trying to cut me off. "Knock it out of gear! Knock it out of gear!" he shouted, but it was obvious that I needed a free hand before I could do that and I didn't dare release my grip on the reins.

As Fred ran towards the digger, crossing the line of fire, Katrina walked out of the field, eyes fixed firmly on the farmyard as if me and Fred were images on a screen, part of a life that had nothing to do with her.

Fred watched her go and then shaking his head as if to dislodge a thought he suddenly found a superhuman burst of

44

energy: he grabbed hold of the digger and, with one huge effort swung himself up, coming to stand behind me with all the agility of a man half his age. I couldn't turn my head to look at him; I could only pull back on the reins for all I was worth, praying for Bonny and Star to respond - but they galloped on, too blinkered to react. Fred didn't hesitate; he reached across my lap and yanked the gear lever back towards him. The noise of the machine stopped immediately. Then he jumped back down onto the ground, ran up the right side and caught hold of Star's head as she galloped on, plunging and kicking, bearing down on her like a rodeo cowboy, her antics lifting his feet clear off the ground. "Whoa lass, whoa there, Star."

Bonny began to slow, finally coming to a halt halfway down the field. Star gave one last defiant kick at the chains and then she stopped too. Sweat was running freely down the horses' flanks as Fred took off his jacket and placed it carefully over Star's head. "Right," he panted, still keeping a tight hold. "Leave the reins and unhitch them, Star first and keep talkin' so she knows where you are and what you're doin'." I did as Fred asked then, talking softly under his breath the whole time, he led the horses out of the field and back to the stable.

More than half an hour passed before I could think of doing anything since my legs had turned to jelly. Later, I crisscrossed over the field, picking up the damaged spuds and tossing them into buckets while Fred inspected the damage done to Ernie's potato digger. He didn't mention the visitor and I didn't have the courage to bring it up, so we carried on as if nothing had happened, side by side, picking up potatoes, the peace eventually returning to the Derbyshire autumn day.

As far as I was aware, Fred's daughter never came to Ball Beard Farm ever again.

Chapter Five

Late March 1976

I fall out of bed and wake with a violence that jolts me upright. I'm shaking and my breathing is fast and shallow. I clutch at the bedclothes with my fists curled tight. My knuckles are white and the sheets are damp with my sweat. I'm crying again and I can taste the vomit in my mouth. I know the terror is waiting for me, lying in the darkness in the space under my bed. I fight against the bed sheets tangled around me, lashing out with a free arm against the monster creeping forward out of the gloom. I knock over the bedside cabinet and the alarm clock hits the wall. I free myself from the sheets and scramble quickly back onto the bed where I crouch on my knees, trembling as the sweat pours from my body. I fight to slow my breathing and close my eyes as a headache throbs. I pray again for these feelings of desolation and despair to go away but last time it was hours before I felt normal again and so I sit, staring into the early morning light as the minutes tick by. A black despairing wave of depression washes over me, wave after wave, dragging me backwards and forwards, like a lifeless body washed up on the shore. I say the words aloud: "*I am 26 years old and I am losing my mind.*" I don't know why I've suddenly starting having

47

these awful nightmares and I don't know why I've lost four days of my life – and I have no idea what's happened to Fred.

I close my eyes and wait till my breathing slows and then I speak softly to myself, reciting a familiar list of words that I know will help me get on with my day. The words act as a calming rhythm as well as a gentle reminder that I can cope - if I only try hard enough:

Get out of bed

Feed the dogs

Get washed

Get dressed

Make a cup of tea, eat a slice of toast.

Twenty years later, when police call at Ball Beard Cottage to arrest me, those same words are still acting as a comfort, only now I have the list written out and fixed to the wall where I can see it.

August 1966

I might have been headstrong but I wasn't a rebel. When my 'O' level results arrived in the post just before my 16th birthday I was more pleased at Dad's reaction than I was with the B and C grades I'd managed to achieve.

Dad slipped a second white envelope in front of me.

"What's this?" I said, watching his face as he smiled at me. I was half hoping for a small cheque made payable to Miss J Holt in exchange for all my hard work and which I'd already decided

I'd use as a down payment on a new saddle for Apache, the pony I'd bought to keep Lucky company.

"This, my girl, is very important. Ingleby's, a firm of solicitors in New Mills, has a vacancy for a junior clerk and this is your appointment for an interview. I know Miss Stevenson, the office manager, and she has arranged to interview you before they advertise the position. You have a chance here, Janet, to secure a job with excellent prospects."

I wanted to ask him how I was going to manage to work at Ball Beard Farm if I was going to have to work nine to five in an office every day but I'd tried to bring the subject up last week and Dad's reaction had been very clear: no daughter of his was going to spend more time than was necessary up to their knees in muck.

"They will be looking for someone who is neat, tidy and articulate," he said, looking at me over his glasses. And I nodded, knowing I would try my very best to prove that I could be all of those things.

I gave a good account of myself in the interview. I might not have been neat or particularly tidy, but I could be articulate when I wanted to be. Three days later I was informed by letter that I had been offered the position of Junior Probate Clerk at a starting salary of £14 a week. Dad was thrilled, Mum was delighted and I accepted my destiny with as much daughterly good grace as I could manage. I was going to go to work as a probate clerk and I was going to make my parents proud, just as long as they didn't ask me to give up working at Ball Beard Farm completely.

Chapter Six

Fred Handford mowing with Hero and Bonny

March 1972

I dragged my old Barbour jacket out of the van and threw it on over my office 'uniform' then dashed across the farmyard, past the farmhouse and the ruined shippon, skidding to a halt alongside the dry stone wall of the pig sty.

"The cow's out in the meadow again, Fred, did you see it?" I gasped. The jacket hung down to my knees like a filthy waxed mini skirt, splattered with cow shit and pig muck. As soon as I pulled it on I felt the world of Ingleby's disappear in an instant and I was back in the world I preferred; working the land that I loved.

I waited, having driven up in my rusty van just as I did every evening, for Fred to touch his cap in acknowledgement, but tonight he could barely look at me. I waited while he swept the pig muck to one side, hoping he would eventually mumble his gruff hello and follow me to the meadow with his dog, Ned by his side, ready to leap into action and round up that errant cow but he didn't; he just carried on sweeping, silent and closed.

"Hello, Janet here to Planet Fred, are you receiving me?" I joked – but I was worried now that it was something serious that was distracting him: perhaps Bonny's new foal, Hero had been taken ill or the bank manager had been making demands again, questioning the extent of Fred's overdraft.

Fred turned slowly to look at me and as soon as I saw his red-rimmed eyes I knew.

"It's mother," he mumbled. "She's dead."

I thought back eight years to the first time I'd seen Fred's mother sitting in the living room in her chair, watching me venture into the farmhouse after I'd knocked on their door and I thought it was a miracle that she'd lasted this long. I waited for Fred to speak again but I suppose words were the last thing on his mind so I left him alone and busied myself with my usual jobs, knowing he'd come to terms with the sad news in his own good time.

But over the next few weeks Fred's concern increased. He discovered that his mother hadn't prepared for her death and had given scant thought to what this would mean for Fred and for the farm.

"There was no Will," he said gruffly, a few weeks after the funeral. He pulled his cap lower as if he could hide from the reality

51

of the situation. "My brother Tom and sister, Winnie wants their share right away; Mags says I can have 'er quarter since she's got her own farm to worry about."

"That's good o' Mags," I said softly, stuffing my hands in my jacket and looking out towards the fields. I thought of Fred's older sister and shook my head. What a pity Fred hadn't married someone of Mags's disposition; a lover of the land, a hard worker, someone who thought nothing of rolling up her sleeves and getting stuck in.

"Aye, but where am I goin' to get the money to pay off t'others?"

My heart skipped a beat. I knew where this was going.

"I'm goin' to 'ave to sell Ball Beard, aren't I? Nothin' else for it."

I couldn't believe what Fred had just said. "You can't sell Ball Beard," I snapped, shaking my head. "What about the horses and the cows, what about the foals you were going to breed and the new silage mix you were going to try? What about everything?" I glared at Fred, too horrified to add to my list of why nots. But Fred just stared into the distance, his grey eyes full of a bleak and wintry certainty.

What would Fred do without Ball Beard Farm, where would he go? I realised with a jolt that we were both thinking exactly the same thing.

"I'm sorry." His words sounded hollow and cold, just like the March wind blowing down from the hills and I felt my pity disappear as I kicked the wall in frustration.

"It's not fair!" I shouted. "No-one loves Ball Beard Farm more than you, no-one. They can't make you do it; they can't!"

"They can lass. You're a probate clerk; you should know." He pulled his cap down lower and stared at the pig sty floor.

"But why should you have to give it up for those that don't care? What'll happen to Bonny and Star? What about Dick; he's been ploughing the fields at Ball Beard for almost 25 years? Where would he go? And what about Hero? He's too young to sell; he's not broken yet." I felt the hot daggers of tears and rubbed my face, anger flushing my cheeks red. "No-one would care for this place like you – no-one."

But even as I railed against the injustice of it I knew there was nothing I could do. It wasn't my fault Fred's mother hadn't left a Will. I grabbed a broom and started brushing the farmyard as if my life depended on it: it was better to reserve all my energy for physical work, instead of this stupid emotional drama; it was getting us nowhere. I brushed like a dervish, attacking the pig shit until the cobbles were cleaner than they'd been in weeks.

For the next two hours Fred and I worked side by side as usual; milking the cows in the large shippon, feeding the pigs in the sty, discussing the price of potatoes and the cost of hay and sharing a cup of tea in the farmhouse only this time, there was no black clad witch sitting in the rocking chair, watching us both with her beady, current-like eyes. It was while we were sitting at the table, having a breather, two chipped cups full of tea in front of us, that I made a suggestion.

"Why don't you ask the bank manager for a loan of £3,000? That's all you need isn't it?"

Fred said nothing.

"Other people get loans all the time; why not you?" I added, oblivious to his silence.

"It's not that simple," he growled, suddenly banging his cup down on the table. "You've no idea, lass. The bank wants profitable accounts and you know I've never bothered with that sort of thing." His glare froze on his face and I watched him with wary eyes, just as I would an angry horse. This wasn't a side of Fred I had seen before and I had no idea how to react.

And then, like a thunder cloud, his fury lifted and he reverted back to the Fred I knew: silent, diligent, consistent. I watched him get up from the table and step into the yard before following him. The subject was closed – for now.

I told Dad the news when I got home but for once, I didn't want to hear his pragmatic words; I hoped instead for righteous anger and a rising up with me against the injustice of it all.

"These things happen Janet…" was all he said, before adding that it was actually none of my business. And of course, I knew he was right but that didn't stop me wanting to make it my business.

"Well these things *shouldn't* happen; it's so unfair," I cried. "The farm is being valued tomorrow for probate," I added. Then I recalled Fred's expression as I'd driven out of the farmyard and I felt the bitterness return like a bad taste in my mouth. The gritty stubbornness in Fred's eyes had been replaced with a look of total defeat.

The next evening I drove up from New Mills and parked the van at the farmyard gate. I walked towards the farmhouse, just as I did every day of the week, and went into the gloomy living room. Nothing had changed since the first time I'd stepped over the threshold eight years ago; the floor was still covered in straw and muck, the shot gun still stood propped against the wall, and the single cold tap bringing water into the house dripped on into the sink. I spotted the Brown Betty teapot on the table and put my hands around its fat belly, guessing from the warmth that Fred had been gone about half an hour, possibly on his way to check that the newly planted potato crop hadn't been damaged in last night's storm, or he could be leaning on the gate complaining about the price of livestock with Ernie Castleford. Fred was a creature of habit; he lived by the seasons, and he would probably die by the seasons, preferring to do the same thing at the same time of year - every year. That's how it was in farming; a life of routine and habit. Fred's whole world comprised Ball Beard's 40 acres and I'd never once heard him express resentment at the hard work required to keep it running smoothly. He never spoke to me of being weary or lonely and he certainly never discussed his financial situation, in fact, money was rarely talked about and yet, I knew it wasn't all plain sailing. There were times when Fred would pay a small fortune into the bank after selling some cattle or a few pigs, only to earn nothing at all for the next four or five months. That's how it was in farming; that's how it had always been.

I gulped down a few mouthfuls of lukewarm tea before setting off towards Round Wood, feeling a small shiver of concern as I crossed the farmyard. I remembered Fred saying once that if things ever got so bad he'd got *a plan*.

"What do you mean *a plan*?" I'd asked him, intrigued and only half serious.

"I'd tek meself off to Ernie's land and I'd throw meself down one o't mine shafts."

"But the drop'd be a good 300 feet. You'd never survive the fall and if you did, the water'd sweep you away good and proper. Not even a deep sea diver would be able to get you out of that one, Fred."

And he'd given me such a look from under his cap.

"Oh," I said, shaking my head. "That's the whole point is it?" I decided to call his bluff. "And how bad would things have to be then, Fred? No Christmas card from Mrs Robinson down the way? Molly refusing to give you any milk? Me deciding to hang my wellies up for good?" I laughed. "As if!"

Fred tapped his cap and smiled. "Aye, lass. As if."

But as I trekked off up the hill towards Round Wood I felt my concern turn to dread. What if the thought of having to sell Ball Beard Farm was enough to send Fred over the edge?

Chapter Seven

Molly with her calf, Buttercup

March 1972

I could see him, standing with his back to me, facing the dramatic view down into the valley. His body was angled towards The Torrs, the gorge carved by the rivers Goyt and Sett, on which the town of New Mills stood like a fort, where cotton mills thrived in the 18th century and where walkers now came and sat in teashops and pubs. In the fading winter light I could just make out the sandstone ruins of the cotton mills and the outline of Stockport in the distance but I could tell that Fred wasn't looking at the view. He wasn't a man to stop and stare at the scenery; he was more concerned with the state of the dry stone wall at the boundary. I watched him bend low to give the stones the once over and as he did so Ned licked his face, tail wagging in a furious rhythm.

"Down boy," he said, not without affection, before standing up again and tightening the string around his waist, a subtle tug, as imperceptible as the movement Dad would make when adjusting his tie.

"Fred!"

Fred turned and nodded his greeting, his hand rising in a salute. I could see the strain of his mother's death still etched on his face.

"The valuer's bin," he said, as I fell into step beside him. "Once I've got the report I'll be putting the farm on the market." He squinted into the wind. "You never know, lass, someone might buy Ball Beard and want to keep you on."

I peered up at him, trying to gauge his mood, but my hair kept whipping across my face like a blonde veil.

"My Dad said you might be able to arrange with your relatives to pay them in instalments."

"Nay, they won't wait; Winnie and Tom are both champing at the bit. And I've told you before, the bank wants profitable accounts before they'll give me a loan and I can't give 'em that."

I pushed my hair back but it didn't make any difference.

It was now or never.

58

"I've got about £900 saved, you can have it all. You can ask the bank manager for the rest. He might listen if you're only asking for £2,000 instead of three. You can't sell Ball Beard Farm, Fred it's been in your family for generations."

Fred didn't falter. He carried on walking. The sky above was turning a deep steel grey; the green of the grass seeping into the soil. He stuffed his hands into his jacket, pulling it down over sharp shoulder blades that threatened to cut through the ancient tweed. "I don't need it, take it," I said.

Fred's cap suddenly jerked forward and I wondered if he'd nodded at me.

"Right," he said with a growl. "Just see the bank manager and ask 'im for £2,000. No problem." His stride grew longer. I was running now to keep up. "You think he'd give that money to the likes of me, eh? I'm not a man as works in an office; I don't sit at a fancy oak desk, I dunna have a salary."

'*Like my father, do you mean?*' but I didn't say it. "That doesn't matter, Fred. We've got to do something. For goodness sake, fight! Don't you want to keep the farm and the horses and your way of life? What else is there? What else can we do?"

"I've told ye, I could never get a loan."

"You could try…"

"You know how harsh these Derbyshire winters can be; you know how it can be months sometimes with me not earning a penny. It's the same wi' all farmers; I'm no different. Mother didn't leave a Will and that's that. I have to do what the law says.

59

Winnie and Tom are entitled to their share."

"But they have no interest in Ball Beard Farm."

"No, but they've a right to their inheritance."

The frown grew deeper, the anger more evident until my concern about what Fred would do next became more worrying than his deep-seated irritation with me. I had no more answers to offer so I did the only thing I could think of: I asked him about Round Wood. It was a clumsy diversionary tactic but it was a subject that had been playing on my mind for years and I couldn't think of a better time to bring it up.

"Why is it called Round Wood when there are no trees up here?"

Fred appeared to take the change of subject in his stride. Who knows, perhaps he was relieved not to have to talk about money for a while because, as he told me the story, I felt the strain lifting. "There used to be trees, lass, plenty of 'em; there was a small circular copse just over there." He pointed in the distance. "I can tell you a version of the story we tell to tourists and then I'll tell you the truth if you like?"

I nodded.

"Local historians round 'ere say that all the wood was sawn down in't second world war. They say that Round Wood was directly below the flight path o' German bombers who used it as a navigation tool on their way to Manchester's bombing raids." Fred pushed his cap up a notch. "And since it was so important to the bombers, it had to go. All the wood was removed and, hey presto, the Germans didn't know where they were any more."

"And that's not true?"

"Course not, lass."

"How do you know?"

"Cos my father, Tom Handford, cut it down." I saw a smile flicker on his face as if the telling of the story was just as interesting for him as it was for me. "It was the winter of 1947. The snow was so thick on the ground vehicles couldn't get up to the villages. Come March we were all freezin' as well as starvin' since there was no coal for heat, so people started walking up through Ball Beard Farm to Round Wood and sawing off a bit of firewood here, a bit there. Father didn't object; he knew that without heat there'd be more deaths but the number coming up the hill became a flood so Tom decided to take the law into his own hands; he rallied a work party o' 10 men, walked up to the top one freezing Sunday mornin' with axes and handsaws and set to felling the trees. It took four days to fell and cut the trees into manageable pieces. Then they split 'em and cut 'em and stored them in the farmyard to dry out. I remember Tom payin' the men with as many eggs as we could gather and a barrel o' cider between 'em."

"But why make up the story about the bombers?" I asked.

"Well, it's more romantic than saying it was the fault of one man, isn't it lass?"

"But without your dad's actions you would have frozen to death yourselves."

"People don't see it like that round 'ere," he snapped.

61

"They like to pin the blame on someone in particular for anything they see as …initiative. But as I see it, Tom was just doin' what everyone else was doin'; he just did it better."

I nodded.

"Feelings run deep in these parts," he added. "And there's no point explainin' to 'em if people don't want to listen. Grudges go back generations, lass, generations." Then he pulled his cap back down on his head before falling silent again.

I knew Fred was right. My brother had recently married and ever since the wedding Dad had refused to speak to Pete or his new wife. I had no idea what could have caused the family rift since Dad had always seemed the most rational and reasonable of men; as a father he could not be faulted, but as a father-in-law, well, it seemed he was just as fallible as the next man. The close knit villages of The Peak District were full of such tales; brother refusing to speak to brother, mother ignoring daughter, and I was a little dismayed that the Holt family had now become one more in a long list of families for whom estrangement was a fact of life.

I didn't know if it was the talk of families falling out that suddenly got through to him or the fact I'd included myself in his problems but something in Fred's expression changed; subtle at first, I saw the creases on his forehead release their grip and his pace slowed.

He stopped walking and turned to look at me. "It might work…"

"What?"

"It might work if you …" He stopped but I urged him on. "It might work if you could pay some o' your wages into the farm business every week, so we 'ad a regular income. Then I think the bank would agree to a loan." He touched his cap and set off again, towards the farmhouse this time, his expression grave.

"Then that's what I'll do," I said striding after him. "You can have the £900 and then, and then…I give my mum £4 a week but I save nearly all the rest. You can have £10 a week." I jogged along beside him, eager to hear the problem was now resolved but I could see that there was something else on his mind. He stopped again, this time taking even Ned by surprise.

"Would you like to become a partner in Ball Beard Farm, lass?"

"What?"

"You 'eard. If you're goin' to be puttin' money into Ball Beard you need to make sure your interests are protected. We should become equal partners – assuming we don't go bankrupt first." His expression was still grim but his eyes looked less haunted. I turned briefly to look behind me. In the gathering darkness I could just make out the outline of the semi-detached houses below us, the street lights dotted along the suburban roads like oversized orange lollipops and the River Goyt snaking through it all with its sinister, black trail. There were no skylarks above me singing their tune this time, but the feeling I had in the summer of 1962 when I'd trekked up to this very spot, was exactly the same.

"Yes," I said with certainty. "I'd like that Fred; I'd like that very much."

And he nodded as if to say that that was that then; the deal was done.

We made the agreement formal in so much as we had a contract drawn up at Ingleby's and I became an equitable partner. I never held an equal stake in the farm but that was more than enough for me. Thanks to Fred's offer I'd realised my childhood dream: I was officially a farmer and nothing would ever make me happier than that.

But looking back now, I wonder if I would have been as keen to leap in if the gypsy's curse had been cast *before* I signed the document rather than *after*.

I was strolling into the farmyard, two weeks later, still feeling a foot taller than my four feet 10 inches, when I heard the unusual sound of angry voices. The cursing echoed around the yard as I jogged around the corner where I saw a furious Fred, standing his ground and arguing with one of a group of gypsy travellers who'd arrived a few weeks earlier. They'd asked for some grazing and Fred had agreed to them staying on his land providing they paid in advance. They had complied with his request and had paid for the field as well as a supply of hay for their onward journey. It was now obvious, listening to the animated conversation, that they were leaving today and, in preparation, had spent the last few hours in the barn packing their sacks with hay for the journey. Fred told them they could have 10 sacks for which they'd paid him 10 shillings in total and Fred had pocketed the money, satisfied he'd got a good deal.

But at four in the afternoon, when they still hadn't come out of the barn, Fred had wandered in and watched, amazed, as they each took a handful of hay, twisted it round and round as tightly as possible, tied it into a knot and then pushed it down into the sack. They'd been at it for two hours and had filled just six sacks, each of which weighed about a hundredweight.

Now, most men I know would have been furious and would have accused the travellers of deceit, taking much more hay than had been agreed but Fred had come out of the barn, laughing his head off. It wasn't the fact they'd pulled the wool over his eyes with the hay that was making Fred angry; it was something else entirely.

The argument was heating up. Fred was shouting at the traveller, a small man with dark skin and very white teeth. The man had arranged to buy three of the cockerels that Fred kept in pens in the field. A price had been agreed and the traveller had come to collect the birds. Fred had caught the first cockerel and quickly dispatched it with a twist and pull of its neck but the traveller had thrown his hands in the air shouting, "No, no! I buy them alive; they must be alive!" He demanded that Fred comply with his request but Fred would have none of it, pointing out that the sale was for dead birds, ready for plucking. The explanation, in broken English, was that it was the traveller's religion that dictated that the birds had to be killed in a certain way and ended with him thrusting the bag in Fred's face.

I watched Fred as he stepped forward, pushing the little man hard on the shoulder. "Don't tell me what to do, mate. I don't give a sod about your religion; I've reared these birds and looked after 'em meself and I'm not having you cartin' 'em round the countryside fastened in a bag. Anyhow, I know 'ow you bloody foreigners kill 'em: you hang 'em up and slit their throats then leave 'em flappin' and bleedin': the poor little sods. I'm not having that; you 'ave 'em dead or not at all." Fred advanced slowly on the traveller, his fists clenched by his side. I watched, fascinated. I'd never seen Fred so angry. The traveller shouted back: "We had an agreement."

"Stick your agreement up your arse!"

The traveller stared, black eyes bulging and began to chant at Fred, words I didn't understand, in a language I didn't recognise, before adding with a quiet menace: "There my friend, I have put a curse on you, on your family, on your cows and on all of Ball Beard Farm." Then he turned abruptly and walked away across the lane.

"Good for you, you're no better than these 'ere animals. Now shove off and don't come back!"

Later, sitting at the kitchen table over a cup of tea, I could tell that Fred was still incensed. "Did you hear all that?" he asked. "I welcomed 'em onto my land - which is more than anyone else would do round 'ere - I gave 'em a field for their ponies, let them take me for a fool with the hay and then they have the cheek to start ordering me around with me own bloody livestock." Fred took a large swallow from his chipped cup as I watched the anger slip from his features. "Well, there you go, lass; you're now a partner in a farm with a curse on it. Welcome to Ball Beard Farm."

And we laughed so much I had trouble swallowing my tea.

1972 with my pony, Apache and trap

Chapter Eight

15 March 2010

I stood at the entrance to the consulting rooms and stared at the plaque on the wall: *Dr Belinda Browne-Thomas, Chartered Counselling Psychologist, BSc(Hons), PhD, MA, AFBPsS, CPsychol.* I knew that anyone with that amount of letters after their name was bound to charge a small fortune for their services. I'd told Mary that my budget for sorting out the nightmares was £800 but Mary had warned me to be open-minded.

"These things take time," she'd told me on Tuesday evening after our usual game of badminton with Carol and Claire. "You can't expect Dr Browne-Thomas to come up with all the answers straight away; you've had all this locked inside you for 34 years so I'm guessing it's going to take quite a bit of coaxing to get it out again."

"Well, if it's not coaxed out after eight hundred quid then it's staying there," I said. "I don't care what you or Dr B-T tells me, I'm telling you I've got the nightmares almost under control and I don't want those particular horrors coming back to haunt me like they used to. I need my beauty sleep, Mary."

Mary tried not to smile. "I'm not letting you leave Ball

Beard Farm with your five ugly mutts and a caravan until I know you've got this sorted. What sort of friend do you take me for?"

"A meddlesome one?"

"One who cares," said Mary, firmly. "Sounds to me like you've got these nightmares under control while you're in a place you've lived in for 40 years, but what about when you set off for pastures new? What about when you leave Ball Beard Farm for good? Listen to me Janet: you should get to the bottom of this once and for all, especially now you've told me you can't remember what you did for four days either, I mean, what's all that about?"

"What do you mean; *what's all that about?*"

"Well, that's just it; you can't remember can you?"

"Well, I must have been carrying on as normal for four days since no-one else seemed to notice any different. I don't remember Mum or Dad passing comment on me losing my marbles; mind you, Dad was too ill to notice and Mum was too busy looking after him to pay much attention as to whether I was frothing at the mouth or not."

"Didn't anyone say anything to you at work? I assume someone in your department in the solicitor's office would have commented if you'd been particularly distressed?"

I went quiet.

"What?"

"I wasn't actually at Ingleby's in 1976."

"But I thought you joined the firm in the late '60s and you didn't leave until…well, until you went to prison in 1997."

"I had six months out when I worked full time at the farm."

"You never told me that."

"It never cropped up." I shrugged. "Don't forget, we didn't meet until 1979 and by then I was back at my desk and had been for two years. After Fred asked me to become a partner and our finances bucked up I resigned from the practice. Everything seemed to be going well; I mean, we weren't about to become millionaires any day soon but we were doing okay - but then he disappeared and things got really difficult. I had to do all the work on my own and the joint bank account was frozen, so I had to go back to work at Ingleby's, I had no choice. Fortunately, Miles let me have my old job back."

"Didn't you inherit the farm?"

I gave a wry laugh. "No, of course not. I only had an equitable interest in the farm based on what I'd paid in to it over the years. Fred's daughter, Katrina inherited as next of kin and it usually takes seven years before an estate can be settled in these sorts of circumstances; when there's - when there's no body. Fortunately for me, Katrina managed to sort it in five years but that still meant I had to struggle until 1981 not knowing what the hell was going to happen."

Mary looked at me, trying to take in what I'd said. "But people thought you had something to gain from Fred's disappearance, didn't they? What about that pamphlet Mags is supposed to have written – the one accusing you of having a hand in her brother's disappearance?"

70

"I haven't seen any such pamphlet, let alone read it so I can't comment. For all I know it could just be more New Mills gossip."

"We should get hold of a copy," said Mary, pursing her lips. "That sort of thing shouldn't be allowed."

"But I've told you, when Fred disappeared, Mags was very supportive; the whole family couldn't have been more helpful. They'd come up here at harvest time or any other time for that matter, when I needed them for calving or foaling. I couldn't fault them. The pamphlet – if it exists – was written more than 20 years *after* Fred disappeared."

"So what made Mags turn against you all of a sudden?"

"It was after I went to prison. Implicating Mags' granddaughter, Debra, in my illegal activity wasn't my finest moment. Mags never forgave me for that although, bizarre as it sounds, Debra did."

Mary looked at me with what I can only describe as acute irritation. She was thoughtful for minute or two before carrying on with her train of thought. "What did his family make of Fred's disappearance back then? Did they have any idea where he'd gone?"

I shook my head. "Fred was separated from his wife, Nan, and his daughter Katrina had been living down south for years so I never heard from either of them – except once, when Katrina agreed to sell the farm to me. Fred had very little to do with his younger sister Winnie, apart from paying over her share of the farm when their mother died." I frowned as I thought back to the past. "Fred's brother Tom died not long after his mother passed away so that only left Mags and she was busy with her own farm across the valley. As I said, when Fred disappeared Mags was full of sympathy for me; she and her family did everything they could to help but after I...well, after I went to prison, that all changed."

Mary looked away. "I know. It must have been awful for you."

"There's not a day goes by when I don't regret what I did..."

"You mean the affair with Miles?"

"No, not that."

"Stealing the fifty thousand from Ingleby's, you mean?"

"*No*, implicating Debra. I can't believe I was so stupid. It must have been terrible for her, having to stand up in court and defend herself. I mean, of course she didn't have anything to do with the fraud, that was all my doing; Debra would never do anything like that."

"Well, you shouldn't have passed her that cheque then, Janet. Of all the stupid things to do, you worked in a solicitor's office; you should have known about money laundering."

"I wasn't thinking straight."

"I'll say."

"It's all water under the bridge now," I said sadly.

"Except - nothing's really resolved is it? You don't know where Fred is, you don't know why you're having these nightmares and you don't know why you lost four days of your life. What conclusion did the police come to?"

I looked uncomfortable.

"They must have said something," she pushed.

"Well, yes. There was a suggestion of suicide."

"Why?"

"They said they found '*evidence of disturbance*' at a mine shaft on Ernie Castleford's land which I understood meant they believed that Fred had thrown himself down there, never to be seen again but I don't know - there was no suicide note and for the life of me I can't imagine Fred ever leaving his animals, no matter how bad things got and things weren't that bad for us financially at the time he went missing…" I shook my head. I was fighting back tears now and those familiar feelings of despair were beginning to wash over me. I fought with the desire to scream at Mary and tell her to shut up: I could do without all this, really I could.

"I presume they interviewed everyone, including you?"

I nodded.

"And that was their conclusion was it: suicide?" Mary was bemused. "Well I guess it's too late now to check up on these things; I suppose the file will be buried on some rubbish tip somewhere or…"

"No," I said, interrupting her.

Mary looked at me as if expecting bad news.

"That's just it, Mary, the file is still open.

I looked again at the shiny brass plaque on the wall before

opening the door and presenting myself to the young receptionist who took one look at me and frowned. I felt my hackles rise. *'Get over yourself, Barbie doll,'* I thought to myself. "Janet Holt for Dr Browne-Thomas," was what I said instead. I looked at the immaculately turned out young woman. *'I used to have hair your colour - except mine was naturally blonde'*, I muttered before catching a glimpse of myself in the mirror behind her desk: grey, short hair lying flat on my head, curls cut off long ago, wearing a washed out, shapeless sweatshirt and ancient jeans. I realised I'd dressed for the farmyard not a medical consultation.

"Dr Browne-Thomas will see you now," said the receptionist, recovering her equilibrium and I immediately felt my anger subside. I'd forgotten what effect my appearance could have on other people since I rarely left the farm these days.

I turned in the direction the receptionist indicated and immediately spotted a woman a little younger than myself standing in a doorway, waiting. She wasn't smiling but she didn't look unwelcoming either, just...observant. She had thick, wavy grey hair and penetrating eyes and appeared to be scanning me in a subtle, practised way. "Dr Belinda Browne-Thomas," she said, holding out a hand.

"Janet Holt," I said, feeling like one of Mary's five-year-olds on the first day at school.

Dr Browne-Thomas led me into her consulting room and indicated a chair for me to sit in. I very nearly asked where the couch was but something held me back: I had the distinct impression that humour might not be appropriate in this situation, at least not yet.

The doctor smiled then sat down opposite me behind a plain wooden desk, pen in hand, poised over a spiral bound notebook. I glanced at the page. The date was written in neat, even handwriting across the top but apart from that the page was blank. The rest of the room was as bland as a cheap hotel room but strangely, I felt the lack of character quite soothing.

"What can I do for you?"

I hesitated. For some reason I'd expected more preamble than this. "Well, my friend, Mary, suggested I come to see you," I said. "She's not happy about me going travelling until I sort out these nightmares that I've been suffering for 34 years."

"And would you mind telling me a little bit about the sort of nightmares you have been experiencing, Janet?" Her voice was soft but firm. I felt as if she was guiding me to a response rather than simply asking me a question, if that doesn't sound too fanciful a notion. I hesitated then decided to take the plunge. I was paying quite a lot of money to be here, after all.

"Nearly every night since 1976 I've been waking up crying, screaming and gasping for air. I imagine a - a red door and I've got to get through it, but I can't." I stared at the doctor, challenging her not to believe me but I could see she was making no judgement whatsoever about what I was telling her. I forced myself to go on.

"I keep stretching and reaching out for the latch but it's too far away and then these - these creatures appear and I know they're going to come and get me; gargoyles, monsters, hideous things that make your skin crawl and your blood run cold - and I start screaming at them to leave me alone, to *get off me*, *get away from me* but they don't take any notice and then they follow me; telling me over and over that I'm going to die... and then I'm suffocating - there's hay and straw all around me and I'm drowning in it, it's dragging me away from the door and I'm screaming and clawing my way back to it because I know I've got to go through it or, or these monsters will be right and I will die but I can't get there and…and…" I was gasping for breath, the words falling over themselves to get out. A sob escaped; a great wrenching spasm, gripping me then letting me go again. I couldn't breathe. I'd just plunged myself straight back into a nightmare; a nightmare I couldn't wake up from because I was already awake. What had I done? How the hell was I going to get out of this? How on earth…?

"I don't know what to do. I don't know why I'm having these nightmares, I don't know why, I …"

I stood up and pushed my chair back. Mary had been wrong. There was no point dredging it all up again; no point at all. I'd just about got them under control and now they were back. Oh God, they were back! I flew to the door, my fingers scrabbling for the handle when a firm voice spoke to me from behind the desk.

"Have you seen this door before, Janet?"

I paused.

"Have you ever seen a door like this door in your

nightmares?"

My fingers closed around the cool metal. I could reach the door; I could leave the room if I wanted to.

"No," I said. "Not that I can remember."

"You say these nightmares began in March 1976?" Dr Browne-Thomas' voice was soft and soothing. I felt concern in her voice rather than curiosity and I realised in a moment of clarity that I *did* want to go on; I wanted to tell her. I wanted to tell her about Fred, I wanted to tell her about Ball Beard Farm, I wanted to tell her that Fred had disappeared on 19 March 1976 and that his body had never been found and I wanted to tell Dr Browne-Thomas that Fred's sister, Mags, wanted nothing whatsoever to do with me. It was all inside me and now I wanted to let it all out. I could feel a sense of unburdening myself even as I imagined saying it but I wasn't sure I could do it. I let go of the door handle and turned, taking a tissue from Dr Browne-Thomas' outstretched hand and sat slowly back down in the chair.

Chapter Nine

15 March 2010

Dr Belinda Browne-Thomas told me it was perfectly possible to forget what I'd done for four whole days and still go about my business in a normal manner which was a relief to me since I told her I thought I was going barmy. She called it a fugue state. Apparently fugue states can be caused by a particularly stressful episode in a person's life. She also told me that my recurring nightmares were probably linked to this, although I don't know how she could say that with such authority; she'd only just met me.

"In March 1976, when your business partner, Fred Handford disappeared, did you receive any counselling?"

"No," I said, taking a deep breath.

"Did the police or anyone else suggest you get professional help?"

"No," I said again.

Dr Browne-Thomas' eyebrows rose, creeping closer to each other in the middle of her forehead. She jotted down notes in her spiral-bound notebook but said little, just a nod here, a nod there; encouraging and subtle.

"Do you have any idea what could have happened to

Fred?"

"They say he committed suicide."

"Is that what you believe?"

"I know - knew - Fred better than anyone, and I know he'd never leave his animals or the farm without – without making provision for them."

Dr Browne-Thomas asked me about my memory loss.

"When I woke up on the morning Fred disappeared I knew straight away that something wasn't right. I felt groggy, as if I had the beginnings of a cold, and I had a right headache. I pulled the covers back on the bed and went to put my slippers on as usual but my toes touched something cold and wet instead. There was a pair of muddy wellingtons right there on the carpet."

"Was that unusual?"

"Of course it was; Mum kept a clean and tidy house. But there was other stuff too. I couldn't remember what I'd done on the farm, or what I'd had for my tea, or what I'd watched on telly last night; nothing." I paused and looked up at Dr Browne-Thomas as if the doctor should be able to answer these questions for me. I thought of my mother's words; '*Nothing's so broken it can't be fixed, Janet*' but maybe that wasn't true any more - what if my memory - and my mind - was beyond repair?

The doctor gave me an encouraging nod. I gripped the tissue hard in my hand and took a deep breath before continuing.

"I kept thinking that everything would come back to me but the more I tried to remember the more I seemed to forget."

"What do you mean, Janet?"

"I'd forgotten what I'd done the day before, and the day before that, and the day before that and…after Sunday it's a total blank."

Dr Belinda Browne-Thomas' eyes were watching me with all the intensity of a camera lens.

"I know I'll never find out what happened for those four days. That's why I'm more concerned with the nightmares. My friend Mary said I can't leave for Scotland until I've sorted them out."

There was another nod, slower this time, more thoughtful. "I understand, but you might find that one helps the other."

I considered this before carrying on. "I tried to concentrate on what I had to do at the farm that day. I knew that the door to the shippon needed mending because Dolly, one of our young heifers, kept escaping and Fred and I …" I winced. "Fred and I needed to sort it out. I told Mum I didn't feel like having any breakfast and then I remember saying to Dad, *It's Sunday today, isn't it?*' He put his newspaper down, took off his glasses and he told me straight: *"We'll have no more of this nonsense, Janet; we're not in the mood for any more of your jokes."*

Dr Browne-Thomas looked on as a tear slid down my cheek.

"You were close to your father?"

I nodded. "I told him I was sorry. I knew he was still weak from his stroke; any upset left him breathless and I could tell I'd

80

upset him. I felt guilty."

"We all upset those we love occasionally, Janet."

"You don't understand - he never wanted me to be a farmer; he hated it when I gave up my job at Ingleby's."

Dr Browne-Thomas put her pen down on the desk then clasped her hands together as if she was about to say a prayer. "You may find it helpful if you consider the idea that everyone has the power to choose their own path in life; consider the fact that you have a choice."

I glared at her. "That's not true. Sometimes you..."

"We all have choices, Janet."

I hesitated but decided not to challenge the doctor's concept for now. "I looked at Dad's newspaper and I could see printed right there in black and white: *Friday 19 March*. And I thought to myself: what's happened to Monday 15 and Tuesday 16 and Wednesday 17 and ...and what have I been doing for four whole days?"

I waited but I knew the doctor couldn't possibly have an answer to that question. How could she, she hadn't been at Ball Beard Farm 34 years ago, delivering calves, mucking out pigs, picking potatoes, ploughing the fields. Only Fred and I had done that.

I bit my lip and carried on. "I made up my mind to go to the farm and get cracking with the jobs but even as I was thinking about going up to Ball Beard I felt this awful panic. My hands started to shake, I felt sick. I remember Mum shouting after me as I was leaving the house not to be late; we were having sausages for tea and she said she was going to put some in a dish for Fred."

"Was Fred welcome in your family?"

"I think Mum felt sorry for him. He was the same age as Dad. He never saw his ex-wife or his daughter, as far as I knew."

The doctor picked up her pen. I stared at her, expecting her to say something, but she was quiet and then, something suddenly snapped inside me. "This conversation is a little one-sided, isn't it?"

Doctor Browne-Thomas glanced up but said nothing and I was immediately contrite. I plunged straight back in.

"I...I set off on foot across the fields. As I got closer I found myself picking up speed, until I was running to the farm: I don't know if I was running towards something or running away from it but all I knew was I had this compulsion to look over my shoulder; I had a feeling that something terrible was about to happen and it was literally weighing me down and squashing me into the ground.

"The footpath took me over Ernie Castleford's land and I could see Ernie in the distance. I didn't want to stop, I just wanted to get to Ball Beard as quickly as I could, do what I had to do and then come home again, but he'd think I was being rude if I did that so I had to stop for a chat and while we were talking he said a really strange thing to me: he asked me if I'd managed to get hold of the heifer I'd been chasing across the fields a couple of days ago. He described her to me: the blue roan with horns. '*She came*

82

down that field like shit off a shovel,' he said. '*And the next thing, lass, you were coming down't field after it!*'"

I looked at the doctor. My voice slowed down, just like Dad's used to do. I was choosing each word carefully now before I let it out. "The only blue roan on the farm was Dolly, the heifer, the one that kept escaping through the broken shippon door, but I had no recollection of chasing her round the field, no recollection at all." And as I said the words I felt my heart pound in my chest, as if I'd been running up towards Ball Beard Farm for the last half an hour instead of sitting in a comfortable consulting room.

"How are you feeling, Janet?"

I shook my head. "The farmyard was completely quiet. I thought Fred must have finished his early morning chores and gone in for his breakfast so I opened the back door into the harness room and Fred's sheepdog Ned shot out like a bullet, nearly knocking me over. Fred never went *anywhere* without Ned. '*Fred*!' I shouted, but there was no answer. I put my hands around the teapot on the table. Fred liked his tea and in this freezing weather the kettle was never off the stove but there was no sign of a brew being made in the last hour. And then I turned round and that's when I saw Fred's cap hanging on the hook on the back of the door."

Dr Browne-Thomas looked up, her dark eyes alert. "Is this significant?"

"Fred never went anywhere without his cap," I said. "We used to say that - that hell would have to freeze over first before he'd take it off his head." I rubbed angrily at my eyes.

"And then - and then - you'll probably think this is totally, bloody stupid."

Dr Browne-Thomas said nothing.

"Fred had a calendar; it was a Christmas present from one of the neighbours. It had a picture of a Shire horse ploughing a field across the top and Fred would turn over the plastic pages every day so that he knew what date it was. Only I could see that it hadn't been turned since - the 14 March. I'd never seen the calendar one day out, never mind five. And then it occurred to me. What if he was lying injured somewhere? What if he'd had a stroke, like Dad, and was lying in bed now, too weak to move?" I looked at the doctor with a half-hearted belief that she would be able to answer that question now and give me the excuse I needed not to carry on.

"I opened the door to the hallway and then I looked up the stairs. I'd never been upstairs before but I told myself to get a grip. I went slowly up the stone steps, one at a time, trying not to think of him lying there, helpless, but then the bedroom door appeared in front of me and I had no choice; I had to push it open. The hinge creaked so loud I nearly jumped out of my skin. I forced myself to go in. I was petrified, really petrified."

I stopped and rubbed my eyes again; vigorous movements: to see the image or to block it out, I wasn't sure.

"But all I saw was a single bed - Fred's bed - and it was empty. A blanket had been drawn back as if someone had just got up. I walked over and I touched the sheet. It was cold and damp.

There was nothing much in the room. A bed, an old wooden chair, a small chest of drawers. That was it. Fred wasn't there.

"I went back downstairs and I stood in the kitchen, looking at the calendar. I couldn't get the date out of my mind: *14 March*. Why had the page been left on 14 March?"

Doctor Browne-Thomas put her head to one side and waited. I felt anger inside me, ebbing and flowing at random.

"I looked down at Ned. *"Come on boy, where's Fred?"* I said and true to form he trotted off, but it was obvious he couldn't find Fred's scent. I followed him around, searching the buildings, the barn, the pigsties, the lofts, the hen houses but there was nothing. And then I noticed Marjorie, our only milking cow, standing there in the shippon with a full udder, milk dripping from her teats. Why hadn't Fred milked her? I grabbed a bucket and a stool and relieved her of her burden as quickly as I could while I wondered what the hell I should do next."

"And what did you do next?" asked Dr Browne-Thomas.

"I put Ned back in the farmhouse and was about to set off home when I thought I'd better throw some hay to the cows before I left. Then I saw Dolly."

"The escaped heifer?"

I nodded. "Except the broken shippon door was now mended and hanging on its hinges like new. And then I knew – I knew that I was losing my mind. I threw the rest of the hay to the cows and I set off home. I needed to talk to Dad. I remember telling myself over and over as I ran back down to New Mills:

Dad will know exactly what to do; Dad will know exactly what to do.

Chapter Ten

19 March 1976

I burst into the kitchen in Low Leighton Road, an icy blast of wind following me through the door. Mum stopped pouring the tea and turned, cup in hand.

"What is it, Janet?"

"It's Fred. I don't know where Fred is. He's disappeared; he's gone. It must be bad, Mum, really bad. Ned was locked in the farmhouse - his cap was on the back of the door - I don't know where he is. What if he's dead?"

Mum put the cup down and led me to a chair. "Now then love, are you sure he's not with Ernie?"

"He's not with Ernie," I said firmly. "I know he's not with Ernie."

I understood now that the dread I'd felt that morning was justified. I'd been right to panic. Fred was gone.

"He could have called in to see his sister, Mags, at Greenacres. I'll ring her shall I? That's what your Dad would do if he could. Fred might be there right now, having his lunch." But the more Mum talked, the more I could feel the drama seeping into our warm and cosy kitchen: even she couldn't keep it at bay.

A phone call to Fred's sister revealed nothing.

"Mags says she hasn't seen or heard from Fred in weeks but it didn't sound like she was worried about him, in fact she was quick to move on from Fred and asked me to pass on her thanks for the jodhpurs you dropped off for Debra the other day."

I stared at Mum blankly. *'What jodhpurs?'*

"Apparently they're a great fit, which I must say is a bit of a surprise to me, love, since, last time I looked, Debra was a good six inches taller than you. Janet, what's wrong? You're as white as a sheet."

I couldn't remember going to Greenaces Farm any more than I could remember what else I'd done over the last four days.

Mum sat down next to me. "Now listen, love, don't worry about Fred, I'm sure we'll find him. Do you want me to phone the police? Is that what you think I should do? Shall I call now or…?"

"Now," I said. "Call them now, Mum, please." I let my head drop into my hands. I glanced at the calendar on Mum's wall, just in case, but no, there it was again: Sunday 14 March, the day my world seemed to have stood still and I felt the fear that had stalked me all the way up to Ball Beard that morning come crashing back down again onto my shoulders.

Detective Sergeant Browning of Derbyshire Constabulary told Mum he'd meet us at the farm later that day, which I felt should give me enough time to organise my thoughts. I knew I had to come up with a reasonable description of what I'd been doing for the last four days. I had to convince the police that I had no idea what had happened to Fred and the more time I had to do that, the better it would be. I couldn't afford to be vague and I couldn't afford to be too specific either, but above all I wanted them to be worried enough to conduct a thorough and complete search of the area. Fred wouldn't have gone far, I knew that, and with enough people searching for him, I believed it was only a matter of time before they found him. I sipped half-heartedly at a cup of tea while Mum busied herself getting ready to come with me and then I put my head round the sitting room door to say goodbye to Dad, my heart filling with sadness as I saw him propped up on cushions. "I'll see you when we get back, Dad," I said, hoping my words would give him comfort.

He nodded at me over his glasses. "I'd like to come too, but...." I shook my head and told him it didn't matter and went to give him a kiss on the cheek. I could tell that he was having a bad day. He indicated to me that he wanted to tell me something so I leant in closer. "All the hard work you've put into Ball Beard Farm, Janet, I know I haven't always approved but it's gone well, I can see that and I know that Fred's grateful to you for all you've been doing..."

I put a hand on his arm. "I know, I know, he was only saying the other week how good I am at milking and ploughing now and how I've got the pigs eating the new swill like it's some sort of nectar." I could see a flicker of amusement in Dad's eyes and I wanted to go on and tell him more but I couldn't, there wasn't time.

"We won't be long," I said before letting go of his arm and moving reluctantly out of the room.

I pulled the front door to behind me and spotted Mum, waiting for me in the van, perched on the passenger seat with her handbag on her knee. I swallowed hard and felt the last of my confidence ebb away like the final grains of sand slipping swiftly through an egg timer.

I drove slowly and carefully, the rhythm of the short drive going some way to help clear my mind but by the time I pulled up in the farmyard the panic was back again and the question was going round and round in my head: Where was Fred? Where was Fred?

I could see Fred's sister standing off to one side by the shippon, talking to a police officer. Something Mum had said on the phone to Mags earlier must have persuaded her to come up to Ball Beard Farm after all. I wondered if it was the mention of the police that had persuaded her to drive up from Greenacres because I knew, as sure as eggs is eggs, that if officials were going to get involved then Mags would want to be there; she'd want to make sure that anything that went down in writing was recorded in a manner that suited the Handford family - and suited Mags most of all.

"You say that you had no reason to believe that Mr Handford would leave Ball Beard of his own accord without informing a member of the family, is that right, Mrs Handford?"

"It's Mrs Naylor," said Mags, her tone informing and

admonishing at the same time. "I married into the Naylor family in 1937. I've been widowed these past 13 years."

Sergeant Browning nodded politely. "So, do you have any idea what could have happened to your brother? We've already had a chat with Mr Ernie Castleford of Lane End Farm and he told us your brother had appeared distracted. He said that Mr Handford might have been concerned about his finances."

Mags Naylor shook her head vigorously. "Definitely not."

"Mr Castleford went on to say that Mr Handford had even, on occasion, spoken of, and I quote, '*doing away with himself*' if it all got too much. Had things got too much for him, Mrs Naylor?"

Mags looked indignant. "I don't know what you mean by that. I was left a widow at the age of 46 with no pension and four mouths to feed. I was told I was young and healthy enough to work and that's exactly what I did. That's what Fred did - because that's what we all do." Her voice echoed round the farmyard. "And I know that Fred would never leave Ball Beard Farm without making provision for his animals."

"I see. Mr Castleford mentioned an accident that Mr Handford had last year. What was the nature of that accident, Mrs Naylor?"

"He fell off a horse, I believe." Mags stroked the side of her cheek and looked towards the farmhouse. "Where's Ned?" she asked suddenly.

"Mrs Naylor. How badly was your brother hurt? Was he admitted to hospital?"

Mags glared at the police officer. "It wasn't a bad fall, Sergeant - as far as I can remember. I visited Fred in hospital but he checked himself out almost immediately. He recovered quickly. It wasn't serious. Now, where is Fred's dog and why isn't he out in the fields trying to find my brother?"

"Actually Mags, Fred's accident *was* serious," I said, stepping forward. "If you remember, Paddy bolted while he was pulling the flat cart on the way over to Chinley." I looked directly at the police officer, his eyes flashing at me in the brittle March sun. "Fred had hold of the head collar, Sergeant - he was trying to teach the young horse the route to the corn merchants. A sheep jumped up onto the bank alongside the track and startled the life out of Paddy. The horse bolted and Fred was dragged half a mile down the lane, right into the village. He banged his head so hard he had to have 42 stitches. His skin was hanging off; you could see part of his skull."

Sergeant Browning flinched slightly. I took a deep breath and glanced over my shoulder. Mum stood silent, listening carefully to everything that was being said. "And Ned doesn't know where Fred is, I've already tried that one."

Sergeant Browning cleared his throat; he wanted to assert his authority but, for some reason he appeared to be floundering. "How long ago was the accident?"

"Nine months," I said. "I noticed a change in him almost straight away. Before the accident Fred was always optimistic about the farm and about our future. Afterwards, I'd come up to

Ball Beard of a morning and I'd find him slumped in his chair, thinking gloomy thoughts. He was a different man after the accident, a different man."

"You never mentioned this to me before," said Mags.

"I didn't think it was my place to discuss Fred behind his back," I said quickly.

"Mrs Naylor, when was the last time you saw Mr Handford?"

Mags looked over the police officer's head towards Round Wood and sighed. "A while – but you have to understand, Sergeant, we don't have time to go traipsing round Derbyshire whenever the fancy takes us. Fred knows we're there for him if he needs us. My son comes up every year to help with the harvest and a Sunday lunch is always on the table - for him and for Janet."

"How long, Mrs Naylor?"

"A couple of weeks; two, maybe three."

I said nothing.

"Quite possibly more, but it was very difficult after Nan and Fred divorced. Fred wasn't much of a socialiser. He could be a little…taciturn."

Sergeant Browning made a few notes then turned back to me. "Miss Holt, you appear to be the only person who had regular contact with Fred Handford. When did you last see him?"

"Eighteenth of March. It was a normal day," I added quickly.

"Had he spoken to you of any particular worries?"

"We talked about the crops and the animals, nothing more."

"Were you in a personal relationship with Fred Handford?"

"Certainly not," I snapped. "He was ... he and I are business partners, Sergeant." I saw – or rather felt – Mum and Mags edge closer to me. "We entered into an agreement five years ago. I lent him money and I paid in regular payments from my job as a legal executive until I resigned and began working here, full time, five months ago."

"I told you that was a bad idea," said Mags softly. "Just put extra pressure on you both, didn't it?"

Sergeant Browning looked from me to Mags and back again. His pencil hovered over his pad. "Now, please think about this carefully, Miss Holt; do you have any reason to believe that Mr Handford might have committed suicide?"

I stared at him, eyes focused in shock. "No, there's no reason I know of for Fred taking his own life, none at all."

I felt my legs buckle underneath me. Mum stepped forward and caught me just in time.

"Stop officer, can't you see you are upsetting my daughter," said Mum, suddenly finding her voice. "Please - let's all go into the farmhouse and have a cup of tea. We don't know yet if Fred's simply gone out for the day; he might be home soon and all this worry'll have been for nothing." My arm went rigid. "Come on now, love, a cup of tea'll do us all the world of good."

"I'm not going in there," I hissed. "I'm not going into that farmhouse."

94

Mum looked helplessly at me and then at Mags. The look of defiance on Mags' face had been replaced with one of concern. It was obvious Mags didn't know what to do either. Sergeant Browning stood staring at the three of us until, distracted at the sound of footsteps coming across the yard, he turned and immediately forgot about the tea.

"We've been scouting around and we think we might have found where it happened, Sarge." A young constable half spoke, half gasped out the words.

Where it happened: where what happened, I thought frantically.

"We found some evidence of disturbance at the top of one of the mine shafts on Ernie Castleford's land."

"But that's about 10 foot off the ground isn't it?" asked Sergeant Browning.

"Yeah, our guess is he's climbed up on top and thrown himself down the shaft. It must be a 350 foot drop or more; no-one's going to survive that Sarge, he'd be smashed to a pulp."

Sergeant Browning didn't look at us. "Sounds like it could be the evidence we need," he said, flipping his pad closed and popping his pencil into his top pocket.

"Evidence of what?" We all turned to look at Mags. "What are you saying, Sergeant? That my brother left Ball Beard Farm - a farm, incidentally that has been in our family for three generations - and took himself off to some disused mine shaft on his neighbour's land, climbed to the top and – threw himself down? Is

95

that what you're saying because, if so, I would very much like to know why. Wouldn't you like to know why, Janet?"

The police officers turned to look at me.

"Well?"

I shook my head. "I agree with Mags," I said eventually. "I can think of no reason why Fred would kill himself - no reason at all."

"And you're forgetting one very important thing, Sergeant: my brother's cap is still on the back of the farmhouse door. Fred would never go out in freezing weather without it; none of us ever saw him, rain or shine, winter or summer, without that cap on his head."

Chapter Eleven

CONCERN is growing about the safety of a New Mills farmer, who disappeared over a week ago. After extensive searches police have been unable to trace him.

Mr Fred Handford was last seen on Thursday last week, at their farm, Bailbeard Farm, off Laneside Road.

Police were alerted on Saturday when 56-year-old Mr Handford had not returned home to the farm and they started making inquiries as to where he could have gone.

known relatives and friends and, on Sunday, New Mills and Buxton mountain rescue teams were called out. It was thought that Mr Handford might possibly have gone out to do some job and been hurt.

Extensive searches were made of the farmland, adjoining land and the moorland above the farm, Ollersett Moor, but without success. Police now have no idea where he could be and a police spokesman said, "We are gravely concerned about his

would be very risky and a team could come across dangerous obstacles. The shafts are unsafe and could cave in. Many are probably filled with water or various types of gas.

Police have been in touch this week with the Coal Board but are reluctant to seek assistance from a rescue team until all other lines of inquiry have been exhausted.

At the moment, said a

High Peak Reporter Thursday 25 March 1976

March 1976

I'm walking quietly towards the door, my feet barely touching the ground; I'm floating, drifting along, quietly and peacefully. I feel no fear. This time the door doesn't threaten me, it beckons me to come in. I reach out a hand and take hold of the latch. There's no resistance. I push slowly and hold my breath, peering into the darkness. I want to go in but I have to wait for my eyes to adjust first, the darkness is impenetrable and as I wait the silence begins to suffocate me. I take a step forward, then another step, holding my hands out in front of me then...BANG! My heart pounds. The light from the doorway vanishes and there's a solid wall of black. I stretch my hand backwards, searching for the latch but there is no latch. I scrape frantically, digging grooves into the smooth wood until I feel the blood drip from my fingertips.

BANG! A dull light in the distance grows closer, lighting up a second door. It gapes at me like a huge, red, toothless mouth: the sound as it opens is the very sound of Hell penetrating my soul. I stand petrified as a figure appears in the doorway. It beckons to me, arms floating closer to my face. I put my hands up to protect myself and try to close my eyes but I can't; the face is still there, staring at me, inches from my own. I can see the features now, they're coming into focus but I twist and turn, refusing to look. Oh God, no! The face is mine; I am looking at myself, I am staring into my own eyes. I scream and scream and scream until the noise wakes me up and I feel the bile rise in my throat, the tears stream from my eyes and the panic grips my body like a vice.

On Thursday 25 March I picked up Dad's copy of the High Peak Reporter and felt my fingers turn to ice as I gripped the edge of the paper. The headline told me what I already knew: the search was still going on for the missing farmer. I read the report through twice more, hoping to find something buried in the words; a clue to his whereabouts. '*Mr Fred Handford was last seen by his [business] partner at 6.15pm on Thursday last week, at their farm, Ballbeard (sic) Farm, off Laneside Road.*

Police were alerted when 56 year-old Mr Handford had not returned home to the farm and they started making enquiries as to where he could have gone. New Mills and Buxton mountain rescue teams were called out.'

I stared again at the words. I'd told them that I'd last seen Fred alive on Thursday 18 March. Well, what else could I say? I couldn't remember seeing Fred that day but I'd told the police that I had. And then the divers had gone searching for Fred's body and I remembered what they'd said when they told me that the mine shaft was too deep to penetrate. They'd told me that the constant flow of water running down the shaft was like a 'waterfall' which would have washed the sides clean. And they'd told me that the water at the bottom of the shaft was at least 20 feet deep and flowing fast into Yard Mine, a shaft that hadn't been worked for over 80 years. It was no surprise to anyone when they said it was too dangerous to send a diver down, so they'd used high density lighting instead, lowering it into the shaft on ropes and pulleys. But they found nothing; no clothing, no body, nothing. If Fred had wanted to be swept away, never to be seen again, then he'd made a bloody good job of it.

Moorland hunt for farmer

By STUART WALSH
POLICE and mountain rescue teams were today searching for a missing farmer on desolate moorland in the New Mills area.
Forty-five-year-old Mr

Fred Handford was last seen on Thursday.
He disappeared from the isolated Bow Beard Farm, New Mills, leaving behind his horse and cart, and dog —and the hat he always wore.

A police spokesman said: "Neighbouring farmers said he never went anywhere without them.
"He is a single man and lives in a fairly isolated spot. He has not been miss-

ing for two days and we are worried about him.
Mr Handford is 5ft 10in, slim with a scar on the right temple. He has short hair and is believed to be wearing a tweed jacket, fawn trousers and gumboots.

Manchester Evening News Monday 22 March 1976

Chapter Twelve

9 April 1976

The police asked me to come in for questioning. I was fairly sure they thought I'd got something to do with Fred's disappearance; I'm not stupid, I'd heard the rumours circulating in the village.

"This is Detective Sergeant Browning interviewing Miss Janet Elizabeth Holt at 2.30pm on 9 April 1976. What is your date of birth please, Miss Holt?"

"Twenty-eighth of August 1950."

"Address?"

"Fourteen, Low Leighton Road, New Mills."

"How long have you known Mr Fred Handford of Ball Beard Farm?"

My voice didn't waver. "I first got to know Fred in 1964 when I was 14 and I was looking for grazing for my pony. I used to visit the farm and help out at weekends and then in 1972, after Fred's mother died, he and I went into partnership together. Things seemed to be going reasonably well, or at least I thought they were."

"And was your relationship with Mr Handford purely a

business relationship or were you involved with him personally?"

I looked up at Sergeant Browning. I knew my gaze was steady and my voice, when I spoke, felt as icy as the day Fred disappeared.

"No. I knew there was gossip in the village, if that's what you mean, but Fred never made any advances towards me and he never made any suggestions of that nature. He was old enough to be my father: our relationship was a business partnership and nothing more. I knew about the gossip but I ignored it."

Sergeant Browning nodded but I could tell he didn't really believe me. "What about his state of mind when he disappeared, Miss Holt, had Mr Handford seemed more concerned than usual in the last few days? Mr Castleford, your neighbour, seems to think there might have been money worries."

"As far as I'm concerned, this was not the case. Fred was occasionally moody but in a day or two he'd be right as rain again. He'd had the accident with the young horse, following which I suggested, more than once, that he see the doctor to get himself checked out but Fred always replied that he didn't have time. He told me to mind my own business."

"Mind your own business?"

"If you want the precise words, Sergeant, he told me to fuck off."

"I see. And why did you suggest that he went back to his doctor?"

I pushed the hair back off my forehead and sighed. "Last

101

summer, a few weeks after his accident, I came up to the farm as usual and asked him why he had dried blood all over his shirt. He told me the blood was as a result of taking out his stitches."

"The stitches in his head following the accident?"

"Yes, he'd taken out his stitches himself – with a pair of scissors." Sergeant Browning looked at me as if, once again, he didn't believe me. I glared at him. "That was the sort of man he was; tough, no-nonsense…"

"His sister called him taciturn."

"Yes, if you like. He didn't suffer fools; he was a man who loved his farm and he loved his animals. He didn't have time for anything else, not even a trip to the hospital. You won't understand that sort of thing Sergeant; unless you're a farmer yourself."

Sergeant Browning didn't take offence. "Did Fred Handford have any enemies?"

"None that I knew of. Fred wasn't much of a socialiser and he didn't have many friends - but he didn't have any enemies either."

"What about his wife and daughter?"

"You would have to ask Mags about that."

"Did you ever see either of them at the farm?"

"Once, I think. I may have seen Katrina at the farm once – but that was 10 years ago."

"Was their relationship a close one?"

"No," I said, staring at the clock on the wall.

"I want to go back to the rumours, Miss Holt. You do

102

realise that a lot more is being said about you and Fred Handford; that you and he were close in more ways than one? There are some who suggest that you were having an affair with him and that you had fallen out and..." Sergeant Browning paused. "Is this true, Miss Holt?"

I looked directly at Sergeant Browning. "I know what you're getting at Sergeant and I'm telling you it's ludicrous, bloody ludicrous."

"Were you responsible in any way for Fred Hanford's disappearance?"

I glanced up and bit my lip. "Responsible? What do you mean, responsible?"

"I think you know what I'm trying to say." His voice had an accusing edge.

I put my hand to my mouth and took a deep breath. "I didn't kill him, if that's what you mean."

"You were set to gain financially, though, weren't you?"

"No, not at all. Fred hasn't left a will and things are very difficult for me at the moment. I will probably have to go back to work at the solicitors. I'm hoping there'll be an opening there for me soon. Our bank account has been frozen. Katrina will eventually inherit the farm, when and if she can obtain a..." I sat quite still. "When she is able to obtain a Presumption of Death certificate."

Sergeant Browning looked neither pleased nor disappointed. "No suicide note was found, Miss Holt."

"I'm aware of that. That's what's so strange. That's why I'm thinking he can't have committed suicide. I keep thinking Fred's going to walk back into the farmyard at Ball Beard tomorrow and tell me everything's fine and he'll ask me how the cows are doing and he'll ask me how the pigs are going on and then he'll ask me about the crops in the fields and I'll pour him a cup of tea and we'll carry on with our business just as we've done these past 12 years. I've known Fred Handford since I was 14 years old Sergeant and I never had him down as a man who would give up on the farm; never in a million years."

Sergeant Browning narrowed his eyes as he looked at me. "Is there anything else you would like to mention regarding Mr Handford's disappearance, Miss Holt?"

I nodded. "I don't know if this is relevant but, on 19 March, when I was searching for Fred in the farmhouse, I noticed a half bottle of whiskey was missing from the shelf in the kitchen, next to the calendar. Fred hadn't touched it since the Christmas before last. Fred rarely drank and I remember wondering why the whole bottle had suddenly disappeared."

"I see. That's interesting." Sergeant Browning appeared to be putting two and two together. "Did Fred ever mention to you that he had considered taking his own life?"

"Only in the same way he had with Ernie. We thought he was joking, but if he had wanted to do it then he would have known which mine to choose."

"What do you mean?"

"He was very interested in the local pits. He knew where to go to get…" I hesitated. "He knew where to go to get coal without paying for it, Sergeant. He'd come back with a bag full every now and again. He didn't think of it as stealing since no-one else was mining the pits round here. He was just using his initiative." *Just like his father before him*, I almost added.

Sergeant Browning made a final few notes before signing off the statement then he followed me to the door. I looked up at him; he was about twice my height and twice my weight.

"I know what you're thinking, Sergeant," I said, suddenly turning round to face him. "But as my Mum always used to say, appearances can be deceptive. Just because we worked together every day of our lives doesn't mean we were close. Fred and I loved Ball Beard Farm, nothing else, just Ball Beard Farm."

Sergeant Browning glanced down at me before stretching over my head and opening the door. I walked out, without a backward glance, into the calm suburban street. I knew he didn't believe me but I also knew he couldn't seriously accuse me of anything either: Fred had disappeared but there was no body and I had no motive for murder. It was thanks to the gossipers in New Mills pointing their fingers at me that the police suspected me. I'd heard people say I'd been having an affair with Fred and I'd heard others say that there was another farmer fighting it out with Fred for my affections and that we'd got rid of Fred together. And which farmer was I having a bit of hanky panky with then? Ernie Castleford? It was too ridiculous for words. There was no possible explanation for Fred's disappearance – only suicide. The problem was I had no idea why Fred would kill himself and if *I* didn't know why he'd gone and jumped down a mine shaft, what chance did the police have of uncovering a reason?

Chapter Thirteen

March 1977

I looked at my face in the mirror. "Everybody looks like this at five in the morning," I muttered, trying to convince myself that grey bags under my eyes, skin as translucent as wet tissue paper and hair like a bedraggled Yorkshire terrier was normal – well it was if you had a full time job as well as a 40 acre farm to run.

I heard Mum's voice next door, hushed and concerned. Dad had suffered a second stroke three weeks ago.

"Fancy a cuppa, Mum?" I whispered.

"That would be lovely," said Mum with a tight smile, before turning back to Dad and tucking in the eiderdown under his emaciated body. "I'll be down in a minute. I'll make you some breakfast."

"No, you stay with Dad; I'll sort something when I get to the office. Did you get any sleep?"

Mum shook her head.

"I'm sorry Mum, I wish I could do more …"

"Don't you worry love, you've enough on your plate and besides, it's only me he wants."

I wasn't sure that was true but it was certainly what Mum believed. "I might be late tonight, Sandy's about to calve and she seems a bit out of sorts. I said I'd meet Margaret, the vet, up at the farm after work; she said she'd check her out and put my mind at rest." I waited for a response but none came. "I'll call you after lunch to check how Dad's going on."

Minutes later I was pulling on my jeans and dragging a comb through my hair, putting my concern for Dad's health to the back of my mind, not because I wanted to, but because I had to. Then at 5.15am I was driving at breakneck speed up an empty Laneside Road, just as I did every morning, glancing at my watch every few minutes.

The cows and the pigs were all inside, still on winter rations, so they needed feeding; and then there was the shippon to clean and the ponies to be fed. There were doors to be mended and fences to be fixed, muck carting, muck spreading, ploughing, planting, chain harrowing, rolling and walling; the list was never ending and as everyone knew in farming, each job had its own seasonal time limit. I shook my head and nearly laughed out loud at the ridiculousness of it all: why, only last week I'd decided to write down all the jobs that needed doing and got as far as 30 before giving up. "No wonder I look like an undernourished dwarf," I said out loud, glancing at myself in the rear view mirror. "Hi ho, hi ho, it's off to work we go."

I pulled up in the farmyard, opened the door of the van and plonked my foot down, right in the middle of a puddle, the freezing cold water splashing in over the top of my boots and soaking my toes. "Bloody 'ell," I muttered before leaping over the next six puddles to the farmhouse door.

As usual, Ned was there to greet me with an exuberant bark of approval, just as eager for his breakfast as he was for human company. Then I turned to the calendar, glancing at the Shire horse as it pulled the plough patiently across the field, never quite reaching the other side. I closed my eyes and took a deep breath. The nightmares only came when I was asleep, but the memory of those nightmares was as close to the surface as ever, ready to rear up and attack me at the slightest provocation. I stared at the date as I turned the page: *18 March* - almost a year to the day since Fred disappeared.

My hand strayed to Ned's head as I lowered myself into Mrs Handford's ancient rocking chair. "I can do this," I said out loud. "I can do this, Ned, no matter what anyone thinks. I shall keep Ball Beard Farm going until Fred comes back; any day now he's going to walk into that farmyard out there and ask me how I've been, and then we'll carry on as if nothing's happened. I don't care what anyone thinks: it's not my fault he's gone. I tried to persuade him to go to the doctor; I tried till I was blue in the face. You can take a horse to water, but you can't make him drink, isn't that right, Ned? I can't talk to Dad and I can't talk to Mum but I'm telling you now, he'll be back; before this summer's out, Fred Handford will be back where he belongs, with me, at Ball Beard Farm."

I rubbed my face and stood up again, steadying myself with a hand on the kitchen table then I pushed the hair back off my forehead only to see, out of the corner of my eye, Fred's battered flat cap, hanging on the back of the door. I cried out loud, a hand flying to my mouth, the image as shocking and as brutal as a knife in my heart. Why the hell hadn't I removed his cap before now? Why hadn't I thrown it down the mine shaft, just as I'd threatened to do a year ago? Ned must have nudged the door to; I'd forgotten it was there. I walked across the room and flung the door back, hitting the wall so hard the cap flew to the floor, landing on the dirty flagstones like a hideous squashed fly then I took one last look at it before turning away, my heart beating furiously in my chest. "I can do this," I said out loud. "I can bloody well do this."

The wind outside hit my face with the force of a gale but, keeping my head down, I forced myself across the farmyard, striding towards the shippon as the memory of last night's nightmare swirled above my head like a storm cloud. I had to check on Sandy, that task had priority now. Margaret was coming up this evening to see that all was well but, before then, I had to make a pen so Sandy was comfortable as she prepared to calve.

As soon as I pushed the door open I could tell something was wrong. The chill outside had permeated the walls of the shippon, turning the straw beneath my feet to an icy crisp. I saw the mound on the floor and even before I stepped closer I knew what it was; I knew that Sandy's calf had been born in the night and I knew it was dead, suffocated with its own membrane.

110

I stood and stared at the lifeless lump, anger and disappointment dragging me down so low I almost fell to my knees. This was all my fault. "You stupid fucker, Janet!" I screamed. Fred wouldn't have cocked up like this. He would have known to leave the cow loose and she would've been able to lick her calf clean. I'd misjudged it like an idiot and now look at them both. "I'm bloody useless I am; useless and fuckin' worthless." Sandy mooed gently as I bit my lip but all I could do was turn to get the wheelbarrow. I didn't have time to feel sorry for myself: I had to ring Margaret now and cancel her visit, and then I had to do what I had to do before going back home to change and driving to work. Today I had to get Miles' authority for the course I was about to sign up for: it was time to get serious about earning more money and the only way to do that was to study for further qualifications, although, God only knows where I was going to find the time.

By 10 o'clock that morning, I felt as if my head was about to explode. How many times did I have to explain to the bank manager that the overdraft would be reduced when my salary went in and not a day before? I sat at my desk at Ingleby's and let my head fall into my hands. Oh, why did Fred have to disappear and why was running the farm so bloody difficult without him? And why, oh why wouldn't these nightmares stop?

There was a knock on the door. I looked up just as the handle turned and for one brief, stupid moment I thought it was Fred come back to see me. But as soon as I caught sight of the sleeve of that immaculate tweed suit I knew it wasn't him at all. I struggled to pull myself together; it wouldn't do to appear unprofessional in front of my boss.

I stood up, placed both hands on my desk and took a deep breath.

"Good morning Miles."

"Morning, Janet. I'm hoping you can update me on how probate is progressing on Edward Bolton's will. His son said he could come in tomorrow if…" Miles paused, his intelligent green eyes scanning me for clues. "He said he was free to sign the document on Monday if that was convenient for you. I understand you had initially suggested today." He was watching me with a peculiar expression on his face. I knew my hair was wilder than usual and my clothes more dishevelled. "I know Mr Bolton is a busy man, so I am assuming you will accommodate his request. But then I'm sure you know all there is to know about being busy. How is Ball Beard Farm doing by the way?" His expression conveyed professional concern; his body language seemed to be saying something else.

I nodded and leant more heavily on my hands. "Fine," I said.

He took another step towards me. "Jean tells me that you have been a little distracted of late."

I turned my head. "Jean?"

"Yes, your secretary tells me you have a lot on your plate; your father's health, the farm, Fred's disappearance …the gossip in

112

the village."

"I don't listen to gossip."

"No, and you'd be absolutely right not to but, if you're worried about something I would prefer it if you told me. I am your employer, Janet. If you need some time at home or…"

"It's not that," I snapped.

"Then what is it? When I invited you to rejoin us it was because I knew what a diligent worker you are. You also know that I was particularly disappointed when you resigned last year." I heard the emphasis on the word 'particularly'.

"If there's anything you need to tell me, Janet, anything at all." He put his hand on the desk next to mine. I glanced down at his clean finger nails and smooth skin before almost whispering the words.

"It's a year," I said, finally. "It's a year since Fred disappeared."

He nodded.

"But the police are no nearer finding out what's happened to him. They're saying that he committed suicide but there's - there's no body, so no-one really knows if that's true and the bank account's still frozen and Katrina can't do anything with the farm for seven years so I have to keep going no matter what - but I don't know if I can. I've got cattle to feed and fields to plough and walls to mend and pigs to muck out and, oh God, the nightmares; they come every night and then in the morning it feels like I've had no sleep at all." I picked up a pen and moved it from one side of my desk to the other. I'd never spoken about the nightmares before. Part of me was shocked that I'd told Miles while another part of me wasn't shocked at all. There was something about his natural authority that invited my confidence; as if by sharing the horrors of my nightmares Miles might be able to make them bearable.

"What do you dream about?"

"I'm trying to get through a door; I'm trying to escape…"

"From what?"

"I'm not sure, but when I get closer I realise that it's…" I gripped the table and took two more deep breaths. "That it's…that I'm…that I'm running away from me - and I'm petrified."

Miles almost laughed. "That doesn't make sense, Janet. Why would you be trying to escape from yourself?

I shrugged. I had no idea.

"It's nonsense," he said quietly. He'd moved closer and was standing next to me now. He put his hand on my shoulder, squeezing me tight so I had to turn to look at him. "You are confident, assured, and very sweet, but you are not in the least bit frightening."

"Perhaps there are some people who don't agree with that analysis?"

"Janet, I've worked with you for 10 years; I think I know you well enough to pass comment. No-one wants to escape from you; in fact, most people I know would prefer to get closer to you."

I narrowed my eyes. "I am beginning to think that Fred Handford had a strong reason to get away from me."

114

"And I believe you are over-complicating the matter."

"What do you mean?"

"It's obvious to the police that the man committed suicide, so why doubt it? The fact Fred's body was never found tells you nothing. Fred probably knew what he was doing; he threw himself down the deepest mine shaft in the area because he wanted to do the job properly."

"But why didn't he leave a suicide note?"

"I take it Fred was a man of few words?"

I nodded.

"Then I think we can assume that Fred thought it was no-one's business but his own if he wanted to take his own life."

"Really? And how would you feel if your business partner buggered off without a word to anyone? I'm sorry," I said, suddenly aware that I was speaking to my boss. "I didn't mean…"

"It's perfectly all right, Janet, emotions – and all that. Carry on."

"And then there's the gossip going round New Mills: even Mags is starting to look at me sideways now and she knew Fred as well as I did. Neither of us can come up with a reason for him doing such a thing. And as for the nightmares; well, putting up with them every night is enough to make me think I really am going off me rocker."

"You are not going off your rocker," said Miles, looking at me with the smile he used in court, appealing to the magistrate to see things his way. "I know how much pressure you've been under

115

these last 12 months: who in their right mind wouldn't suffer a few bad dreams as a result of that?"

I wanted to explain to him that what I was suffering from wasn't a few bad dreams, but mind altering images so vivid I was frightened to go to sleep, the effects of which were starting to affect my judgement. The nightmares were literally sapping my energy and whittling away at my self esteem. It was no exaggeration to say I was physically exhausted with the effort needed to appear sane in the 18 hours I was awake every day – you only had to look at me.

"You can come to me whenever you want," he said, the grip on my shoulder softening. "I have your best interests at heart and I want you to know that."

Miles' words had the strange effect of loosening my muscles; I felt that if he pulled his hand away now I would probably fall forward and collapse at his feet. "I admire you, Janet; I admire the way you fight for what you want. In fact I've always admired you."

I felt my eyelids grow heavy. Miles' handsome face and green eyes blurred in front of me. I tipped towards him, feeling as weak as a day-old heifer. I could smell the clean, fresh aroma of starch mingled with aftershave but all I could think about was how much I wanted to lie down, right now, under my desk, and go to sleep – and that thought didn't budge from my mind, even as he kissed me softly on the cheek.

Chapter Fourteen

1977

"Janet, are you busy?" Miles knocked and walked in to my office without waiting for a response. I looked up at the sound of his voice and felt a familiar, dramatic pull in my chest. Miles' features were extremely pleasing on the eye; it was like watching my young stallion Apache parading himself around the fields in full view of everyone, his head turned to show his equine beauty to its best advantage. I'm not being fanciful, but there was a certain animal quality to Miles that I liked.

I smiled at his vanity, his artfully brushed hair concealing a centrally located bald spot but framing a handsome, high cheeked face. All in all, he could afford to be confident.

"I intended to propose lunch today but I've just remembered that you signed up for the legal executive course which means, I suppose, that you can ill afford the luxury of an hour away from your desk." He smiled to show he was joking then coughed slightly and pulled his shirt cuff down from under his tweed jacket to show that, on second thoughts, he might not be. "Remind me, what subject are you immersed in at the moment?"

"Conveyancing - but I am allowed to eat, you know."

Miles raised an eyebrow at me. He could never make up his mind if he disapproved of my manner or not. I was the only one of his employees who addressed him like this; all the other girls in the office simpered slightly when they spoke to him. I think he found that irritating - but normal.

"In that case, how about 1.30pm?"

"One thirty's fine. I'll nip to Geo's and pick up a couple of tuna sandwiches, shall I?"

"Not for me: ham and mustard, fresh fruit salad and one of Geo's fabulous coffee cakes if you don't mind. Meet me in my office; I've got a proposition to put to you, one I'm hoping will fit in with your other commitments." Miles hesitated then, uncharacteristically, let his impatience get the better of him. He stepped fully into the probate office, pulling the door quietly behind him. "How's Walter?"

I was pleased but surprised at his concern for Dad. "Not good, why?"

"I have a conference in Manchester next week. I'd like you to come."

"I see. Well that might be difficult. I've got two new calves to see to, fence painting and a field to plough this weekend." But even as I was speaking I had to admit that a legal conference might be a welcome change from my usual schedule of probate followed by pig shit. "But if it's only one night..."

"I'm sure your mother could cope and besides, I thought you'd got rid of some of your more demanding animals." I almost smiled. Miles was not a farmer, but he sometimes liked to pretend that he understood the ins and outs of my world. "You've halved the number of livestock haven't you?"

"Yes, but I haven't halved the workload. I've still got the cows, the hens, the crops, the horses…and then I've got the ILEX legal course to study for now and my clients to consider, and, don't forget, there's my social life to squeeze in somewhere along the way."

Miles held up one long-fingered hand, as if he was stopping the traffic. "Your social life? Well, if you come to Manchester with me next week you can combine work with …pleasure." His green eyes looked at me closely. "And any time you save in the process you can then spend either at Ball Beard Farm doing whatever it is you do up there or, you can put in a few hours with ILEX. How does that sound?"

I laughed. "Well, if you put it like that, I suppose I've no choice."

"That's settled then. I'll get Jean to book you a single room for Friday night, shall I?" Miles tipped his head to one side and waited with his hand on the door as if he expected me to answer that question with: *'don't worry about a single room, let's book a double, shall we, and save the firm some money'* but I had already turned back to the work on my desk. I didn't have time for his none-too-subtle innuendo.

In Manchester the following week I dutifully sat through a three hour seminar on the Administration of Justice Act, taking

119

notes on the changes that Ingleby's would have to implement following recent amendments to the Act. The seminar dealt with how to protect the interests of a surviving spouse if a partner died intestate.

"If only Fred had left a Will," I said with a wry smile. "Settling his estate would have been much less complicated." I was sitting opposite Miles in the hotel restaurant, enjoying the chicken Kiev almost as much as I was enjoying the company.

Miles leant across the table towards me. "Ah yes, but it wouldn't have helped you, would it, Janet? You have to be married to be a spouse, remember?"

I dropped my knife with a clatter. "What did you just say? A *spouse* - that would never have happened," I hissed. "How can you even say that?" I glared at him with a fury that took both of us by surprise. Miles recoiled as sharply as if I'd slapped him across the face.

"I'm sorry, I thought...."

"Fred and I were business partners, nothing else, just business partners."

"Yes but the Administration of Justice Act states…"

"I know what it states and that's not the issue. For your information, I've never had a relationship with another man; not Fred, not anyone."

"You've never had…" He glanced at the next table. No-one was paying us any attention. "You've never slept with another man?"

I shook my head.

"You've had boyfriends I take it?"

"Of course I've had boyfriends; I've just never had sex with any of them." I met his gaze, blue eyes duelling with green, until Miles finally gave in and looked away.

My anger hovered over us like a thundercloud, the closeness of the previous few hours almost evaporating in the heat. I stared at my plate of unfinished food, my newly trimmed blond hair like a neat halo around my head until Miles sighed in defeat. "I'm sorry," he whispered and I nodded, not quite ready to accept that he was speaking the truth.

It was a full two hours before he could placate me enough to join him for a nightcap in his room by which time I think he was too exhausted to remember why he'd invited me up there in the first place. We fell asleep, lying next to each other on the bed, his feet entwined in mine, my head nestled on his arm. By the time I woke up in the morning, Miles told me his arm was completely dead.

Miles lay on the bed while he watched me get dressed. He said the smooth skin on my body made him think of a time when the whole world was younger and more innocent and I told him to stop being so fanciful. He said that the lace of my knickers reminded him of a spider's web which I thought was daft too – but quite poetic.

"How on earth can anyone as delicate as you find the strength to farm 40 acres of land, rain or shine, 365 days of the year? How do you get up at 5am every morning and put in four hours of backbreaking physical labour before arriving at the office, clean, fresh, and smiling?"

I ignored him. "Isn't it about time you got up, sleepy-head?" I said: a much simpler question, if you ask me. I pulled a clean white shirt over my head, undoing just the top two buttons to save time then toyed with the idea of bending over the bed and kissing Miles good morning. But I knew if I did that he might try to persuade me to get back in with him and it was already 7.30am; I didn't have time. I could feel the pressures of the day starting to crowd in already and it was time I phoned Mum to check how Dad was doing.

"Did you sleep well?" Miles stretched towards me and almost succeeded in grabbing my arm. I turned to look at him, lying on the bed like a cat who'd just got the cream. I looked at the slant of his cheekbones, the fullness of his lips and the slightly louche floppiness of his hair and realised how ridiculous it was that I should be falling in love with Miles Ingleby: he wasn't my type at all. He looked like a matinee idol; someone Mum might swoon over in the cinema, not a man who could help me muck out the pigs or harvest the potatoes. I couldn't think of a man less suited to a farming life than Miles.

"I had a wonderful night's sleep," I said, realising with a jolt that it was true. There had been no nightmares last night, in fact I hadn't dreamt of anything except kissing the man in whose arms I had lain from midnight until seven this morning and because of that I felt rested, relaxed and almost cat-like myself.

"You ready for another day of legal analysis?" I teased.

Miles groaned. "I'd rather analyse your body any day of the week."

I laughed and took a step closer to the bed. "But if I allow you to do that I might be setting a precedent and I think you'd agree, Mr Ingleby that would be dangerous. You are my boss after all and we're here to discuss changes in the law."

I stared down at his bare chest and broad shoulders and felt desire pass through my body like a bolt of electricity. I was shocked at this sudden ability to flirt. I'd never managed – or wanted - to do that before.

He lifted a hand in a sort of request while he let his eyes drift down from my face, over the two open buttons of my shirt. I took his hand in mine and felt his warmth on my skin, then took a step closer, the cool of the bed sheets brushing against my bare leg. I could hear him breathing; a gentle rhythm, lulling me, reassuring me, his breath a whisper of warmth on my thigh. I bent lower and kissed him on the lips.

"Janet," he whispered and I nodded, pulling my shirt back over my head and slipping into bed beside him like a cat coming to curl up beside the fire, stretching luxuriously in the heat. I kissed him, my eyes closing as I let him guide my hand beneath the sheets. I knew then that there would be no legal discussion today. Miles had been right: we didn't need that single room after all.

Afterwards, we lay together side by side, our bodies

pressed against each other, our mutual heat cooling on our skin. I felt my eyelids grow heavy and nudged my hand closer to Miles, wanting to hold on to him as I drifted off to sleep but his palm lay still and his fingers didn't seem to want to wrap around mine. I tried again; worried that I could feel a reluctance nudging between us in the bed, as cold and sharp as a frost-tipped blade of grass. I shivered but remained still.

I lay on the bed, the twisted sheets wrapped around our limbs like flimsy leg irons, holding my breath until he spoke and when he did I felt the bed fall away, tipping my world on its axis, throwing me into an abyss - only this time I wasn't dreaming; this time I was awake.

"You didn't need to lie to me, Janet."

He sounded like an efficient lawyer - nothing more.

"I don't know what you mean."

"I wouldn't have minded; we all have a history. God only knows how many sexual partners I'd had by the time I was 27."

"I said I don't…"

"Please, no more." I felt him shrug his shoulders as he lay next to me. "I don't think less of you. Do I know the chap? Was it one of your farming fraternity?"

I froze. "I was a virgin before this morning, Miles. I've never been with another man; I've already told you that."

"Really?" I heard the doubt in his voice. "That would make this morning very, very special if that was true."

"It is true."

124

"Is it?"

"Yes."

He sighed deeply and then, as if he'd made a decision to believe me even though he didn't, he slid his hand across the bed. My heart stopped pounding and I was able to close my eyes and listen to his breathing as he fell asleep, his head against my shoulder, his leg wrapped around my body.

This time I stayed awake. I was scared that the nightmares wouldn't leave me alone and today I didn't want to think of the lonely horrors that had haunted me for the last 12 months. I felt safe with Miles and I knew he would protect me. I felt sure of that fact.

But of course Miles couldn't protect me from reality. In 1979 Dad finally passed away and so began Mum's long downward spiral into depression.

In 1981 Fred's daughter, Katrina, succeeded in getting a Grant of Letters of Administration to her father's estate, based on the presumption of his death on or after 18 March 1976 and I made enquiries about buying her out. No-one was more surprised than me when the bank agreed to give me a loan.

The day the loan was approved I took a moment to reflect, up on Round Wood, remembering when I'd looked down from this very hill almost 20 years ago. I thought now of Fred and the circumstances that had led me to become the owner of the farm, wondering if there was the faintest chance he was still alive. I knew that if he did return I would give Ball Beard Farm to him without question but something in my heart told me that this was never going to happen. Instead I began to make plans; I vowed to increase the cattle numbers and maybe one day renovate the farmhouse. Fred would approve of that. The farm was holding its own, but without Fred to help me I knew it would always be a fight to survive.

Chapter Fifteen

8 April 2010

"Tell me, why did you decide to seek help, Janet?" It was the day of my second appointment with Dr Belinda Browne-Thomas and she was looking at me with those distinctive dark eyes.

"As I've already mentioned; I've got this meddlesome friend, and she insisted that I come to see you before she'd let me go off travelling with my caravan so I didn't really have a choice."

"We all have a choice, Janet."

"You don't know Mary. She won't even let me go to the supermarket on my own these days; she's worried I'm going to have a breakdown at the check-out but I told her the only reason I'm likely to lose my marbles in Tesco's is if they stop stocking my favourite yoghurt."

Dr Browne-Thomas raised her eyebrows but didn't smile. "I would also be interested to know why you chose to see a professional about your nightmares now, after 34 years."

I thought about that for a moment. "I think it's too late to find out why Fred disappeared," I said sadly. "And I don't think I'll ever discover what I did for those four days in March 1976 but, as I say, I'm planning on selling the farm and if there is anything I can do about the nightmares before I leave then I'm prepared to give it a go."

Dr Browne-Thomas looked thoughtful. "I believe a treatment known as EMDR may be suitable for you."

"What's that?"

"EMDR is a psychological treatment method that can help in the retrieval of forgotten traumas. It was first developed by an American clinical psychologist, Dr Francine Shapiro in the 1980s. Eye Movement Desensitisation and Reprocessing is essentially guided eye movement. I would move my hand in front of your eyes, like so," Dr Browne-Thomas waved her hand slowly in front of my face, like the Queen waving to her subjects. "I would do this while encouraging you to relive a specific experience, one that could help in understanding your trauma and go on to explain your nightmares. The EMDR therapy brings the inaccessible details of the experience to your conscious mind while the method - the hand movement - allows you to resolve the old experience and cancel its traumatic nature."

"What do you mean: cancel it?"

"In the sense that if the treatment is successful you will be able to recall the event voluntarily and feel the pain of the old experience - but you will be in control. In effect you will be able to determine whether or not to re-experience the event and to what degree. You will have a choice."

I waited for a moment before speaking. When I did my

128

voice was quieter, less sure. "As I've already said, doctor, I don't see how you can get to the bottom of something I have no knowledge of. How can you make me remember something from 34 years ago? I don't mean to be rude but all you're doing here is wafting your hand in front of my nose."

"The movement will be much more rapid," said Dr Browne-Thomas with a slight smile. "The idea is that I will get you to focus on the trauma, not on the eye movement. Your repressed memories should come back to you spontaneously. It may not happen instantly, but you should see the results within three or four sessions."

I looked away. "And how much will all this cost?"

Dr Brown-Thomas told me that her charges were £120 an hour. She also told me that each session usually lasted no more than 60 minutes.

"At this stage would you like to hazard a guess as to what's causing my nightmares?"

"It's too early to say with authority but I would guess the trauma of Fred's disappearance and your arrest 20 years later may have something to do with it."

"My time in prison had nothing to do with Fred."

Dr Browne-Thomas nodded. "No. Well, the treatment should give you all the answers you need."

"I still don't see how it can. If I can't remember something now, how will I remember it in the future?"

"The physiology of the brain indicates that the EMDR

technique does not do anything extraordinary to the mind, the brain simply retrieves the memories. I like to use the analogy of storing those memories in a filing cabinet, or, in your case perhaps, keeping them in a bucket."

"A bucket?" I suddenly realised that this was Dr Browne-Thomas' attempt at a joke. "Oh, I see, you mean like a *bucket* on the *farm.*"

The doctor nodded. "Yes, but I ought to say too that in order to resolve the trauma you have to process the information in full consciousness and relive it."

I was nervous again now.

"Yes and the mental pain and reaction can be as strong as, possibly even stronger than it was during the original experience. EMDR does not reduce the degree of the affective experience."

"What do you mean?"

"In reliving it you are likely to feel the pain of the old experience vividly; in fact the feelings you recall will probably stay with you for the rest of your life…"

I felt more panic at those words: *the rest of my life.* But Dr Browne-Thomas merely nodded reassuringly. "We can work together to ensure that you are able to control that experience at will, so that eventually you will be able to determine whether or not to re-experience the event and to what degree."

I thought of my nightmares and felt my blood run cold. "I've just about got all this under control, Doctor. If the nightmares come back as bad as they were a few years ago…"

"I understand."

"What if I can't control them? What if my brain doesn't react like everyone else's?"

Dr Browne-Thomas nodded again. "The treatment advises that you choose a 'safe place' before we begin. This safe place will be used to bring closure as and when you need it or to help you tolerate a particularly upsetting session."

"What sort of 'safe place' would you recommend?"

"It could be a place where you've felt happy in the past, with your parents or your wider family; it might be one of those moments when you felt a significant happiness with friends, or it might simply be a place that gives you the greatest feeling of comfort."

I thought for a moment. There was no doubt that I'd felt safe during the years I'd spent growing up in Low Leighton Road but somehow, all that seemed too long ago now, part of a life I could barely recall. I thought then of my closest friends. I always felt happy when I was with them; I loved our regular nights in the pub and the ridiculous games of badminton we shared every Tuesday, but, as to where and when I felt happiest, there could only be one place.

"Ball Beard Farm," I said with certainty. "Ball Beard Farm will be my safe place."

"Good," said Dr Belinda Browne-Thomas. Then she consulted her diary before handing me a leaflet. "We will sit in this position." She indicated my chair opposite her desk with both hands. "I will ask you to think of your safe place, and then if you become upset during the treatment I will ask you to go back to Ball Beard Farm in your mind. I will ask you to watch my hand as I encourage you to think about the nightmares and I will ask you to talk about whatever is on your mind." She looked pleased. "We may achieve a lot in one session or, it may take two or three."

"That sounds simple enough. Do we start now?" I asked.

"Not today. I want you to be absolutely sure that you wish to proceed. I want you to read the information through and I want you to understand that the therapy can be upsetting and I want you to know that I can't give any guarantees."

"Nothing can be more upsetting than the nightmares," I said, suddenly serious.

"And I can't guarantee that the nightmares will stop," said Dr Browne-Thomas.

We were both silent for a moment. No guarantees, then.

"I can see you on 12 April for the first treatment and you may bring a friend with you if you wish."

"A friend?"

"Yes, someone to go home with; someone to support you."

I shrugged. "I don't think I'll need anyone to hold my hand, if that's what you mean. It all sounds pretty straightforward to me. I'm more than happy to go ahead with the treatment and I'm free to meet up again on 12 April."

That night Mary and I met for a drink in the White Horse.

"If you want me to come with you when you go to see Dr.

Browne-Thomas I will, I'm teaching all morning but I can come after that," said Mary.

"No, it's fine. I don't see any problem – unless, of course, Dr B-T discovers I've got a super brain and wants to experiment on me."

Mary didn't laugh. "Well, all I'm saying is if you need me then ring."

"Don't worry; I'm sure it will be *something and nothing*, as Dad used to say."

Mary looked sceptical then decided to change the subject. "How's the sale of the farm coming on?"

I shifted in my seat. "It should all be sorted by the middle of June."

"Really? And have you planned where you're going yet?"

"I've already told you: I'm going to the west coast of Scotland – for a holiday. I'm thinking of setting off in the middle of the month; I'll drive till it gets dark so hopefully I'll get most of the way before the dogs start sending me round the bend with their barking."

"You're really doing this, then?"

I nodded. "Why wouldn't I?"

But the irony hadn't escaped me: in selling Ball Beard Farm I was selling my 'safe place' and I had no real idea of what was going to replace it when it was gone.

Chapter Sixteen

1982 Rose standing on the site of United Utilities' new pipeline at Ball Beard Farm

1981 – 1984

Mary and I go back a long way. We met in 1979 walking our dogs up on Round Wood. I was a 29-year-old part-qualified legal executive/ farmer having a secret affair with my boss and she was a 19-year-old trainee primary school teacher madly in love with David, her fiancé but for some bizarre reason we hit it off straight away.

"Tell me again, who's Annie?" asked Mary as we slogged away across the fields one freezing cold morning three years later. The rain was slanting down from a muddy sky but it didn't stop us taking what was becoming our regular Saturday hike. I'd brought an aging and creaky Ned along with me while Mary brought Bess, her scatty mongrel. The dogs got along all right and provided there weren't too many stops along the way we were usually back for bacon butties and a pot of tea by 10 o'clock.

Today we'd set off through the farmyard as usual then cut through the bottom field, before trekking up to Round Wood and turning south towards Bluebell Wood, all the time Mary had been trying to ask me about Annie but hadn't had a chance because the dogs kept running off after rabbits and I had to keep whistling them back.

"Annie is Rosanna's foal," I said eventually.

"And who's Rosanna?"

"Rosanna is Rose's foal who was out of Star and - before you ask - Star was the offspring of Apache and Bonny. Apache was the stallion I bought when I was 16 years old and Bonny was one of the original Shire horses at Ball Beard along with Dick; she came with the territory, if you like." I smiled. "I take it you like horses then?"

"Oh yes. You're so lucky, Janet, having all this..."

"All this what: all this hard work? Or the chance to hang around outside in all weathers and have the driving Derbyshire rain play havoc with my beauty regime? I'm covered in pig shit and cow muck most of the time, you know, or else I've got my head in a bucket of swill. Although, I suppose on a good day I might be building a dry stone wall or planting spuds. I go to work at

Ingleby's just so's I don't forget what it's like to wear a skirt and to show off my legs."

Mary's eyes were shining. She'd recently been appointed reception teacher at Furness Vale Primary School and in the process had reverted to a rather touching childlike state herself. "But you must see some amazing things. Have you ever seen a calf being born or… or milked a cow?"

"Yes and yes, many times." I looked at Mary closely; she was 21 years old and obviously still believed in that romantic notion of farming where the sun always shone, the birds were always singing and no-one ever had to shoot a diseased animal. But I also saw a sincerity in Mary's eyes that was surprising. "And it's rewarding, of course it is; that's why I love it so much."

Mary nodded slowly. "I'd really like to….help out at the farm one day – if you wouldn't mind. I was thinking of an Easter project for the children and if I could experience it all first hand…"

"Okay," I said, shocking her with my lack of hesitation. "What about next weekend? You can ride Annie if you like - and if you want to know what it's really like being a farmer you can have a go at milking Marjorie. She's getting on a bit now but she still gives me a few gallons a week."

"Oh, I've milked a cow before," said Mary, smiling at me through her rain soaked hair.

"In that case you'll know exactly what to do."

The following Saturday was another grey and drizzly day. I was in the middle of the farmyard cleaning out the pigs and feeling

136

like a watercolour version of myself, the dirty colours of my surroundings all bleeding into each other; grey on slate, beige on green, brown on black. At the sound of the vehicle coming up the lane I turned around quickly and leant on my brush, making sure I was facing the oncoming car but when I realised it was Mary I relaxed again.

"Drive on," I shouted over the sound of the engine. I pushed the hair out of my eyes with a muck-streaked hand. "Pull in round the corner, in front of the gate but watch out for the potholes – and the gigantic yellow diggers."

Mary stopped the car and waved back at me through the open window. "What are the diggers for? Are you planning on doing a bit of gardening, Janet-style?" She laughed at her own joke.

Mary was able to laugh but Fred would have had a heart attack. Not only did Ball Beard Farm have its own tractor now, thanks to me, but I'd just given permission for three mechanical diggers to take up residence next to the covered reservoir, in the field at the far end of the yard. These diggers were enormous, powerful pieces of machinery, capable of excavating five tonnes of soil in one go and I could just hear the anger in Fred's voice at seeing them on his land, poised like a herd of yellow, long-necked monsters: *'What's goin' on 'ere, Janet? I've told ye; no mechanisation at Ball Beard Farm while I'm still livin' and breathin''* But then, just as he was about to storm over and see the men off his land I'd tell him that United Utilities was intent on providing a better water supply in the High Peak area and to do that they needed to bring water from Higher Disley, laying a pipeline across our land in the process - and for which they were paying handsomely. At the mention of extra income there was a slim chance Fred would have come round to the idea, but in all honesty, I doubted it.

"How long are you planning on having the gardeners in for?" asked Mary, glancing over at the bunch of young - and not so young workers.

"Twelve months; it's a big job," I said, recalling the conversation with the foreman. "We're not talking about a crop of potatoes here, Mary; we're talking about burying a metal cylinder 20 feet underground. But once they realised they couldn't get the machinery down the bridle path they had to pay me for access, so I can't complain." We both chuckled as I told her about the poor clerical officer at United Utilities who had been under the impression that the yellow monsters were capable of gaining entry down a path barely wide enough for a horse and cart. Fortunately for the clerical officer I'd given them access over the farmyard – and been paid £2,000 for my pains.

"I've brought a picnic and a flask of tea. You mentioned that you've no electricity in the farmhouse. I wasn't sure how you coped when it came to making a brew."

"I've got the range but, to be honest, I rarely use it these days. Mum's usually got a pot waiting for me when I get home but thanks, that's very - organised of you." I laughed as I bent down

138

lower. "Do you always come this prepared? Actually, don't answer that, of course you do; if you're not deputy headteacher by the end of the year I'll eat my hat."

Mary blushed in that self-deprecating way she had before telling me she'd just seen Miles driving down the lane as she was coming in. "I waved at him," she said with a giggle. "He probably wondered who on earth I was. Will you tell him I was just being friendly; I wasn't…well, you know…I wouldn't want him to think I was flirting with him." And then she blushed even more.

"I know," I said with a wink. "He's a bit handsome; can be distracting at times, tell me about it."

I saw the look of confusion on Mary's face but she said nothing more before winding the window up and driving to the far end of the yard. I couldn't believe how close a call that had been; I must remember to warn Miles to be more careful in future. He'd only popped in for an early morning cup of coffee, but how many other bosses did that on Saturday morning with their staff? No, I was pretty sure Mary wouldn't be so keen to see me if she knew that I was having an affair with my boss, and a married man to boot.

By the time she walked back into the yard I'd finished sweeping and was deciding what task to give her first when I realised she was standing as still as a statue, gawping at the view.

"Isn't this a beautiful spot?" she said, waving her hands around like a conductor.

"I suppose it is; I haven't looked at it properly in years."

"Once you've gazed on that beautiful scenery I'm sure all's well with the world at any time of the day or night." I glanced at the hills towards Chinley then thought of my nightmares and wondered if Mary couldn't be more wrong. "This view probably explains why you're so laid-back," she added, unable to pull her eyes away. "Do y' know, the only time I've seen you ruffled was the time you nearly thumped that driver when he cut you up in the high street and parked in front of us, blocking our way. Do you remember? You slammed on the brakes, got out of the car and…" Mary glanced at me then checked herself. "Well, I suppose everyone has their off days, don't they? And he was so rude to you when he got out of his shiny BMW." She was gabbling now.

"I can't remember much about it," I said with a frown. It was true, I couldn't. All I could remember was my anger and my inability to control it.

"Oh, it was all over in no time," she said quickly. "It was something and nothing." She gave me a comforting pat on my shoulder.

"*Something and nothing*," I repeated, but it wasn't nothing; I'd almost lost control and I couldn't remember why.

"What have you got planned for me today?" asked Mary, her voice bringing me back to the present. I looked her up and down. She'd come prepared, just as I'd expected she would; she was wearing an old pair of jeans, spotless wellington boots and a huge Arran jumper. In fact she looked like a younger, neater version of me.

"Marjorie's waiting for you in the shippon," I said, handing Mary a bucket. "But be careful, you'll have to watch her."

"What do you mean; *watch her*?" asked Mary, suddenly wary. "I thought you said she was old."

"Well, she's old but she's no pushover. Don't worry. I'll stand guard. Just take the bucket and keep talking softly to her, that way she'll know you don't mean her any harm."

I could tell that Mary would do exactly as she was told – because that's what Mary always did. She took the bucket then marched purposefully towards the shippon, eager to prove to me that she could milk a cow just as effectively as she could control a class of five-year-olds.

"Righto, Marjorie, it's only me - Mary. Now don't you worry about a thing; I've just come to…." I watched as Marjorie's tail flicked from side to side. She tried to turn her head to get a good look at the stranger, the chain around her neck sliding up and down the boskin and clinking against the shippon's uneven stone wall but it was too short to get a clear view. Mary hesitated but I nudged her closer, handing her a stool and indicating the best place to put it down. Once more Mary did as she was told, balancing her bottom on the smooth wood and placing her knees gingerly under Marjorie's fat belly. Then she took hold of a front teat, ready to begin.

"You said you've done this before. Was it recent?"

Mary shook her head. "No, I was about six at the time; it was on a friend's farm."

141

I grinned but said nothing. Marjorie sensed a hesitation and took her chance; stepping forwards and kicking the bucket straight into the dung channel, tipping Mary backwards off the stool.

"Hey!" Mary thudded down hard on the stone floor. "There was no need for that," she said, rubbing her backside through her jeans. She turned to look at me. "What did I do wrong?"

I picked up the bucket without so much as a smile and handed Mary a clean one. "Nothing. You just have to tell her who's boss, that's all."

Mary almost snatched the second bucket from my hand. She sat down on the stool with a little more force this time, determined to get it right. "Now then Marjorie, come on, you give me some milk and I'll give you a pat on the backside, that's fair isn't it? It's nothing you don't do for your owner so you can do the same for me too, can't you?"

Mary took hold of the teat again. She pulled and squeezed just as I'd instructed - but nothing happened. Marjorie lifted a back foot. "Behave," I said and poked her in the rump. Marjorie put her foot back down on the floor and Mary pulled at the teat again. This time a drop of milk dripped out of the end and fell into the bucket.

"It worked," she shouted. "I'm milking Marjorie!"

"Brilliant, what did I tell you? Nothing to it. You'll have this week's quota in the bucket in no time."

Mary nodded then peered over the rim. "Well, maybe not a week's worth," she said, thin-lipped. "Possibly not even a day's worth, if I'm honest."

Twenty minutes later the bottom of the pail was barely covered and I was fidgeting with boredom. I stepped away from Marjorie who was standing quietly now. "Keep trying. I'm going to collect the eggs. I'll be back before long. Don't forget, you've only got a few hours before nightfall and you wanted to ride Annie today, so come on, Mary; put some effort into it."

Mary glared at me over her shoulder and I caught the look - amusement mixed with exasperation - that was to characterise our friendship for the next 25 years. I also saw Marjorie observing her with those liquid brown eyes, the look of innocence on her bovine features almost masking her guile. As Mary went to squeeze her teat again Marjorie made no mistake this time, she lashed out with her hoof and hit Mary squarely in the chest then she kicked out sideways, hooking her arm and throwing her backwards into the dung channel. A second violent kick sent the milking stool sailing over Mary's head and crashing into the wall. Mary gasped in shock before struggling to her feet, rubbing her arm and cursing. She looked at the pail, lying on its side, a tiny puddle of milk forming forlornly on the concrete. Then she stood for a minute or two, hand on hip, making sure nothing was broken until I thought I was going to bust a gut keeping my laughter in.

"Oh blimey, you'll never make a milkmaid, Mary," I said, tears blurring my vision. "I hope you're not as incapable with horses as you are with cows."

Mary was patently cross. "You're not blaming me for this are you? Stubborn brute."

"What, me or the cow?"

"Both." A smile inched across her face. "Oh blimey, I think I need that cup of tea now. I'll go and get the flask." She tucked her hair behind her ear and limped towards the doorway. "I look a sight, don't I?"

"Not too bad," I said, wiping my eyes. "I wouldn't say you looked as if you'd been dragged through a hedge backwards exactly…"

"Oh, well, that's good then."

I stepped to the side, anticipating a swift swipe from Mary's good arm. "You look as if the hedge has fallen on top of you."

"Right, that's it, that's the last time I help you with your chores," she shouted, chasing me out of the shippon and throwing a handful of hay at my head at the same time.

"Stick to being a primary school teacher," I laughed as she ran across the yard. "It's not as dangerous and the money's better."

"I will," she shouted back.

But it was a downright lie. Over the years Mary did more than attempt to milk Marjorie; she helped out at farmers' markets and at harvest time, she turned up at weekends and after work in the spring, in the summer and in the depths of winter too, ever present and armed with her rucksack full of sweets and flasks of strong tea. If there was a motherless calf Mary would volunteer for feeding duty, a bottle of warm milk at the ready, keeping me company through the night; if there was a field of potatoes that needed harvesting she was there too, bringing David with her until he too was almost a permanent fixture at Ball Beard Farm. The truth was, Mary wasn't just a friend, she was an asset and although the nightmares were never discussed between us she became innocently adept at helping keep the worst of them at bay.

Chapter Seventeen

1971 me, far right, eating ice-cream with friends before setting off on a sponsored ride across the High Peak area

December 1985

It's funny, isn't it, the things you remember? I remember this particular Saturday in December because it was a lovely, balmy winter's day; warm enough for Miles to wear one of his cashmere jumpers instead of his overcoat. Miles had told his wife he was going to pick out a goose for Christmas dinner and he'd asked me to go with him. It was one of those days when we tried to pretend that we were a normal couple but it ended up being one of the strangest days I can remember, filled with flashes of insight and hindsight – none of which were mine.

"I'll need a 20 pounder at least," he'd said as we drove over to Kate Barton's farm near Buxton.

"That's a big bird just for the four of you," I said, trying to keep the irritation out of my voice.

"Extended family," he said as he turned his BMW north. "Christmas isn't Christmas without your family around you, is it?"

I thought of Mum and me on Christmas morning and then I thought of Miles and all his relatives, standing round the Christmas tree and singing carols like some perfect tableau out of a Dickens novel and gritted my teeth.

Crown Hill Farm is almost double the size of Ball Beard Farm but, acre for acre, nowhere near as productive. The rumours in the area blamed Geoff Barton for this failing and they would be right. I knew his wife, Kate, and she was only human; running a B & B single-handedly, feeding Geoff and their three strapping sons as well as doing all the book-keeping and housework was enough work for a small army of people, not one woman. She did it all without complaining and yet her family found time to criticise her for everything she did: if the tea wasn't on the table quick enough, if the farmyard wasn't clean enough, if the garden wasn't producing enough vegetables for the roadside stall. The barracking and the lack of respect from the four of them had turned Kate from a rosy-cheeked farmer's wife into a depressed hag with more than a passing interest in the supernatural. This was her escape from the harsh reality of her day-to-day existence: she dared to believe that there was life after death. I'm convinced it was the only thing that kept her sane.

I knew about the money stuffed under Kate's mattress for a 'rainy day' and I knew about the harsh treatment she was subjected to at home but I didn't know just how much Kate liked to communicate with the dead. If I'd been in the room when Kate spoke to one of her spirits 'on the other side' then I certainly wouldn't be trekking up here now on the lookout for a goose.

"I take it the geese are over in the next field?" I asked, as I stood in Kate's sparsely furnished kitchen.

"Aye." Kate pointed through the farmhouse window with a gnarled, arthritic finger. "Field's a bit boggy." She pursed her lips and looked Miles up and down. "Shouldn't think those shoes'll do you much good." She indicated his leather brogues and then eyed his tweed trousers and cashmere jumper suspiciously. Miles stood there like a child in his Sunday best, not saying a word while she gave him the once over.

"Do you have a shed we can drive the geese into?" I asked, forcing Kate to look at me.

Kate almost laughed. "No-o, we've none o'that."

"Then how do you expect us to catch one?"

Kate snorted. I got the feeling that we were the best entertainment she'd had in months. "My 'usband chucks 'em a bit o' corn then grabs their legs. You'll have to do t'same."

She pointed at me as if that was decided, and then she

nodded at Miles. "'E'll stay wi' me. I'll make 'im a cup o' tea. Not much use both o' you goin'." Miles pulled a chair out from under the kitchen table, not needing to be asked twice.

"You payin' for the goose?" asked Kate. Miles nodded. "That's alright then," she said and moved slowly to the kettle.

I turned to leave the kitchen, muttering under my breath, before trekking off up the hill clutching the handful of corn that Kate had so graciously given me, listening out for any sign of the geese.

I stepped over the brow of the hill and saw them straight away; a bunch of well-fed, confident creatures, clustered together in a group. For some bizarre reason an image of Italian widows leapt into my mind. Cursing and honking, competing to be heard, they all turned and looked at me at the same time.

Now, I've raised plenty of geese at Ball Beard Farm over the years, so I know what they're like; angrier than pigs and much slyer than cows. I threw the corn on the ground and watched them waddle towards me, a mass of plump, white meringues on legs. I caught that challenging look in their beady eyes and suspected, rightly as it turned out, that this might take me some time.

When I got back down to the farmhouse - more than an hour later - I was covered in mud from head to toe and Miles was on his third cup of tea. I held out a mass of furious goose to show them both, flapping upside-down in my hands like a huge white, angry bat.

"He'll do, I reckon." I grinned at my audience. There had

been no way I was going to come out of this one a loser.

Kate stepped forward to do the honours. "He'll be ready by Christmas Eve," she said, folding a couple of crisp ten pound notes and popping them in the front of her pinny. "But we don't deliver," she cackled.

I looked from Kate to Miles and back again, suddenly eager to get out of here and back to my own kitchen where it was much warmer and ten times cosier. "Time we got going," I said. "Can't waste all day; I've got my own animals to see to."

Miles stood up, thanked Kate for the tea and led the way back to the car. As we crossed the farmyard his hand sought out mine and I let him take it.

"She was a strange one," he said, nodding over his shoulder and giving me an affectionate squeeze.

I sighed. It was so easy to forgive him. "What do you mean?" I asked.

"While you were outside goose-hunting, Kate informed me that she was a medium."

I frowned and kept my head down. "So I've heard, but I didn't think it was the sort of thing you'd be interested in."

Miles didn't appear to hear me. "She told me that she feels deeply for your loss." He squeezed my hand again. "Did she know Fred?"

"Everyone knew Fred," I snapped.

"She said she'd 'connected' with Fred and that she hoped that what she had to say would be a comfort to you."

150

I opened the car's passenger door and threw myself into the front seat. "You don't believe that nonsense do you? Fred disappeared eight years ago. What on earth would he have to say about it now? What would anyone have to say about it?"

"She said she felt Fred's presence and wanted to pass on a message to you; he said to tell you that he was sorry."

"What do you mean 'sorry'?"

Miles shrugged. "She said, *Sorry, and please look after the animals*."

"Who did? Who said look after the animals? Fred or Kate?" I turned to look at Miles but I couldn't hold his gaze. He was totally oblivious to my discomfort; he was fascinated by what he'd been told and for some peculiar reason he seemed to want to pass on every single word of it to me.

"She said that few people look favourably on you and that you have no friends around you."

"Well, that's obviously not true," I snapped. "Of course I've got friends. I've got you, I've got Mary, I've got Claire and Carol..."

"She also said that the truth has not always been your friend. What do you think she meant by that?"

"I have no idea what she meant," I said, shaking my head and feeling as if I was being cross-examined. I flinched, feeling his hand on my knee.

"You walked in with your prize goose just as she was telling me that sadly, our lives don't always turn out like we planned them and that we can *do things* as a result. She also added – a little disingenuously if you ask me - that she couldn't presume to know the truth."

"*Presume to know the truth*! That's a posh choice of words for Kate!"

Miles ignored my sarcasm. "And then her conversation took an even odder turn when she referred to your teenage years, describing how you used to ride your pony bareback round the streets of New Mills without a care in the world."

"Well, I'm glad you thought that was odd."

"She also told me that she was envious of you. She said she'd wished she could ride as instinctively as you at that age." He paused and leant towards me across the gear stick. "You sounded happy," said Miles, softly. "I wish I'd known you then."

He slowly withdrew his hand and turned the key in the ignition. I looked away out of the side window but I could feel him watching me. I pressed my lips shut and I think he knew, with a rare flash of insight, that I was furious with him, not because he and Kate had shared an intimate conversation – although that was partly it - but also because he was telling me something about myself that I didn't recognise. I felt as if he was describing a stranger to me, and yet it was a description that rang bells deep in my subconscious. There were elements in Kate's description that sounded vaguely familiar. Yes, as a teenager, I did remember riding Lucky around New Mills without a saddle - and yes, I did remember feeling happy.

Chapter Eighteen

1986 – 1990

Mum sold her house in Low Leighton Road. We used the money to renovate the farmhouse so that we could live there together and then I obtained planning permission to convert the shippon, Marjorie's old home, with the intention of turning it into a holiday cottage. I increased the cattle numbers and sold the last of the pigs but I still had to borrow heavily to carry out all the work.

And then Mum was diagnosed with cancer and this, added to the electric shock treatments she'd endured for her depression, meant she was no longer the Mum I knew and loved. She became confused and distressed, silent and uncommunicative. I'd find her alone with her thoughts, sitting looking out of the farmhouse window and saying nothing. I'm pretty sure Mum's experience put me off seeking help for my own problems and that's why I struggled on as best as I could, bottling it all up and trying to ignore my disgusting nightmares. It was the only way.

"Cup of tea, Mum?" I asked, touching her gently on the shoulder. Mum turned her head to look at me, her expression blank. "By the way, I've bought us a lovely piece of haddock for our tea."

"Haddock?"

"And I've got some new potatoes and fresh green beans to go with it. You like green beans, don't you?"

Mum's face lit up with a memory. "Your Dad likes a nice bit of fish."

I squeezed Mum's shoulder. "Dad's not here, Mum. It's just you and me now. We're living in the farmhouse at Ball Beard Farm and you help me collect the eggs from time to time. Mags came to visit yesterday, do you remember? She brought you a cake; a coffee and walnut cake?"

"Mags?" Mum was confused. "Fred's sister?"

"Yes that's right. Fred's sister."

Mum frowned at me, her eyes suddenly focusing on mine. "Where is Fred?"

"I don't know Mum."

"Why can't we find him?"

"I don't know," I said again. "That's what I keep asking myself."

I left her, sitting in the armchair and went into the kitchen to make that cup of tea. This was the third time this week Mum had asked where Fred had got to. The question seemed to be bothering her more and more as time went on. It was as if she wanted an answer before it was too late.

In 1989 Mum finally lost her battle with cancer. In some ways it was a relief since I felt I'd lost my real mum years ago.

154

After the funeral I felt numb and cold, my emotions shut down totally and I don't even remember crying. The fact I was alone now didn't bother me as I felt as if I'd been coping alone for as long as I could remember.

Interest rates soared. I struggled to make the repayments until finally, it dawned on me that I was living in a large, partially renovated farmhouse while there was a one-bedroom cottage on the other side of the farmyard that would suit me much better so I made a decision to sell the farmhouse, use the money to pay off the bank and improve the farm at the same time. I could concrete over the muddy farmyard at long last, buy a tractor and retire the working Shires, then concentrate on rearing dairy heifers with the idea that I'd sell them on to dairy farms. I also wanted to convert to organic production and then, in my spare time, I hoped to introduce a breeding programme for quality show jumpers. Not that I had much spare time - but horses were and always would be a passion of mine – so I had to find a way to fit them into my life in some form or another.

"Good decision," said Miles when I told him I was selling the farmhouse. "Free up the equity. You don't need all that space. It'll be much cosier in the cottage." And he'd winked at me as if his opinion was the deciding factor.

"Since you never stay the whole night with me, Miles, I don't see what difference it makes where I live." I was annoyed at his assumption that he could express an opinion about my life just like that and it bothered me sometimes that he never wanted to take our relationship a step further. After all this time together Miles appeared just as content with the impermanence as he was in the beginning; he didn't crave stability, he craved attention. And he had never, in the 20 years we'd been sleeping together, spent a whole night at Ball Beard Farm. We'd make love, we'd eat together but he would tell his wife that he was working late or seeing clients and he would always leave my bed before dawn. It was this fact that particularly rankled and was creating a tension between us that I didn't trust myself to express.

"Be honest," he said. "You don't really want me to stay."

"What gives you that idea? It suits you not to stay, that's why you don't stay. Don't blame me for your duplicity."

"You mean what we have doesn't suit you too? Don't be coy, Janet. You've got me whenever you want me, you know that; you've got the farm and you've got a demanding job. I don't see how you can fit a full-time relationship into your life. At least with me you don't have to compromise too much. And as we all know, you don't like to compromise; isn't that right?"

I glared at him but said nothing. His anger frightened me. I wasn't ready for our relationship to break down and I could tell that he was tempted to push me just that little bit too far. I'd heard the rumours about Miles and other women, the gossip in the office, but I wasn't ready to listen to them – not yet.

"Mags phoned me last night," I said, changing the subject.

Miles looked puzzled. "Fred's sister?"

"Yes. She asked me not to sell the farmhouse."

Miles whistled softly under his breath. "That's a tricky one."

"Is it? I don't see why. I own the farmhouse."

"Yes but it's been in the Handford family since the year dot. You know what some of these Derbyshire families are like. Sometimes it's difficult NOT to upset a Derbyshire man – or woman."

I refused to meet his eye. I wanted to stay angry for a little longer. "She asked me to rent it out and not to sell it. I told her I couldn't afford to do that. I need the money. I've decided to rear dairy heifers and I need new cattle sheds, plus the farmyard's like a bog in winter; it needs resurfacing." I challenged him to argue with me.

"I'd advise caution," said Miles, more serious now. "It doesn't do to get on the wrong side of someone like Mags. Not unless you have to."

But I couldn't help wondering if it was too late for that.

Chapter Nineteen

1982, Rose and the JCB working in the background

1991 – 1995

I sold the farmhouse for £156,000, paid off my debts and moved into the cottage then made the decision to expand my farming business by rearing dairy heifers, just as I'd told Miles I would do. After selling the first two heifers at market I could see it was going to be a good business. At long last it appeared I'd hit on a profitable idea. Unfortunately, through no fault of my own, this new-found optimism didn't last long. In 1992 BSE appeared out of nowhere and hit me with the full force of a hurricane.

Bovine spongiform encephalopathy, a fatal disease in cattle that farmers around the world have come to dread, arrived in the

UK and immediately decimated the farming community. As first, I didn't worry since I genuinely believed that BSE wouldn't impact too much on my business; it was dairy herds and farmers dealing in barren cows who appeared to be affected the most but the full implications hit me much quicker than I'd anticipated, just as I prepared two more newly calved heifers for sale.

"They're beautiful," said Mary, looking on with admiration.

"Lovely neat udders," I said proudly. "I've hopes of realising as much as £1,400 for each of them. They ooze quality, don't you think?"

Mary nodded. "Will you contact Trevor?" I'd known Trevor for years, he had a 'flying' dairy herd in Cheshire, which meant he would purchase dairy cows and heifers, milk them for one or two lactations and then sell them on.

"It's worked well so far. I'll see how he's fixed," I said as I walked past the farmhouse and turned into the cottage. I had new neighbours now, much to Mags' disapproval. Alan and Judith Gunning both worked long hours as lecturers at Manchester University so I didn't see them or their teenage daughters very much, but they were lovely people and I hoped eventually Mags would come round and realise it was far better that the farmhouse was used as a family home than have me rattling around in it on my own.

"Trevor, it's me, Janet. How's things?" Trevor muttered something non-committal down the phone line. I told him about the heifers I had for sale but when I said he might like to take a look at them there was an ominous silence.

"I can't promise anything," he said eventually. "Movement restrictions: we're at a standstill."

"But these are two of the best animals you could hope for; you won't be disappointed."

"I'm sure they are but my hands are tied. I can't move anything on until it's been tested. Thanks to BSE, older cows are having to go to special incineration plants and they're overflowing with work. I've got to keep animals I'd normally sell on. I've got no capacity."

It took me only a few moments to absorb the full implications of what he was saying. "For how long?"

"I can't say. All I know is I've got no prospects for the foreseeable future. I'll phone you when I hear more. Could be days, could be weeks."

Trevor said he was sorry and passed on a few phone numbers. He wished me luck but I knew with a sinking heart that there was no point holding my breath. I contacted the farms on Trevor's list, all with the same result.

The following week I took two of my heifers to the cattle market at Chelford and entered them in the dairy section without reserve. I had no choice, the heifers needed milking twice a day and at the moment I was having to do all the milking by hand. I already had another two heifers in the shippon with another five due in the next 10 days. It was impossible to keep them all.

160

I stood anxiously at the side of the sale ring, trying not to listen to the farmers around me talking in hushed tones about the crisis and what it meant for the community. I spotted Ernie Castleford on the other side of the ring, his 80-year-old wizened body propped up by his two sons, one on either side and I raised a hand in salute. Ernie wouldn't be buying and it was unlikely he was selling; he was here because he wanted to be part of this real life drama. The BSE crisis was the Peak District version of a Hollywood disaster movie. Months down the line Ernie would still be telling the story to anyone who'd listen; how he'd witnessed two of Janet Holt's best young heifers go at auction for a *bargain price*, a *ridiculous sum*, a *huge loss*, a *record low*…

One heifer sold for £245 and one for £290. I'd lost more than £1,000 on the sale but I hurried away, refusing to think through the implications.

The situation worsened dramatically over the next few months. I was selling heifers as they calved, with prices ranging from £200 to £400. I was losing hundreds of pounds on each animal, but there was nothing I could do. To make matters worse, a government compensation scheme had been brought in to help dairy farmers caught up in the crisis, but I wasn't a dairy farmer – I was rearing replacements for the dairy industry and so I didn't fit into any category that qualified for compensation. I knew I had to improvise or I'd lose the farm as well as the animals so I stopped buying heifer calves to rear and began to take on more work as a dry stone waller instead. There was plenty of work in this part of the Peak District and I thanked my lucky stars that I had the skill to take advantage of that fact. I now had two other forms of income on top of my 'proper' job as a legal executive: farmer and dry-stone waller and Mary was worried. She wanted to know how I was getting through the days with a smile on my face.

"Well, if I don't smile I'll fall asleep," I told her, masking a yawn.

"How much sleep are you getting these days?" asked Mary as she tried to find a space on the table for a casserole dish she'd brought with her for my tea. She began to clear away dirty crockery, piling it into the sink.

"I'll do that," I said.

"I'm just trying to help."

"I know but I can clear up my own mess."

Mary stood and watched me clear a space on the table. "What's that?" she asked, pointing to a small brown bottle which, until then, had been hidden behind a wall of dirty mugs.

"Just some tablets."

"What are they for?"

"Nothing."

"Janet, what are they for?"

I looked up at Mary. "I've been getting headaches," I said.

"What sort of headaches?"

"Bloody painful ones. The doctor said I've got high blood pressure."

"But you're the fittest woman I know; how can you have

162

high blood pressure?"

I shrugged. "Don't know. He said it might be stress. Things have been a bit hairy round here lately, I don't know if you've noticed. He told me my blood pressure was 180 over 120 and that there was a risk of stroke. I've been on them a couple of weeks."

"And how are the headaches?"

"Oh, coming along nicely thanks."

"I'm serious, Janet, have they cleared up?"

"Sort of," I said, looking away. "I'm getting there."

Mary was like a dog with a bone. "How much sleep?"

"Five hours, sometimes less, but don't worry; I've got a plan." I turned and winked at her.

"I think you need one. My David suggested you sell the farm."

I stared at her. "Are you mad? I can't sell the farm!" Mary looked at me as if she was about to say something else but then changed her mind. "It was bad enough selling the farmhouse."

"How much did it all cost?"

I pretended I didn't know what she meant.

"BSE; the heifers: how much money have you lost?"

"About thirty thousand," I said, knowing that there was no point lying; Mary had an uncanny knack of homing in on the truth. "But as I say, I've got a plan. I'm selling off the last of the dairy heifers and I'm going to keep their calves to rear for beef instead. I'm thinking of selling direct to customers and applying for organic status. I haven't got enough land to rear the number of animals you

163

need to make a huge profit but if I sell the beef direct I think it'll be a good way to maximise what I can make on each animal."

Mary listened in silence.

"And in the meantime, I've been doing enough dry stone walling to build my very own Great Wall of the Peak District."

"But it's all so – physical," said Mary.

"I've thought of that too," I said, turning towards the sink. I filled the kettle with water, ready for a cup of tea. "I think Miles might be increasing my salary in the next month or so."

"Really, how come?"

I pointed to an envelope lying in the debris on top of one of the cupboards. "Take a look."

Mary leant across and picked up the envelope. She must have recognised the stamp on the front. "Did you pass?"

"Take a look," I said again.

She lifted out the piece of paper and saw the Institute of Legal Executives logo on the top right hand side before glancing swiftly down the page.

"Sixty-eight percent! Blimey Janet, how did you manage that?"

"I've told you before; I'm a genius! Miles promised me a salary rise and an office of my own if I got through these exams and I'll be holding him to that."

Mary came up to me and put an arm around my shoulders. "We should celebrate: a trip to the pub with Carol and Claire, perhaps?"

I grinned. "You do know that in three years time there's a good chance you'll have to genuflect when you see me?"

"What do you mean?"

"Well, if all goes well, I will be awarded a Fellowship of the Institute of Legal Executives."

"Ooh, get you," said Mary. "A Fellow indeed and I always thought you were a woman - or at least a very small version of one."

"Blinking cheek," I said, thrusting the mug of tea at her.

Mary laughed. "No, seriously, you deserve it. You've worked so hard, Janet. I couldn't do what you've done, never in a million years. I don't know how you've managed to find the time." She raised her mug in a salute and I clicked mine with hers.

Sadly, our celebration was premature: I never did make Fellow because in three years time I was in prison.

Chapter Twenty

12 April 2010

At the age of 27, just before I began my relationship with Miles, I'd finished with my boyfriend, a farmer named Mitchell Steele. He was serious about me and he'd asked me to marry him. I knew he cared about me but for some reason I persuaded myself that he didn't really want a wife; I told myself he wanted a bookkeeper and a farmhand instead, someone to have sex with and someone to give birth to his children and so I said no to marriage. Looking back and with the benefit of hindsight, I wonder if I finished with him for a completely different reason, one that had more to do with what happened in March 1976 than it did with any notions of equality and it was this thought that was running through my mind on the morning of my third session with Dr Belinda Browne-Thomas.

The sun was shining so brightly I knew I wouldn't be able to see properly on the drive over to Hyde so I rooted out a pair of sunglasses from the back of a drawer in the mobile home and tried them on for size. Jelly nearly had a fit. "It's only me, you daft dog," I soothed, but she was petrified at the transformation so I took them off again and watched as she tentatively began to wag her tail.

The other four dogs were locked in the shippon next door; which was fortunate, because I wasn't gone for two hours as I'd anticipated, I was gone for six. I didn't get back to Ball Beard Farm until late that evening – until the paramedics had signed the release form - and by that time poor Jelly thought she'd been abandoned.

I climbed into my battered blue pickup truck and looked at my reflection in the rear view mirror. I laughed; I didn't recognise myself with the glasses, but then given the peculiar turn my life had taken recently I wasn't sure I recognised myself *without* the sunglasses either. I was puzzled by this sudden desire to sell the farm; it wasn't like me to want to leave the place I'd lived in and loved for most of my life. I was about to turn 60 in August so perhaps you could say I was about to retire, but it didn't feel like I was retiring; it felt like I was running faster and faster, like a hamster on a wheel or a fox running to keep ahead of the pack. I didn't know what would happen if the wheel stopped turning or if the pack finally caught up with me, all I knew was that I was seeing a psychologist because Mary had asked me to and if, as a result of that, the nightmares stopped then that must be a good thing, surely?

I sat down in Dr Browne-Thomas' consulting room, expecting and receiving her usual greeting. "Good afternoon, Janet. What can I do for you today?" It was as if she was waiting for me to take the lead rather than guiding me.

167

"I thought I ought to tell you a bit more about my life, doctor. And then I'm ready for the EMDR treatment we discussed last time. I've read the leaflet." I waved it in front of my face then dropped it on the desk. "I know it might not work, but I'm prepared to give it a go."

Dr Browne-Thomas tipped her head slightly to one side "And what was it you wanted to tell me?"

"On my way over here I was thinking about the men in my life. There haven't been many, but they've all made an impression, one way or another." A nod from the other side of the desk encouraged me to go on.

"First and foremost, there's my Dad: a man ahead of his time in many ways; he wanted me to have a career just as much as he wanted my brother to get a job with prospects. That's a bit unusual, don't you think?"

The doctor gave a slight smile.

"Then there's Fred, a man who didn't hesitate to offer me a partnership in his family farm; a stroke of luck, you might say, but again, not usual round these parts. And then along comes Miles, the most educated man I've ever met; clever, charismatic, charming, a partner in a law firm, married with two children and I fall for him hook, line and sinker. I should have known he was trouble from the start, shouldn't I? I should have known he was just like the Mitchell Steele's of this world – only more handsome."

Dr Browne-Thomas' eyebrows rose as one. "You thought

that perhaps your judgement had become flawed in choosing to have a relationship with Miles?"

"Of course."

"And yet, you told me last time we met that you didn't think that Miles - or your time in prison – was the cause of your nightmares. Is that correct?"

I nodded. "I'm here because I want to sell up and leave Ball Beard Farm as soon as possible and I can't go until the nightmares are sorted. I promised Mary."

"And would I be right in saying you are the sort of woman who keeps her promises?"

I was surprised at the warmth in her voice. "Yes, but that's not always a good thing is it? When Miles finished our relationship I vowed to get my revenge - and I kept that promise. When he finished with me I made sure I took away what was most important to him." I hesitated. "But he deserved it. He might have been educated and able to hold down a good job but he's no different from the farming families I know in Derbyshire where the men are bullies, taking what they want from the women in their lives and giving nothing back." I thought of Kate Barton's husband at Crown Hill Farm and looked over the doctor's shoulder. "I'm ready," I said suddenly. "I'm ready for the treatment."

Dr Browne-Thomas leaned across the desk towards me. "Do you remember what I said to you about a safe place, Janet?"

I nodded.

"You should think of your safe place and, if you become

upset during the treatment, I will tell you to go there and that will then help you to cope. You told me that Ball Beard Farm would be your safe place. Keep that in mind and everything will be fine."

Dr Browne-Thomas held up a hand in front of my face. I glanced at it, barely paying it any attention - but then it began to move. The hand loomed large; I looked along its length and noticed that it was sprinkled with freckles and that the skin was thinner where it pulled tight across the knuckles. The hand was pale, and looked surprisingly soft, I could see the blue veins just below the surface. It was moving now, gently back and to in front of my eyes and I was looking at it but I wasn't thinking about it. I had to turn my head slightly to keep it in my vision but, even so, it was difficult to look away, the rhythm was hypnotic, the effect liberating.

"It was a Sunday," I said, softly. "Sunday 14 March. On the Saturday, I'd been drag hunting with my friend, Ann Benson. Ann would lay the trail and I would go with her."

Dr Browne-Thomas listened as I recalled the day 34 years ago when my world seemed to have stood still. The sun streamed in from the window behind her head.

"I rode Apache up to Ann's house and then we went over to Werneth Low together with the trail. It was a beautiful day. The horses were as excited as we were and I remember laughing a lot.

"Ann was a brilliant rider and I wanted, more than anything, to be able to ride as well as she did. There was one particular hedge on the trail and I thought to myself; *I'm going to*

170

clear this. If Ann can jump it, I can jump it. And Ann went galloping towards the hedge with me following. I watched her gather Mission Boy, ready for take-off and I followed close behind but somehow she misjudged the distance - which wasn't like Ann at all - and she took a tumble. I was too close to adjust Apache's stride and he sailed over the hedge, crashing into Mission Boy and throwing me off onto the muddy grass. I landed in a heap on top of Ann, trying my best not to let go of Apache's reins. I managed to stand up but we were laughing so much we could barely get back on our horses.

"We went to the pub afterwards and probably had a bit too much to drink. While we were there I asked Ann if she wouldn't mind helping me clip Apache later that week 'cos I couldn't manage it on my own – he was a little sod and he would never stand still for me. So she told me to come over the next morning - on the Sunday - and after saying our goodbyes I rode home. I felt so happy. I felt as if my life couldn't get any better. It was about 6.30pm and I was wondering whether to go up to Ball Beard Farm to help Fred but I couldn't bring myself to go because he'd been so miserable and gloomy lately; always picking holes in things, always moaning, and I didn't want him to ruin my good mood. So I went home and bored Mum and Dad instead with my tales of the day before we all settled down for Morecombe and Wise on the telly.

"On the Sunday I went up to Ann's and we clipped Apache together as planned. Ann's mum was cooking dinner and she asked

171

if I'd like to stay: she was what I'd call a 'rough cook' – she'd often have a lump of fatty mutton on the go, boiling away on the stove but I didn't stop, I came home instead. Mum was doing tater pie, the best meal in the world."

My voice caught in my throat. The cosiness of my memories was about to change; the sun was about to disappear. It was as if, Dr Browne-Thomas said later, the world had suddenly shifted on its axis. I could barely hear my own words.

"After dinner I set off for the farm. On the way up I mused over Fred's change in character since his accident and the effect his mood swings were having on me: I still loved the farm, of course I did, but Fred's despondency was beginning to make working with him more of a duty than a pleasure. I wished he would go back to the old Fred; the one I'd always known: humorous, steady, hard working and I hoped that today, Sunday, 14 March, would be the day he shrugged off this oddly depressive attitude.

"Everything was quiet and Fred was nowhere to be seen so I started to check on the animals. I didn't understand it; it looked as if Fred hadn't attended to the sow's new piglets because I could see that two of them were dead. Why were the piglets dead? That wasn't like Fred; he was usually so careful with the animals. I sorted out the sow and made her comfy then went round to check the shippons. The little shippon was okay but the bigger shippon hadn't been seen to either so I cleaned that out, took three barrows of muck to the midden and then I went round to the front to get the

172

hay."

The muscles in my face clenched tight as if to force the words back into my mouth. Dr Browne-Thomas could see the tears in my eyes, suspended like tiny blobs of mercury and I think she knew, with a terrible feeling of foreboding - and way before I did – that I was about to plunge into an abyss. And I believe, looking back now, she was powerless to stop it.

Chapter Twenty-One

March 1996

My organic beef business was going from strength to strength. I was transporting cattle to the local abattoir then selling in the New Mills area as well as delivering further afield in a new refrigerated van. I had a long list of customers and it was gratifying that my gamble had paid off. I was also overflowing with dry stone walling work. For the first time in 20 years I was making good money. I was also managing to put in a full week's work at Ingleby's. Looking back, I don't know how I did it; I have no idea how I kept up that level of concentration and sheer physical activity. With hindsight, I suppose it was all too good to be true.

"What are your new neighbours like?" asked Mary, nodding across the yard to the farmhouse.

"Lovely," I said. "And the cottage is perfect for one. Don't know why I didn't move out years ago."

"Because the cottage was a derelict barn until you got off your backside and renovated it," said Mary with a laugh.

The truth was, Mary was completely bemused by my energy; she would often tell me she was exhausted just thinking of how much backbreaking work I'd done on the conversion and I suppose - if I thought about it - she was right: I don't know how I managed it myself looking back. "Shame you haven't got a nice man to share it with though," she added, nudging me in the ribs.

I feigned indifference. "Just because David's a lovely husband who massages your feet when you ask him, doesn't mean to say I need a husband too." I nudged her back.

"No, but, even so..."

There weren't many subjects that were off limits when talking to my friends but they all knew that 'men' was one of them. Mary had been married now for almost 10 years and it suited her, but marriage wasn't for me. They knew I'd given Peter Taylor - the wealthy widower from Disley- short shrift and even handsome Walter Barker had been given the elbow after just one night in the pub. I'd told them he wasn't young enough for a spring chicken like me which was absolute rubbish – and they all knew it was rubbish. I suppose Mary just wanted me to be happy and because she was happy and married she assumed I had to be married to be happy too.

It was after 5.30pm and I was tidying my desk ready to leave for the evening. I'd been given an office of my own, just as Miles had promised, after passing my ILEX exams and so I spent most of my working day alone now. I missed the company of my colleagues but it meant I didn't have to be quite so vigilant when Miles popped in to see me: a kiss across the filing cabinets had become part of our normal working day, but it also meant I didn't get to hear the office gossip any more.

175

Miles didn't usually knock on my door and this evening was no exception.

"Are you off then?" I asked, looking up at him with a smile. Twenty years ago I'd kissed Miles for the first time. Since then he'd been everything to me; everything, that is, apart from my husband.

He pulled the door to behind him. "We need to talk, Janet." I was about to make a joke when something in Miles' expression stopped me.

"Okay," I said instead, stepping out from behind my desk. I stood in front of him, close enough to put my arms around him if he'd asked.

"I'll be in Stockport full time from next week," he said. "Business has been difficult, I think you know that. We'll be making a few redundancies."

I stared up at him. I wasn't surprised at what he was telling me but I was surprised at the lack of warmth in his voice.

"I know that. We had a meeting," I said carefully.

"And Marian's coming with me," he added.

"I expected she would be; she's your secretary," I said with a frown.

There was the smallest of pauses before Miles added, gratuitously, "You do know we've been seeing each other, don't you?"

I felt a rushing sound in my ears. The floor rose up to meet me and then fell back down again. I steadied myself with a hand on my desk. "I don't know what you mean," I said stalling for time.

He leant towards me slightly. "I think you do," he said. "I think you know that things have been getting a little stale between us, Janet. Do I have to spell it out?" He said it again. "Marian and I have been seeing each other."

"I don't understand. When? I mean how could you? I thought we…"

"What? You thought what? That we were a couple? We might have been once in your rose-tinted past - but now? I don't think so."

I stared over Miles' shoulder then adjusted my gaze until I was focusing on the painted Lincrusta on the walls of my office behind his back. I stared at the heavily embossed panels, thick with paint, as if I was seeing them for the first time and I realised with a sudden jolt that I hated it. Why had that fact never registered with me before?

"I've been hinting for weeks," he said cruelly. "But you haven't been listening, have you? Any other woman would have got the message by now. Why haven't you?"

Did he expect me to answer that? I looked into his green eyes but I saw nothing but impatience and frustration; he seemed angry with me for some reason.

"You must know I've been having other relationships." I took a step back as if he'd hit me. "You must know about Sarah and Karen." His voice rose.

"Of course not," I said, breathing in deeply. "Don't you

think I would have said something if I'd known?"

"I've no idea," he said, shaking his head. "I've no idea what goes on in that head of yours any more."

I was gripped with a sudden fury. "You told me you loved me. You told me it was only a matter of time, you told me…"

"We've both said a lot of things over the years," he snapped, cutting me off.

"But I would never say anything I didn't mean."

"I *did* mean them, but now, well, now it's different." He looked sorry for a moment but then the cruelty came back in a rush. It was as if he was punishing me for something. "Do you honestly think you are attractive enough for me never to look at another woman?"

I turned away, stung by his viciousness, then walked slowly back to the chair behind my desk. I knew that if I didn't sit down I would fall down.

"I'm going now," he said. "I'm going." He stood and looked at me but I didn't return his gaze. He took one small step towards the desk.

"What about my job?"

"You're job's safe – for now," he said.

"Why?"

"Because you are an asset at Ingleby's; you always have been. Nothing's changed there."

"That's not what I meant," I said.

He knew what I meant but he couldn't answer me.

178

"I told you everything," I said. "You know *everything*."

Miles sighed. "No, Janet, that's not true."

"What do you mean?"

"Everything's a joke with you isn't it? You laugh your way through life, you work yourself into the ground, you rarely take a holiday and when you do it's only so you can do more work at that bloody farm of yours. It's not normal."

"Oh, and you *are* normal, is that it? It's normal to hide a 20-year-relationship with another woman from your wife, is it Miles? And it's normal to see other women at the same time?"

Once again, he could think of nothing to say. He glared at me, his expression unreadable and then he backed out of the office, closing the door softly behind him.

I sat there for half an hour, waiting for the fury to erupt, waiting for the moment when I would pick up my huge oak desk and throw it across the room just as I'd done once before, years ago, but nothing happened. Instead I sat, dry-eyed, as the reality of the situation slowly revealed itself to me: I had had a sordid affair with a married man for 20 years, a sexual relationship with a man who lived at home with his wife and two children and who had now told me he'd been seeing other women – colleagues of mine in this very office; women I'd had no idea about.

I stared down at the pens on my desk. I counted them out: five pens; there were five pens on my desk. I picked one up and moved it. I couldn't believe how stupid I'd been. He'd told me he loved me and in return I'd told him everything. Or rather, I hadn't.

179

Miles had been right about that; I'd told him only as much as I remembered.

I picked up another pen and moved it next to the first.

Perhaps I should tell Miles' colleagues about our illicit relationship? That would really put the cat among the pigeons, wouldn't it? Miles had always impressed upon me the importance of keeping our relationship secret from the other partners.

I picked up a third pen and moved it across.

My job seemed worthless to me now; all that hard work I'd put in so I could pass my exams and increase my salary. It meant nothing, nothing at all.

I moved a fourth pen.

The farm meant nothing.

I moved the last pen.

I counted them. Five: there were five pens on my desk.

Chapter Twenty-Two

April 1996

I closed the file and pinned the cheque to the front for signature. J Holt was about to receive another gift of £1,000 but I had no doubt that Susan North, one of the partners at Ingleby's, would pick it up this time and realise that J Holt was a fictitious beneficiary. Just reading the cheque would alert her and when questioned, I would tell all. The fall out would be catastrophic but it would be worse for Miles. He would have to explain his relationship with me, the person perpetrating the fraud and, after an investigation, there would be no doubt he'd have to leave the firm of solicitors that he'd helped to build up so successfully.

I walked into the office. My hands were steady. "Would you sign this for me please, Susan?" I asked, sliding the file across the desk. Susan flicked her blonde hair off her face and picked up her pen. She unclipped the cheque then looked up at me and smiled.

"My husband and I had some of your organic beef for dinner last night and extremely delicious it was too. Remind me to put in another order next week, will you, Janet?"

I assured her that I would.

"Well done with your exams, by the way."

I nodded.

"Keep up the good work; who knows, you might make partner one day."

"Oh, I don't know about that. I'm only a legal executive," I said as I watched Susan sign her name.

"But your caseload indicates a much greater responsibility. Experience counts for a lot these days, Janet, especially in towns like New Mills. You're a popular member of staff. Our clients like you."

I looked down at the desk. Susan carried on speaking but I didn't hear what she was saying.

"Is there anything else?" Susan slid the file back across the desk.

"No, I don't think so."

"Don't forget now."

"Don't forget what?"

"Don't forget to remind me about the beef."

I picked up the cheque. "No," I said with a frown. "I won't forget." Then I walked back to my office, each step falling heavy and deliberate on the parquet floor.

I continued to steal money from my employer. Over a period of seven months I appropriated more than £50,000 which, in legal parlance, amounted to 26 counts of theft by false accounting. I left cheques lying on my desk but no-one looked at them; I stood in front of partners as cheques were signed and waited for questions to be asked but none were ever asked. Perhaps it was the fact I'd been a trusted employee for nearly 30 years? Perhaps it was the fact that Ingleby's had become lax in their procedures? Who knows, all I knew was that I would end up in prison. I was in no doubt about that, but I also felt that I'd done sufficient damage to bring Miles Ingleby crashing down with me. There was no way he'd be able to continue as a partner in this law firm once the truth was discovered.

One bitterly cold day in November, just before a meeting of fee earners, I made a decision. I walked into the boardroom, poured myself a glass of water - and waited.

One by one my colleagues joined me. At the sight of Miles taking his place at the head of the table I felt the freezing cold weather outside the office sweep in with him. All the confusion I'd felt when he'd finished our relationship had been replaced now with a cold, solid hatred.

"We will be reorganising the Ingleby offices in the near future," said Miles, at his most assertive. He scanned the row of faces, strung out around the table like beads in a necklace. "As you know our Stockport office continues to go from strength to strength but we have reached the stage when we can no longer ignore the fact that we have to make further redundancies here in New Mills." He turned swiftly and looked in my direction. "Janet, I would like you to consider a position as personal assistant to my fellow partner, Susan North. You can continue to manage your own case load but we need you to take on extra secretarial work so that we may - cut costs."

I stared listlessly over Miles' head. It sounded as if he was speaking to me from an awfully long way away: distant words, distant feelings. I knew, of course, that I had no choice in the matter; I knew that it was either say yes to his offer or accept that I had no job at all - but then I switched my attention, catching him unawares and I wondered if perhaps there was a third option.

"I'd rather take redundancy," I said suddenly. "Don't sack Jean; she's a much better secretary than me. Surely Jean can have the PA position? I'm sure Susan will be able to manage my case load on her own."

Miles looked from me to Susan. He pushed his hair back off his forehead and pinched his chin between his thumb and forefinger. I could tell he hadn't expected this.

"What will you do?" he asked, then, "I mean, a noble gesture but hardly necessary."

"I think it's necessary," I countered. "Besides, Ingleby's will save more money this way. I take it you pay me more than you pay Jean?"

"Of course," said Miles.

"Well, then." I challenged him to disagree. "I'll make sure my desk is cleared by the end of the day."

Miles looked back at Susan who could only shrug, relieved. I imagined she'd envisaged a much tougher battle than this.

"I take it your files are all in order," asked Susan, as we trooped out of the boardroom. She had no desire to make eye

184

contact with me although I felt that she wanted to sound as sympathetic as she could.

"Of course," I said. "Clear, straightforward and unambiguous." I smiled for the first time in weeks. "I don't think you'll find it difficult to find what you're looking for."

When I got home to Ball Beard Farm that evening, I sat in the tiny kitchen and looked at the shoe box in front of me on the table then I turned slowly to look out of the window. The farmyard was swept clean, the mud was gone, all the pot holes had been filled. I shivered and held up my mug of tea to my lips, blowing the steam up into my eyes and waiting until my vision cleared. There were just the hens and the horses left and, thank goodness, I'd found someone to look after them. I was no fool; I knew how this was going to end.

I glanced at some of the receipts in the box; payments for the new roof on the barn, the resurfaced yard, the new tractor. I think Fred would have liked the improvements I'd made around the place although I'm pretty sure he would have disagreed with the purchase of the tractor, in fact I could imagine him furious with me, using a tractor after all these years. Well, maybe this would have been one of those rare instances when I would have disagreed with him; perhaps I would have gone against his wishes, who knows? I looked up at the shelf above the window and stared at Fred's calendar. Just like the Shire horse making its way across the field and still not quite getting to the other side, I'd never know now. It was much, much too late for that.

Chapter Twenty-Three

November 1996

All hell had broken loose at Ingleby's. A whispered phone call from a colleague told me that a discrepancy had been found on one of my files and the police had been alerted.

I put the phone down, made a cup of tea and then checked the shoe box containing all the bank statements, receipts and other papers relating to the stolen £50,000 as well as details of all the items I'd bought with the money. I intended to give the box and everything in it to the police just as soon as they contacted me but in the meantime I had one or two loose ends to tidy up. I picked up a pen and wrote out a list of things I had to do before leaving Ball Beard Farm:

Contact friends, A and M and ask them to take care of the horses

Prepare the cottage so they can move in while I'm gone

Say good bye to Mary.

That was it.

I put the pen down and considered what Mary would say to me when she found out what I'd done. "Stupid idiot" sprung to mind.

It was three weeks before the police knocked on the door: four plain clothes detectives and a WPC. I confirmed that I knew why they had come and handed the box over to them at which point they appeared a little taken aback. They searched the house but found nothing else – I'd already removed the other list, the one that I kept on the inside of the cupboard door, out of the way of prying eyes like Mary's; the one I'd written 20 years ago:

Get out of bed

Feed the dogs

Get washed

Get dressed

Make a cup of tea, eat a slice of toast.

I had a feeling that the list would be just as important in prison as it had been at Ball Beard Farm – apart, that is, from feeding the dogs.

I was taken to the local police station where I was questioned at length and charged with theft. I confessed from the start and told them the reason why I'd stolen £50,000 from my former employer but the officers in charge seemed reluctant to believe me. I was confused about that; I was trying to make it easy for them.

Someone at the station made reference to hell having no fury like a woman scorned and I considered adding another of Congreve's famous quotations to the mix - that you '*must not kiss and tell*' but then realised that that was exactly what I was doing: kissing and telling, that is.

It wasn't long before I realised what was going on: the other partners at Ingleby's were trying their hardest to deflect attention away from the fact that Miles and I had been having an affair. They were extremely nervous of the implications for Ingleby's if the truth became public knowledge: a partner had been having a relationship with a colleague who had gone on to steal thousands of pounds from the client account. It was debatable whether Ingleby's would survive the scandal, let alone Miles.

The police continued to insist that other people were involved in the fraud. I continued to insist that this was not the case. I was allowed home on bail. The police were still not satisfied; they continued to dig - until eventually they found something.

This time, just two officers knocked on the door of the cottage.

"We now have reason to believe that the theft of money from your employer was a conspiracy between you and other persons," they said.

I looked at them blankly. "What other persons?"

"We have discovered at least one instance of money laundering."

"I don't know what you're talking about," I said, truthfully. "I've told you: I was the one who stole the money and I will be going to prison because of that. No-one else is involved."

The first officer hesitated while the second officer spoke up. "In May of this year did you or did you not pass a cheque to

188

Debra Blacklock?"

I looked from one to the other and felt my heart sink. Debra, Mags' granddaughter, owned a livery firm with her husband. I remembered I'd paid her with an Ingleby cheque for Chloe's keep. Chloe was a thoroughbred mare I'd bred myself.

"That cheque, drawn on the Ingleby client account was made payable to Mr and Mrs Blacklock's livery firm. The cheque was subsequently paid into their bank account. We have arrested Mr and Mrs Blacklock on a charge of conspiracy."

I couldn't believe what I was hearing. "Neither Debra nor Ian had anything whatsoever to do with the theft. I gave them a cheque in payment for keeping Chloe at livery with them, but Debra had no idea the money was stolen. I made a mistake. I'm telling you, they knew nothing about this."

But the officers were adamant. This was a clear case of money laundering as far as they were concerned and Debra and Ian would have to go to court to defend themselves.

Chapter Twenty-Four

1997

I don't remember much about the trial, possibly because I don't remember *feeling* much during the trial. If there's no emotion, there's no memory – isn't that the case? Or, is the opposite true: if there's *too much emotion*, there's no memory?

Either way, I don't remember anything other than pleading guilty and taking counsel's advice when it came to ensuring that Debra and Ian should be released without charge.

"It is vitally important that we denigrate your character as much as possible," my barrister said, looking at me intently. "I want the jury to believe that you have not a shred of remorse when it came to taking money from your employer because you wanted, more than anything, to bring about Miles Ingleby's downfall."

I nodded. That was exactly how I felt.

"Conversely, I will make sure the jury feels nothing but compassion for Mr and Mrs Blacklock, who were after all merely friends of yours. You passed a cheque drawn on Ingleby's client account in order to pay for a horse that you kept at livery at their stables - but that is all; they had nothing to do with the fraud."

I nodded vigorously. This had not been part of the plan; the thought of Mags' granddaughter, Debra and her husband, Ian standing in the witness box made me feel physically sick.

My barrister took me at my word – or at my nod – either way he did indeed make me sound like the worst sort of friend a person could possibly have the misfortune to come across. After listening to him talk I felt I wouldn't have given *myself* the time of day, let alone anyone else. I didn't dare look around the courtroom to seek Mary out; I didn't want to see her face because I didn't want to see her disappointment and confusion reflected back at me.

I pleaded guilty on all charges and was sentenced to 22 months in prison. Quite rightly, Debra and Ian were found not guilty of all charges. I felt immensely relieved about that, but I felt nothing about my own fate. I had known all along that this was how it would end. Conversely, when my barrister came to see me in prison he was furious. "The judge wanted to make an example of you," he said, the anger on his face making him look 10 years older than he actually was.

"I must have deserved it," I said with a shrug.

"No – it wasn't just you on that stand." He wagged a finger at some unseen guilty party. "The judge accused you of bringing down the whole of the legal profession. I was expecting nine months at the outside, not two years."

"Twenty-two months," I corrected.

"Twenty-two months." He almost spat the words out.

"I broke the law," I said. "I have to pay the price."

"Your intention in perpetrating this fraud was to bring

about the downfall of an ex-lover - not the whole of the legal profession." I very nearly smiled at his disgruntlement. "There is an element here of you being punished for their incompetence."

I wasn't sure I understood what he was getting at - and I said as much.

"You forged cheques; you did not mastermind a sophisticated fraud in the manner of an experienced career criminal. If Ingleby's had employed due diligence you would have been caught much sooner."

I said nothing.

"And as for not allowing your relationship with Miles Ingleby to be taken into account in mitigation …." He shook his head, this time, I thought, just as much in sorrow as in anger.

"The judge said that Miles was not in court to confirm or deny our affair," I said by way of explanation. I wasn't stupid, I knew my barrister's anger wasn't all to do with how the law had treated me; it was also because his professional pride had been dented, but it was a help – of sorts. Unfortunately, there was nothing I could do. I had been sentenced to 22 months in Newhall Prison and that was that.

I'd anticipated the outcome at the trial and had already left the farm in the hands of Anthony and Mitchell, two gay friends of mine, horse lovers in need of a home. They were going to move into the cottage and bring their own horses with them, looking after mine at the same time. In retrospect, I realise now that this was probably a foolish thing to do since I hadn't drawn up any form of legal agreement but that was because I was under pressure to act quickly. No sooner had the case appeared in the local paper than they were on my doorstep, offering their help. I'd known the boys for years and I trusted them. I know it's easy to say this now, but I should have listened to Mary. As she is often keen to point out to me, I am not the most perceptive of people. I belong to the 'what you see is what you get' school of thought. I had no idea that Anthony and Mitchell were going to neglect the horses and refuse to leave my home on my return. I wouldn't have let them move into the cottage in the first place if I'd known how it was going to end up.

I was taken straight from the court in a van which was not a vehicle designed for those of a claustrophobic disposition. I sat in a steel compartment the size of a small loo, with just enough room to stretch out my legs. As we covered the miles from the court to the prison I felt as if I was suspended in the space above my head, looking down on myself, wondering what on earth had brought me to this surreal stage in my life.

We pulled up. I could hear voices outside but none of them specifically directed at me until the door finally opened.

"You – stand up and get out."

I did as I was asked, aware that I would have to get used to being spoken to like this from now on. I was no longer a decent member of the community: I was a criminal and as such, I was worthless.

Chapter Twenty-Five

1997

I followed the uniformed prison officer through several sets of locked gates, each time watching her out of the corner of my eye as she waved me through before locking the gate behind me. I felt as if I was on a game show; all I had to do was answer a few questions and I'd be free. Except of course I wasn't on a game show and I wouldn't be free for quite some time.

"Stand there," she said, pointing to another officer who was sat behind a desk, staring at me with a pudgy, expressionless face. It wasn't just her face; her whole body was well padded, cocooned in a grey, shapeless uniform, arms bent round her chest like a furry moth with its wings tucked in. I did as I was told.

"Empty your pockets onto the desk," said the second woman. "Then undress and put your clothes on the table."

It was a sign of my humility and my acceptance of the situation that I did exactly as I was told. I took there, shivering and embarrassed by my nakedness as I watched the first officer search though my pockets and trouser legs – for what I had no idea. I was still standing there when a young girl, barely out of her teens, was brought in and ordered to do the same. Then the warden went through an identical process, burrowing into pockets and delving up sleeves.

We were told to get dressed again – which we did – before sitting down next to each other and awaiting further instruction.

"Aye up," she said, in a thick Yorkshire accent.

I nodded.

"Not seen you 'ere before," she added.

"Er no, that's because I've never been here before."

"This your first time in prison, then?"

I nodded and the girl laughed. "Bloody 'ell, this is my second home, this is. Newhall Fucking Prison and Fucking Young Offenders Institution in the county of Fucking Yorkshire." She laughed even more.

"Not *your* first time, then?"

"Me? Nah, in and out for five bloody years." She made it sound like a pleasant shopping trip into town.

"Don't worry yersel'," she said, not unkindly. "It's a breeze this prison lark; you'll soon see, time'll fly by. Just keep this out of trouble and you'll be fine." She tapped the side of her nose and winked at me.

I noticed she hadn't asked me why I was in prison but it didn't take me long to realise that no-one did, it was an unwritten rule, and one none of us ever broke. We were all prisoners and, as such, we were all the same, united in our loss of liberty and, to a certain extent our dislike of the screws - or some of them anyway. It didn't seem to matter what we'd done on the outside because on the inside we were all equal.

"Holt, follow me." The officer from the van set off towards another locked gate.

"Hey, what's your name?" called the girl.

"Janet," I said over my shoulder. "What's yours?"

"Linda." *Bang.* The gate crashed to and I followed. We passed a room full of women, all ages, sizes, shapes and colours, standing, smoking, talking, playing pool and sitting at a table arguing over a game of Monopoly. The noise of their raised voices was like an assault on my ears; the sound battering on my eardrums, reverberating around my head. Arguing, chatting, shouting, crying – I was drowning in sound.

We reached an empty cell.

"Welcome to your new home," the officer said dully. Then she passed me a plastic bag containing tea bags, milk, sugar, coffee and butter. "There's a mug on the cupboard and a hot water machine up the hall. You've got ten minutes to make a drink then I'll be locking your door. Breakfast is at 8.30. Keep your cell clean and tidy and your bed made."

I took the bag and tried not to listen to the sounds all around me: the voices and the echoes of voices, the clank of metal, the squeak of rubber-soled shoes on cold tiled floors. Then I looked around my cell: a bed, a table, a cupboard and, in the corner, a toilet and a sink. I walked back out to the hot water machine clutching my plastic bag and the noise hit me again, rising like a wave and filling my ears with a deafening roar.

196

"Hello, you're new here aren't you?" A tall woman with long black hair smiled at me. "I'm Liz." She held out a hand, expressing concern that I might be feeling a bit lost. "Don't let it upset you; we're all in this together and if you want anything, don't be afraid to ask."

I was touched by her offer of friendship and, because of that, failed to take in her emaciated appearance, pale complexion and eagerness to please. Looking back, it was just like my gay friends, Anthony and Mitchell all over again: I didn't spot the signs.

"Is that your ration pack?" She pointed at the plastic bag. "Could I borrow a packet of butter and a sachet of coffee - some bastard's nicked mine?"

"Yes, of course, take a few. How many of these do we get?"

"Oh, you get a bag every morning - they throw one in when they unlock first thing."

"In that case, take the lot," I said, "I can wait till tomorrow. Just leave enough for a cup of tea."

Liz smiled, extracted three items and handed them back to me before screwing up the plastic bag in her hand and walking off. I took my drink back to my cell and stood there as the door banged shut, followed by all the other doors: a one-note mournful symphony. I never did get used to that sound.

The next morning I was taken to the refectory by another inmate. As we walked across the yard she asked me if I'd heard all the commotion during the night. I'd heard nothing, which was ironic given how sensitive I was to the noise levels during the day. I could only assume that exhaustion had blunted my senses.

"A girl called Linda – came in yesterday – she topped herself last night. Cut herself with glass."

I listened, horrified. "I came in with a young girl called Linda; short blonde hair, broad Yorkshire accent?"

"That's her," said Susan.

"But, she was telling me yesterday how easy prison is."

"This is a young offenders' institute, love. You'll see them on the wings, swaggering about, swearing and acting tough but it's them you hear crying in their cells at night. They're the ones on suicide watch. All the tough stuff, telling you prison's a breeze; it's just an act."

"But where would she get the glass from?"

Susan pointed down her body with a stubby finger. "She's probably pushed it inside - smuggled it in. There's always a way if you're determined."

I felt sick to the pit of my stomach but I knew I had to put this information to the back of my mind and forget about it. It was a tragedy but it wasn't something I could do anything about. It was one poor girl; a victim of the system. I was older than her and I was stronger.

I followed Susan through the echoing corridors and into the refectory and made my way along the counter picking up a tray, a bowl of cornflakes and two pieces of toast before spotting Liz's dark head on the other side of the room, chatting at a table with three other inmates.

"Hi, Liz," I said, walking up to her. "I've not received my ration pack this morning; do you think I could have a packet of butter for my toast?"

She barely looked at me. "Fuck off," she snapped.

"But Liz, it's me, Janet, remember; we spoke yesterday."

She turned her head. "Are you deaf? I said fuck off or I'll ram your bloody toast down your fuckin' throat."

I walked back to my table and sat down feeling thoroughly dazed. "Did you hear that?"

Susan nodded, stirring sugar into her coffee. "Listen, you don't do drugs do you? No, good, then keep right away from Liz and her cronies. They're drugged up a lot of the time, and when they're not high they're dealing. If they want something from you they'll tell you anything you want to hear: they'd kill their own mothers for their next fix."

I shook my head. "And my ration pack?"

"We get one pack a week, and it has to last, so don't give anything to anyone."

I couldn't believe I'd been so naïve. I told Susan what I'd done. "You'll need to catch on a bit quicker than that. Look, here's a bit of butter." She dropped a tiny blob onto my slice of toast. "When we get back to the wing come to my cell and I'll give you anything I can spare."

I'd barely begun eating when a bell rang and everyone

started filing back to the wing. I joined the throng, feeling like a child lining up after playtime. Susan took a ration pack out of her drawer and picked out a few items.

"Take these; they're all I can give you for now. When you get moved to your wing you can speak to the screws; tell them your pack was pinched - they'll get you another."

"Won't I be staying here?"

She looked at me as if I was mad. "God no, you'll be assessed and, provided you're not a psychopath, you'll get moved – probably to F Wing. Then you'll be given a job and, if you're a good girl and behave yourself you'll be moved to E Wing and, when you've been here about 20 years and they trust you, you'll go onto Enhanced. That's dead posh that is; you'll get your own cell and the door is left open all day so you don't have to wait for Association before you can talk to people." She made it sound like a trip to the Caribbean. "I've never made it there. I always get into trouble." I was just about to ask her what sort of trouble she got into when I heard doors banging all along the wing.

"Quick, it's lock up time."

I nodded my thanks before hurrying up the corridor to my cell.

I never saw Susan again; perhaps, just as she'd described, she'd been moved to another wing herself or even another prison, but what she told me was correct: the next day I was interviewed for assessment - and what happened next took me completely by surprise.

"I see from your address that you live on a farm, would that be your father's?" asked the officer. When I told him that it was my own farm and that I'd raised beef and dairy cattle as well as horses he seemed unusually pleased.

"Brilliant," he declared, thumping the desk. "Would you be willing to work on the farm here? We're short of suitable inmates; you'd be a godsend, and…" he looked me up and down. "You'd get perks; plenty of time in the fresh air."

"Yes, I'd like that," I said, my words completely inadequate for how I felt.

"I'll see if we can hurry you through the system." He looked down at the papers on his desk, the warmth disappearing just as quickly as it had appeared.

"Right, that's all, Holt, what are you waiting for? You can go back to your wing now." And he dismissed me before I'd had time to absorb the good news: he'd obviously got what he wanted.

Chapter Twenty-Six

1997

I changed out of my green prison issue trousers and into my jeans, then pulled a comb through my hair and peered at myself in the mirror stuck at an angle on the prison wall. Did I look okay? I couldn't be sure. The glass was smudged and had a slightly convex appearance so what I saw was the puffy-cheeked grimace of a human hamster rather than a 47-year-old woman. I pinched some colour into my cheeks: I wanted to look my best.

Mary was coming to see me today for her first visit. There was still an hour to go before she arrived but I had no idea how the visiting procedure worked and I didn't want to be late. I'd been told I could have two one-hour visits per month and I was hoping Mary would tell me that she would be happy to use up my allowance with her visits alone. Let's be honest; who else was going to come to see me? I was so excited at the prospect of meeting up with my best friend again I hadn't been able to finish my breakfast or my lunch.

I sat still for a moment on the edge of my bed, listening to the cacophony of noise coursing down the corridor and flowing into my cell. I couldn't get used to this echoing wall of sound but at least it kept the memories of my nightmares at bay: during the day the noise seemed to fill my brain with its demands and I had no room for anything else. My nightmares were back with the force of a hurricane since arriving at Newhall. God only knows what the screws must have thought as I shouted and screamed in my sleep, the terror jolting me upright in my bed. They never mentioned it to me in the morning but that was probably because I wasn't the only one expressing my dismay once those doors were locked. Most of us had nightmares and most of us didn't want to talk about them, so we screamed about them instead. I knew mine were different, though; my nightmares hadn't changed in 20 years.

At 2 o'clock an officer opened my cell door and took me down to the visiting block. My body was searched as a matter of course and then I was taken into the visitors' room where thirty tables were arranged like desks in an exam hall; one prisoner per desk, no paper, no pens. I sat down and looked at the clock: it was 2.03pm. I fidgeted in my chair until 2.10pm.

One of the prison officers walked past my table. "Excuse me officer, are the visitors arriving soon?" She turned and snapped at me as if I was a bothersome child. Edra, a fellow prisoner, leaned across and spoke in a whisper.

"Sharon says they've found drugs on one of the visitors. Let's hope it's not my Mam 'cos I know her and it's just the sort of thing she'd do, stupid cow."

A terrible anxiety gripped my stomach. "Will we still get the full hour?" I whispered.

"We'll be lucky if we get any visitors at all," she hissed.

One of the officers glanced over her shoulder but said nothing. I leant forward, resting my chin in my hands, disappointment and frustration coursing through my body. I'd been looking forward to this visit for two weeks and now, through no fault of my own, it looked like it wasn't going to happen.

But at 2.35pm the doors opened. All prisoners looked up as one as a line of bored, irritated or plain furious civvies marched in, each looking for their own wife, daughter, friend or lover. I scanned their faces, noting at the same time that Edra was doing the same and then I saw Mary – just moments before she saw me – and I waved madly at her as if she was standing miles away on the horizon and not looking at me from across the room. The relief I felt as she waved back was indescribable. And then she smiled her usual smile, her lovely round face beaming at me in all its welcome familiarity. I felt as if she'd brought the sights and sounds of the Peak District with her, shocking me out of this suffocating, claustrophobic environment and I stood up, knocking over my chair in my eagerness to give her a hug. One of the officers was by my side in a flash. "Sit down Holt, no physical contact with visitors."

I bit back my anger but did as I was told. Mary didn't even glance at the screw, she simply sat down opposite me, the smile never leaving her face.

"We've got to stop meeting like this," I said and we both laughed.

"Are you okay?" She was wearing her look of concern, the one she had when I told her how many cows I'd be milking that morning or how much work I had on at the office. "I didn't think I was going to be allowed in. We've all been waiting ages," she went on. She waved a hand at all the other visitors in the room but her eyes didn't leave mine.

"Drugs bust; someone's mum," I said dramatically and then we were both laughing again and suddenly everything was all right: Mary was still my friend, I wasn't going mad and she wasn't going to give up on me.

"I guess I haven't exactly been a model employee, have I?" I looked at Mary closely. I wondered if she knew about me and Miles but nothing in her demeanour indicated to me that she did. So goodness knows what she thought of me stealing fifty grand from my employer. I suppose she must have been thinking what everyone in New Mills was thinking: that I needed the money, so I said nothing to disabuse her of that idea. I felt bad enough about myself without hearing criticism from my best friend.

"What about the gossip in the village?" I asked, moving on.

"You don't usually worry about that sort of thing, Janet."

"I know, I'm just curious."

She leaned closer. "Well, since you ask, it's not good. Apparently Mags has written some sort of booklet accusing you of all sorts."

"A booklet?"

"When I asked about it in New Mills on Saturday, I was

told that Mags had written her biography and paid for it to be published so she could bequeath it to the Local History Society." Mary didn't laugh, although I was tempted. "I suppose her life is interesting if you think about it: widowed in her forties, brings up four children on her own while running a farm at the same time. You've got to admire her."

I said nothing.

"But apparently you've got a big mention too; something to do with you and Mag's brother going into business together. That you and he were partners at Ball Beard Farm and that he disappeared in strange circumstances. You never told me about that." Mary looked at me closely as if searching for clues. "Is it true?"

I nodded. There was no point denying it. "I've been meaning to tell you about it for years but to be honest, there's nothing else I can add to what you've just told me. He went missing - and he's still missing."

"I thought I might try to get hold of a copy."

"Hmm, that might be a good idea. If nothing else we can have a good laugh." I tried to smile but couldn't quite manage it.

"Hey, have you seen these?" Mary put some photographs on the table in front of me. I looked down at images of an aging Hero, grazing in the fields, another one of the hens clucking about the clean, well swept farmyard and one of Anthony and Mitchell, standing outside the cottage, the one I'd converted with my own bare hands, looking happy and content. Ball Beard Farm appeared

206

to be thriving without me.

Mary passed me six James Herriot paperbacks and two pairs of jeans. "Your favourite author," she said, before showing me a list of outstanding items that Anthony and Mitchell had passed on to her.

"What would I do without you?" I asked, putting the list to one side. I knew that most of the items on the list would involve money so there was no point reading it.

"You'd probably sleep better at night," she said, quick as a flash. "It must be a nightmare having a friend like me: always on your case, always nagging you."

I looked at Mary closely. Did she know about the nightmares? Did she know that I tossed and turned at night at the foul images in my head? But no, her eyes were full of humour. Of course she didn't know. How could she? She was simply taking charge of everything I needed in order to survive this ordeal and I realised, not for the first time, what a mess I'd be in without her.

We were just discussing how the weekly games of badminton were progressing now that their star player was in prison when a buzzer sounded and an officer shouted out over the din of our competing conversations: "Times up, ladies and gentlemen. Make your way to the doors now, please."

I looked at the clock in disbelief and felt an anger rise up inside me so violent I could physically taste it.

"Send me another visiting order," said Mary, touching me on the shoulder as she stood up. "I'll bring some more books next time and anything else you need."

My smile was slipping. "Well don't come bothering me too much, I've got a lot on, you know." I stood up too and then we hugged – I didn't give a damn about the screws and their stupid rules.

Mary eventually let me go and walked slowly to the door, giving me one last wave before slipping back to freedom. I wiped a tear from my eye then turned and followed the other women back to the wing. All I could do now was count the days to her next visit.

I counted - and I waited and while I ticked off the days I worked in the prison gardens like a model prisoner expecting a move to Enhanced at any moment. One of the first tasks I'd been allotted was digging over a small plot of ground, ready for planting and I welcomed the peace and the chance to do some physical hard work, setting about the task with enthusiasm but when Shirley and Val, the civilian officers in charge, came back to check on me they burst out laughing. "We're planting primroses here, Janet, not a dead body!"

I stood back and looked at what I'd done. "I'm more of a farmer than a gardener," I admitted, leaning on my spade and looking down at the hole which, I had to admit, was far too deep for flowers.

"Well, at least we know you're suited to the job," said Shirley. She chuckled and winked at her friend, who joined in the laughter after giving me a wary glance first. She obviously wanted

208

to check I could take a joke before making me the butt of one; some prisoners wouldn't hesitate to knock your block off as soon as you laughed at them.

Either way, it was a pleasant interlude, reminding me what it was like to be treated like a normal human being again. The ribbing was no worse than the banter we shared on our badminton nights; I'd pick on Carol for her terrible serves, she'd pick on Mary for her speed – or rather lack of it – across the court and they'd all pick on me for my desire to win at all costs. I smiled to myself then went back to my digging, watching Val and Shirley stroll off arm in arm like a couple of ageing lovers.

Moments later, leaning firmly on my spade, preparing the ground for some more flowers, I heard a sound that suddenly transported me back to the wide open spaces of the Peak District, to Ball Beard Farm and the sight and the sound of the greatest love of my life: horses. I stood, rooted to the spot, as memory after vivid memory came rushing towards me. I felt the blood and adrenalin pump through my body as my heart literally leapt with joy and recoiled with sadness at the same time. It couldn't be, surely? The evocative and unmistakable sound of a heavy horse's hooves, clip clopping on tarmac, and the metallic chink of chains as a cart is pulled behind.

I waited until my eyes told me I was right and yes, there I was, standing in the yard at Ball Beard Farm, the hills of the Peak District all around me as I watched with wonder and disbelief while a magnificent chestnut Suffolk Punch marched round the corner towards me. I stared, drinking in the sight of his healthy coat buffed to a brilliant glossy shine and stood, completely unmoving, as the magnificent animal stamped past, head high, ears pricked and I felt an ache inside that was as sad as it was happy. A dark, wiry man in blue overalls - the 'civvy' uniform - held the reins in a curiously clumsy way, his cap pulled down tight over his eyes while behind him sat six inmates, all shouting and laughing and hanging on tight as the cart swayed rhythmically from side to side. The horse's huge head nodded at me as he pulled against the collar, nostrils flaring, mouth champing against the bit. I stared at the chains linking him to the cart and the breeching strap around his hindquarters and bit back my tears. Then, with the hooves still beating out a rhythm in time with my heart, the turnout disappeared round the corner and, unable to bear it a moment longer, I collapsed with a sob as wave after wave of emotion washed over me. Feelings that had been missing or buried deep inside suddenly came racing to the surface; hope, despair, guilt, shame, desire, and disappointment crashed over me in one unstoppable rush. The sight and sounds of the magnificent Suffolk Punch had opened a door into my subconscious and suddenly I was able to look in and see my life displayed in all its shocking detail for the first time. My successes and my failures were laid out for me like pictures on a wall. I could see the hard work I had thrown away; I could see the chances I had missed and I could see the people I'd disappointed. I cried and I cried as tears that had been dormant for more than a year flowed swiftly down my face.

Inmates glanced my way but no-one said a word. It wasn't uncommon to see one of us suddenly overcome with emotion - that was the way it was in prison - but this was the first time it had happened to me.

By the time I got back to my cell I'd cried until my eyes were dry and all I could do was lie down on my bed and fall asleep.

When I woke at five the next morning everything seemed different. I wasn't floating above myself any more, looking down on a different person. I felt, for the first time in a long time, as if I had reclaimed my own body and I was comforted by this but at the same time I was unsettled. I seemed to have gained a deeper knowledge of what I had done - both to myself and to others - and it frightened me. I thought back to the actions I had taken - coldly, calmly and with no apparent apprehension – and I started to tremble. How was it possible? I couldn't understand it. How had I had an affair with a married man for 20 years; how had I stolen money from my employer, implicated a friend in the fraud, gone to prison? The Janet Holt I had once been would never have done all that. I didn't understand it but I knew now that I had the strength to accept it. And I knew one other thing for sure; there was no going back, no excuses, and no justification. I had to look to the future and that meant thinking of the farm. Would I have to sell Ball Beard when I got out of prison, I wondered? But who in their right mind would give me a job? I wouldn't be able to find work in a solicitor's office ever again. I shook my head. No, I couldn't sell. I would simply have to work harder than ever and try to build the farm back up again. I didn't have a choice.

And so, hanging on to that thought, and with some sort of hope taking up residence in my heart, the cell doors opened and I felt able to look to the future with a glimmer of optimism.

Chapter Twenty-Seven

1997

I walked through the prison grounds with Brian, one of the screws, ready for my first day on the farm.

"We've got pigs, dairy cows and livery horses, as well as Frank the Suffolk Punch and they all need looking after. You'll enjoy the work; it's varied and you get the added bonus of the best breakfasts in prison." I liked Brian; he treated all of the inmates the same, he was professional and courteous, unlike a few of the other screws I could mention.

I looked up at the prison gates. It was strange to think I was going to walk out of here – just like that. I'd been at Newhall for only a couple of weeks but already I felt institutionalised.

A thin, middle-aged man met us at the gate and I immediately recognised him as the man driving the cart the day I'd been digging in the prison gardens.

"That's Peewit - the farm manager - he'll show you what's what," whispered one of the girls and then she winked knowingly at me while all the other girls sniggered. I didn't know what they were getting at but I didn't like the look of Peewit one little bit.

"Another new one," said Brian, pointing at me.

Peewit looked me up and down, his eyes lingering a little too long on my body for my liking but then I had to remind myself that my likes and dislikes didn't matter any more now that I was in prison.

"What's your name?" asked Peewit, and I told him. He informed me that my first job was helping Andrea with the milking. "The rest of you know what you're doing – so get on with it."

I followed Andrea past the holding yard. Peewit stood to one side to let her go by then, as she walked up the narrow passageway, he leant towards her, put his hand out and squeezed her bottom.

"What the hell was that about?" I whispered in her ear. "He just touched your bum. He can't do that, he's an officer. Report him. I'll back you up."

Andrea frowned, checking over her shoulder to see where Peewit was before grabbing my arm. "Look, you're new here, right? I'm only going to say this once: Keep that big, fucking mouth of yours buttoned, okay? It's taken me months to get out here. Peewit and some of the girls have an understanding: he cops a feel when he wants and sometimes a bit more and it makes life nice and cosy all round. Some of the girls like having a bit of cock, even if it is old and wrinkly. So, you'd better learn fast, 'cos if you go shouting your mouth off every time you see something you don't like then every single one of us will be taken straight back to the wing and we'll never get out here again. So fuckin' get that into your brain and keep it zipped."

I waited for Andrea to draw breath. "Okay," I said and nodded.

"And if word gets round that you're a trouble maker, some of us will make sure you regret it." The final sentence was whispered with enough menace to make me flinch.

"I just find it difficult to believe that anyone would let a sleezeball like that …you know…but I can see you have your reasons."

Andrea cocked her head to one side and looked at me quizzically. Then as the cows filed past us into the milking area she suddenly laughed out loud as if deciding that perhaps I was one of them after all. "Listen, I've done a lot worse than that on the outside, believe me. Trust me, when you've been here for a few months you might fancy a bit yourself."

I looked over my shoulder and watched Peewit stroll into the milking area. Somehow I doubted that very much. He was barking out instructions at me now; how to handle the cows, how to operate the machinery and I felt anger grip at my insides. I was familiar with it all – I owned a farm for crying out loud - but I'd learnt my lesson and so I just stood there nodding as he demonstrated how to wipe the cow's teats with a cloth and how to attach the milking clusters. I had it in mind that I would punch him in the mouth if he tried to touch me but I knew that would only result in trouble for all the inmates, me included, so I decided to keep him at arms length instead. And that meant listening to him telling me how to milk cows when I probably had more experience than everyone else in this prison put together.

The animals all seemed nervous and jumpy and, watching Peewit in action, it was no surprise. He was too loud, too physical and far too rough when handling their udders. One poor creature was obviously suffering with cracked teats. I walked up to Peewit intending to do what I always did in a situation like this. "Where do you keep the udder cream?" I asked.

Peewit looked at me disdainfully, "You can't put cream on cows' udders; it gets into the milk. Stop being such a bloody clever dick and get those cows milked." And then he shooed me away.

I knew what he'd said was rubbish. Udder salves were used on dairy cows all the time. Apart from the discomfort, a cracked teat attracts flies, slowing down the healing process and increasing the risk of mastitis. I wasn't sure if Peewit was being awkward or whether he wasn't a proper farmer at all but a despicable little pervert, doing this job for all the 'fringe benefits'. I had a feeling it was the latter.

I finished milking the cow and carefully removed the clusters. "There you go girl," I said and gently patted her rump. The cow flinched and dropped her hindquarters indicating in that one movement that she'd probably been handled badly on a daily basis. I was getting a real feel for the way this farm was being run and it wasn't the way we did things at Ball Beard.

Once the milking was finished we hosed and swept the dairy clean then trekked back to the prison for a cooked breakfast

216

before going out again – this time to the pig unit.

As we walked across the yard I thought back to the pigsties at home: Fred and I had provided warming lamps for our pigs in the winter and in the summer we let them root around in the paddock or splash in muddy wallows to keep cool. I didn't for one minute think the animals would be so well provided for here, but what I actually saw took my breath away. This was intensive farming at its worst. I guessed there was about a hundred or so sows all lined up in small pens, some with litters, some waiting to give birth, all of them lying on concrete. Most of them were Large Whites or similar breeds; intelligent, friendly animals, all now reduced to breeding machines.

"I hate this part of the fucking job, it fucking stinks; I can't wait for dinnertime," said Andrea, aiming an accurate kick at a metal bucket and sending it spinning across the floor. At the metallic clanking and crashing the whole building erupted in an array of deafening squeals and grunts, making normal conversation impossible. "You stinking, noisy bastards," screamed Andrea.

I looked around for Peewit but he was nowhere to be seen, then as the clamour died down a tiny, bird-like woman, covered in tattoos and with a badly scarred face tugged at my arm.

"Come over here; I'll show you what to do," she said, thrusting a shovel at me. "Clean each pen out and then pile the muck in the passageway." She pointed to one side. "When you've finished, Peewit will shove it all out into the yard. Mind your legs - the bastards bite." And with that last remark she smirked and

217

walked away to join a group of her fellow inmates who were now gathering round to watch. Clearly they were expecting some fun.

I opened the pen door very slowly and walked in. At Ball Beard, if I was uncertain about a pig's temperament, I'd take a handling board in with me and hold it in front of the pig like a shield. But there were no boards in this shed so a shovel would have to do. The sow stood in the corner, watching me warily and grunting with small, nervous grunts. "It's alright piggy, I'm only going to clean your floor; I'm not going to hurt you." I could see the pig was listening, but as I took a step forward she rushed towards me, mouth open, ready to bite. I lowered the flat end of the shovel in front of her face to block her vision, and she stopped. As she took a step backwards I quietly moved the shovel round to the left side of her head and she automatically moved to the right. She stood against the wall of the pen and I lowered the shovel, keeping it against my legs, just in case, then I touched her back and began to scratch her gently, digging into the coarse coat. She grunted with pleasure.

It wasn't long before her legs began to buckle and I knew then what would come next. She dropped onto the floor and with a few wriggles and squirms lay on her side, exposing her belly and vast udder, just as she would do for her piglets when they were born. I carried on scratching, moving down her side and then on to her belly with the flat of my hand, massaging her udder as she stretched her legs out, grunting in ecstasy. As the minutes passed the sow's grunts became quieter until eventually, she fell into a deep sleep. I stood up, took the brush and swept her pen out, noticing now that four inmates, including Tattoo, were standing silently watching me from over the wall. I ignored them until I'd swept the last of the muck through the doorway, then I closed the door of the pen, came out and gave them a nod. The sow was still fast asleep.

"How the fuckin' hell did you do that?" said Tattoo. None of the women were smirking now.

"You hypnotized the bloody thing," said another.

"No, I didn't. All pigs like to be scratched on their backs and if you're nice to them they don't usually turn nasty. If they do try to bite, just use a board, or a shovel, to block their vision. There's no need to hit them and if you do you'll only make them more aggressive. You know what it's like to be locked up so how do you think these poor sods feel, stuck in a tiny pen all their lives?"

"Yeah, but you made it lie on the floor and go to sleep. Like magic," said Tattoo.

"No, she's just doing what she'll do when she's got her babies."

Tattoo looked over the wall. "How do know all this anyway?"

"I used to have a farm."

Tattoo started to laugh, looking at the other girls and encouraging them to join in. "Well, I reckon you're all right Mrs Farmer."

219

I knew that this was as big a complement as you could hope to get in a place like this and as I watched Tattoo lean over into another pen I could see she trusted me enough to try it herself. She started on a smaller sow, scratching her back tentatively at first and then gaining in confidence. "Look, look, it's working - it likes it!" The other inmates lined up for their turn, all scratching the pig and watching with amusement as it squirmed and writhed with pleasure.

Tattoo came up to me as I started to clean the next pen. "Peewit told us to boot them as hard as we could. We didn't know any different."

"There's only one pig round here that wants a good kicking," I said with feeling.

"Are you volunteering, 'cos if you are there'll be a few of us joining in."

I sighed and looked at Tattoo. I had the feeling that, behind the savage appearance she was probably all right too. "Where is he anyway? I thought he would be in here supervising."

She told me that Peewit was up the yard, dealing with a calving cow and it didn't sound as if it was going too well. I immediately heard alarm bells ringing in my head. I didn't imagine he would be handling that situation with any finesse either.

Chapter Twenty-Eight

1997

I rushed from the pigs as fast as I could, listening to Peewit's obscenities echoing round the yard like a foul chorus line before I caught sight of him. He was standing next to one of the cows as she lay on the ground, his hands on his bony hips looking like a cartoon version of a bandy cowboy, "Bloody useless bitch, should've sent you in years ago," he growled. I skidded to a halt and then inched my way towards two mesmerised inmates who were watching the whole horrible scenario as it played out in front of them.

The cow was attempting to give birth, but something was clearly wrong. I could see the calf's head and front legs, but the mother was exhausted and didn't appear to be straining. Peewit threw a towel at the cow's rump.

"What's happening" I whispered.

"Dunno," said one of the inmates. "The cow's trying to have a baby but it's bin here hours. Old fuckface keeps cursin'."

Peewit looked up at the two girls. "Where's Brian?" he snapped.

"Think he's up in't gardens," said the other inmate.

"Right, stay here. If Brian comes back tell him I've gone to get the tractor to calve this cow. Got that?"

"Yeah, we'll tell 'im."

Peewit marched off. As soon as he'd gone I bent down and rubbed the cow's head, speaking softly. I could see that her eyes were dull, her mouth was open and she was panting, sweat pouring down her neck. Her ears were icy cold and she was trembling violently. I didn't have to be a vet to know this cow was in real distress and needed help. I shuddered at the thought of Peewit rushing to get the tractor. I'd seen this before: an undersized heifer lying in a field trying vainly to give birth to an oversized calf and the farmer using a tractor to drag the calf out. Some farmers – not many, thank goodness - will do anything to save on vet's bills and on that occasion the calf was alive but the tractor ripped one of its front legs clean off. After watching this going on in a neighbouring field back home in New Mills I was violently sick. I imagined the same thing happening here but I also knew the consequences of doing something without Peewit's authority: immediate dismissal from the farm.

"Go and fetch a bale of straw from round the back and bring two sacks," I shouted at the two inmates. They were no more than 17 or 18 years old and clearly uncertain of my authority. "Get a bloody move on! I need you back here in less than five minutes or I'll put you both on report."

They fell for it; nearly tripping over themselves in their hurry to get down to the straw shed as quickly as they could.

222

Meanwhile I bent down to study the calf as it hung half out its mother, its lifeless head touching the concrete floor. It looked to me like a Charolais and, from the size of its two front hooves, it was massive. Peewit had already attached calving ropes. I estimated it would take him at least 20 minutes to get the tractor.

I unbuttoned my overalls and tied them round my waist, then stripped to my t-shirt. I soaped my arm before kneeling down on the concrete next to the cow. She grunted but nothing more since it was clear she had nothing else to give. I inserted my arm gently then followed the calf's body down along its rib cage as far as the flanks, by which time I was almost at my full extent and practically lying on the floor. I could feel a hoof, lying against the calf's flank, where it had no right to be. The hind leg was forward and the hock, the big joint in the hind leg, was jammed tight against the calf's large hips. There was no way the cow could give birth naturally with the calf in that position, it needed to be pushed back and the hind leg moved but I couldn't reach far enough. It needed someone stronger than me and with longer arms.

The girls ran back, panting, bringing the straw and the sacks with them as I'd asked and we covered the cow in an attempt to keep her warm just as we heard the sound of the tractor coming down the yard. I rubbed my arm with the towel and pulled my overalls back on as the two inmates hurried back to their positions in the doorway.

Peewit reversed the tractor then stepped down from the cab. "What the fuck's this?"

"I thought I should cover her with straw - to keep her warm," I said, making sure I didn't mention the other two. "I'm sorry; I should have asked you first, sir." Servility was my only hope.

"You *thought*… you *thought*…" He was shouting in my face now, stepping forward so that his nose was only a few inches from mine. He smelt of tobacco and bad breath and it was all I could do to stand my ground without swinging for him.

"Who the fucking hell do you think you are; the bloody Queen of England? Has anyone told you where you are? You're a con, you don't have opinions, Holt. You do as you're told. Got that?" He stabbed a finger into my shoulder.

"Yes, sir."

"Right, stand back. You might learn something here." He glared at me. There was no mistaking the look of hatred in those cold, pebble-like eyes. He walked back to the tractor and attached a rope to the calf's legs. I wanted to scream at him: '*You'll break the cow's pelvis; get a vet for God's sake*' but I stayed silent. If I didn't it wouldn't just be me going back to the wing, it would be everyone else too. Andrea and Tattoo would never forgive me.

The tractor started up and drove forward. As the rope tightened I turned away. I heard the cow start to bellow, a forlorn hopeless noise then looked over my shoulder at the two youngsters watching the event unfold in front of them, faces screwed up in horror. The tractor stopped. I turned around. The cow was stretched out, silent now, a dead calf lying on the ground behind her. Peewit was walking back towards me, his eyes fixed on mine; his face wearing a smug, self-righteous look of satisfaction. "And that," he said very quietly, "Is how you calve a cow." Then he bent over me, his wiry frame suddenly appearing more ominous than it ought to do. "Who knows how to calve a cow, Holt?"

"You do sir," I said, almost choking on the words. I swallowed my fury. "Could I possibly give the cow a drink of water now, sir?"

Peewit shook his head. "Unbelievable. You still don't get it do you? You're on report, Holt. Go back to the wing, NOW, and tell your wing officer what I've just said: *GO!*"

I trailed slowly back to the wing, wondering if I'd achieved some sort of record. One day on the farm – one solitary day. If it wasn't so disappointing I'd have laughed. Well, all I could do was report to Brian as Peewit had requested and hope for the best.

But Brian's reaction wasn't quite what I'd expected.

"Well, well," he said. "That's one for the books."

I didn't ask what he meant; I didn't have the energy. Brian passed me over to one of the other uniformed screws and I was led back to my cell. Once inside I sat on my bed and waited, doing nothing as the hours passed. My door remained locked; tea-time came and went. I could hear the women on the wing collecting hot water to make tea and coffee before lock-up. I had a drop of water in my flask so I made a lukewarm cup of tea and sipped it slowly, wondering about the events that had led me cock up my one and only day at the farm but I knew I couldn't have stood by and done nothing because that that wasn't an option: it wasn't how we'd done things at Ball Beard Farm.

Chapter Twenty-Nine

1997

I washed and dressed the following morning at 5.30am just in case I was expected to report for duty. I heard Brian come onto the wing and unlock the cells for the other farm workers but he walked past me. So that was it, then, I'd really stuffed it up.

At 8 o'clock all the other doors were unlocked for breakfast. I stood there, plastic mug in hand, ready for mine. I'd missed tea last night so I was starving.

My door opened – and I was greeted by Miss Evans, a uniformed screw. She ushered me out into the corridor.

"Holt, collect your breakfast things then come straight back here," she said. I knew better than to ask why.

"I've been put on report, can you tell me what happens," I whispered to another inmate in the queue for breakfast.

"You're locked up all day 'till you get a hearing with the Governor; no work, no Association, only trips down here to get food."

I explained to the inmate serving behind the counter that I'd fallen out with Peewit, big-style and she gave me a big beaming smile. "Pass your plate back, love," she said. Then she added

227

baked beans, grilled bacon and three slices of toast to my scrambled egg with a small pack of butter on the side. "Now clear off and if anyone asks you why you've got so much for breakfast tell them it was about to be chucked in the waste." I hesitated. I couldn't afford to get into any more trouble. "I've heard all about that Mr Bloody Peewit and it's about time someone drove that bloody tractor right over him."

I smiled, said my thanks and hurried back to my cell.

At 1 o'clock I was collected and marched off to the office where the wing officer, the stern and formidable Miss Wilson, was sitting next to Brian, looking as if they'd been deep in conversation.

"I understand you had some problems on the farm yesterday. Could you tell us what happened?"

My brain was speeding at 100 miles an hour. I told them about the cow attempting to calve as objectively as possible and apologised for using my initiative in dealing with the situation. I said I realised that I should have asked permission. The two officers stared at me impassively.

"The farm manager has accused you of being rude, obstinate and not complying with his orders. He has asked that you are removed from the farm, which would mean you would not be able to work outside on the livery yard or the gardens at any time. Do you have anything to say about that?"

I tried to assess Miss Wilson's mood but it was difficult. As I mentioned earlier, I'm not known for my perceptive capabilities and I was hopeless at nuance. "Peewit told me he was putting me on report, so yes, I do know that." I said, weighing my words carefully before I spoke.

Brian explained that he was in overall charge of the farm and that it was up to him to place an inmate on report, providing there was justification, of course. "However, Peewit is the farm manager and as such I have to investigate any complaint he makes. I get the impression you didn't hit it off with him, am I right?"

I hesitated again and then told them the clash was probably because I had farmed for so many years on my own and so I had my own way of doing things. I feared I might have been too honest even with that small admission, because I noticed the look of disappointment on Miss Wilson's face.

"What exactly would you say was wrong with the cow?" she asked, looking down at a piece of paper on her desk.

"She was having difficulty calving," I replied.

"Yes, I know that, but why was she cold? Why did you need to cover her up?"

I looked from Miss Wilson to Brian and back again. They were giving nothing away. "The effort of trying to calve for such a long period meant she would be sweating and exhausted - then she would get cold."

Miss Wilson persisted, "How long do you think she'd been trying to give birth? In your opinion, should a vet have been called out?"

I hesitated. "Yes, a vet should have been called."

This time it was a triumphant look that spread across Miss Wilson's face. She glanced across at Brian and nodded.

"Right," he said. "On this occasion I am not going to put you on report. I understand Miss Wilson wishes you to work at the livery yard so, from tomorrow onwards that is what you will be doing. We have horses and we need someone with experience. You fit the bill, Janet."

I couldn't believe my ears. "Thank you," I said, "I appreciate that, but can you tell me what happened to the cow?"

"I'm afraid she had to be shot this morning; she couldn't get up."

"And one other thing," Brian continued, glossing over my dismay. "The hours on the livery yard are shorter, so any surplus time is usually spent working on the farm, but that is obviously not the ideal solution for you given the situation. Would you like to do your additional time in the gardens instead?"

"Yes," I said quickly, before they could change their minds.

And that is how I came to spend the rest of my time in Newhall in the stables, looking after Frank, the chestnut Suffolk Punch and Saracen, a spirited half thoroughbred – whose owner just happened to be Miss Wilson.

Meanwhile, following a complaint by a young inmate, Peewit received a formal warning. It was obvious he was no-one's favourite officer – least of all the inmates - and I'm pretty sure there had been suspicions for years that he had been mistreating the animals. I wonder if Miss Wilson had hopes of me substantiating her suspicions and thereby giving her more weapons to fire. Had I known this then I'm sure I would have been much more forthcoming in my interview.

Unfortunately Peewit kept his job as farm manager. The farm had a lot to offer the inmates but not if it was run by people like him and until such time as he was disposed of, it was the animals that had my sympathy.

Chapter Thirty

1998

I looked at the release form in my hand. After serving one year of my sentence they were letting me out on Licence. Over the last 12 months I'd carried on working in the livery yard and the gardens, I'd attended the gym whenever I could and I'd made friends with inmates and officers alike. My nightmares weren't as frequent as when I'd first arrived but they hadn't disappeared completely. All I could say was that I was coping and I hoped I'd continue to cope once I got back to Ball Beard.

While I'd been at Newhall I'd discovered who my real friends were; friends who hadn't judged me, hadn't condemned me or condoned me but had stayed true, helping and supporting me when I needed it most. Mary stood out like a beacon in a storm: I hadn't heard a thing from Miles Ingleby.

I'd pictured this moment in my mind every single day since I'd arrived at Newhall; the day I would be allowed to walk back out of the prison gates. I'd anticipated the feelings of elation and the sense of relief that would accompany this moment and yet I didn't feel elated or relieved at all. Instead, I felt nervous, apprehensive and confused. I'd heard of inmates who couldn't bear to leave prison, who would even commit offences inside to get extra time added to their sentence and when I first came here I thought such stories were fanciful, but now? Well, I could fully understand it. How can someone, inside for say, 10 years, possibly face the outside world? I had no idea.

I'd stopped worrying about the farm or anything else for that matter a long time ago. I realised there was nothing I could do so there was no point thinking about it. My life had settled down into a strict regime of work, meals, gym and bed - but now that was coming to an abrupt end and I had to face up to my responsibilities again. I'd have bills to pay, food to buy, decisions to make. Unlike some inmates I did have a home to go back to, but that in itself was a massive responsibility. I had a bank overdraft, outstanding bills, no job, no livestock and no income and yet I had to find a way to pay back the money I'd stolen from Ingleby's. Prison was a punishment but it was also a shield against many of life's pressures. The minute I walked out of those gates those pressures would hit me again. Oh yes, this sensation of pending freedom was a very strange feeling indeed.

My door was unlocked.

"You've got one hour, Janet. Pack your stuff, you're going home."

I stared in disbelief as the door began to close again. "But there must be some mistake. I've got my release form here; it says I'm leaving tomorrow."

She hesitated, but only for a second. "Don't argue. If you're not ready in an hour you'll be taken down to the gate without your stuff and you'll have to leave it here. Please yourself." The door banged shut.

And so I started to pack. I wasn't really surprised. The screws would do anything to disrupt and confuse us, but I wasn't aware that it also applied to releasing you a day early. But, hey, why argue? I wanted to go home, didn't I?

But what was I supposed to do about *getting* home? Mary had offered to pick me up – but not till tomorrow. I didn't know if I could get to Ball Beard using public transport and I wasn't sure how much money I'd have in my pocket. Over the months I'd saved about £20 but I had no idea if that was enough to get home. All I knew was I was in Yorkshire at the moment and I needed to get to Derbyshire.

I packed within half an hour - not that stuffing everything into two black bin liners constituted packing - then I sat down on my bed and waited.

An hour passed, then two as I paced up and down in my cell. I heard doors unlock for dinner. Someone opened my vision flap and asked if I'd like something to eat and when I said I would I then waited another half an hour before an unknown inmate offered me a tray containing an unappetising assortment of food.

"Sorry - there were nowt left," she muttered and left.

'*And the condemned man ate a hearty meal*' I said to myself as I poked at the lumpy mash, the congealed gravy and half a sad sausage, then I scraped the food into the toilet pan and flushed it away before washing the cutlery and placing it all neatly on the table. You never knew in this place; they might decide to keep me in for something as innocuous as not eating my tea and I wasn't taking any chances at this late stage.

It was another hour before I was taken to the gates for release. Thank goodness for Mary; I'd phoned her at the last minute and she was able to come and collect me after all. As I waited for her to arrive, I watched some of my fellow inmates walking up the road to the farm after dinner. Some of them waved at me and I waved back but it felt strange - as if the friendships I'd made in prison were all set to fade away and vanish once I'd crossed that threshold.

I fixed my eyes on the horizon for a sight of Mary's shiny Nissan Micra almost whooping with joy when it finally came round the corner. I was so pleased to see her I couldn't wipe the grin off my face for the whole of the 60 mile journey from Wakefield back to New Mills.

"Have you had a nice break?" asked Mary, her grin as wide as mine.

"I haven't bought you a present," I said.

"A glass of wine in the White Horse tomorrow night will do just fine," she said, suddenly unsure. "That is if you want to go; if you want to be seen…"

"Mary, I'm not going to hide away for the rest of my life."

"No, but I thought…"

"You're worried about the gossip, is that it? I've told you; I don't listen to gossip. Will Carol and Claire be coming to the pub too?" Mary nodded. "Well, there you go, we've got our badminton quorum; what more do I need?"

Mary shook her head.

"It's Mags, isn't it?"

She nodded.

I knew now what she was getting at. "Did you manage to track down a copy of that booklet she produced?"

"No, but I know plenty of people who've read it." I glanced at Mary but her eyes didn't leave the road. "The thing is, no-one will tell me what it says. The Local History Society said they can't find the copies that Mags is supposed to have given to the Heritage Centre a few years back and I don't know who else to ask."

We both fell silent. All I could hear as we travelled towards Ball Beard Farm was the sound of the tyres on the tarmac and the low thrum of the car's heater blowing air onto both our faces.

"But, to be honest I don't want to know," said Mary eventually. "If you're not concerned about the gossip, then neither am I."

I nodded. "Thanks," I said.

"You're welcome." She chanced a look at me, just to make sure I was telling the truth and I made sure I was smiling. I needed to track down a copy of that booklet for myself. Goodness knows what Mags was accusing me of.

Mary offered to come into the cottage with me but I assured her she didn't need to. "I'll see you tomorrow, then." She looked at me as if I was going to disappear in a puff of smoke.

236

"Don't worry, I'll be fine," I said with increasing confidence. "Anthony and Mitchell have been doing a grand job while I've been away. All I've got to do is persuade them to leave the cottage before I put it on the market." I knew, as soon as the words were out of my mouth, that getting the boys out was not going to be easy but I had no choice; I had to pay my debts.

"And where are you going to live?"

I tapped the side of my nose. "I've got something up my sleeve," I said – although we both knew I had nothing up my sleeve – or up my nose for that matter.

"Right." She looked at me before scanning the farmyard. I had no idea what she was looking for - my fairy godmother perhaps. "I'll get off then."

I nodded and then she gave me one last hug before walking back to her car. I turned towards the cottage and tried the door. I wasn't surprised in the slightest when I discovered it was locked.

Chapter Thirty-One

**Before and after pictures of a farm wall near Buxton,
Derbyshire, rebuilt by me in 2003**

1999

It was six long months before I 'persuaded' Anthony and
Mitchell out of the cottage. In the end I had to shout through the
letterbox that I was going to set the place on fire unless they
scarpered. There was no use me going to the police to get rid of
them since I had a criminal record now and I didn't want anything

more to do with the law as long as I lived. Meanwhile I was living in a caravan parked up in my field, desperately looking for a job.

I'd been out of prison for just two weeks when I received a letter from the taxman reminding me that I owed him £500 and asking for my proposals. My bank manager also wrote me a lovely letter advising me that interest had been accruing on my overdraft for the past 12 months and could I now do something about it please. There had obviously been a public announcement that I was coming home.

I wandered around the empty farm buildings and walked up the field to my boundary wall. Peering over the top I spotted one of the Castleford's cows, tucked up close to her day old calf. Ernie had departed this world a while back now so I assumed the animal belonged to his sons. The cow saw me staring and rose protectively to her feet mooing gently at her baby as she began to clean him; great rasping licks that rocked the calf from side to side and finally roused him enough to stagger to his feet. He wobbled precariously while I continued to watch, the cow's eyes finally closing in contentment as he took hold of a teat.

I must have been standing there for half an hour watching this image of new life before turning and walking slowly back up to the farm, thoughts racing through my mind. I knew I'd made a right mess of everything, but suddenly I felt a glimmer of hope flickering in my heart. I realised I wanted nothing more than to look after the farm; I wanted to tend the land and care for the animals just as I'd always done and I realised I wanted to be a part of it all again; the seasons, the life, the living – and yes, even the death.

I sat down in the kitchen with a cup of tea, knowing what I would do; I'd fight and I'd work hard and, somehow, I'd build the farm business back up again but first, I had to get a job and then I would have to sell my newly reacquired cottage – I couldn't put it off any longer.

Decisions made, I began to feel much more positive. I reached for the local paper to look through the job vacancies – my options restricted to cleaning or factory work - and spotted an advert for packers at a local factory. *All shifts available, including night shifts* it said. I figured that would be the perfect solution: I could work in the factory at night, see to the farm during the day and perhaps drum up a spot of dry-stone walling on the side for good measure.

As I was considering my application the phone rang. I picked up the receiver; it was Mrs Macpherson, an ex-walling client of mine who had been in touch a year ago to ask me to quote for some work on her driveway. As everyone knew in New Mills, I'd been otherwise engaged for the last 12 months and, since she lived locally, she would no doubt have read all about my demise in the papers so I decided it was best to proceed with caution and I asked her how she'd been and what I could do for her. She didn't even pause.

"Do you remember the quotation you put together for our new driveway wall? Well, we realise you've been – unavailable recently - but we were hoping you could fit us in sometime in the next couple of weeks."

"You haven't asked anyone else to do it in my absence?"

"No, because we loved the other work you did for us previously, it was so original, we decided to wait. You can take another look at the job if you wish; you'll probably want to update your quote."

I was, as they say, gobsmacked. "I believe I quoted £850 and I'll honour that," I said, suddenly feeling very humble indeed.

Mrs Macpherson asked me when I could start work and I confirmed that next Monday would be good for me. I put the phone down and shook my head. I couldn't believe it; I had a walling job!

Then I telephoned the number in the paper enquiring about night shifts at the factory and was given an appointment for an interview the following day. Twelve hours later I was offered a packing job, four nights a week, 6pm till 6am and I realised that if things continued to go as smoothly as this the farm would be stocked up with livestock in no time.

The following Monday I began work on Mrs Macpherson's wall, I worked all day, then at 5.45pm made my way to the factory to begin my night shift. I couldn't afford to take time off in between jobs since I knew I didn't dare take my newly acquired good fortune for granted.

I joined six other women on a noisy packing line, the din of the machines making normal conversation impossible. One of the supervisors explained the set up. "I've put you on a slow machine to start with," she said. I looked at the conveyor belt scattered with aluminium plates like hundreds of oversized coins, not convinced at all that this was a slow machine.

"Right," she shouted in my ear, "When you press that green button your machine starts; the red one is to stop it. You have to pack 100 foil plates into the box, 50 at a time. Put them into the plastic bag then put the plastic bag in the box: two bags per box, then put the box on that conveyor belt over there."

I nodded again.

"Can you count to 50?"

I looked at her as if she was joking then nodded for a third time when I realised she wasn't. It was difficult to express amusement – or any other emotion for that matter – with all this machinery as background noise.

"Good, right, any questions?"

For a change I shook my head and the supervisor left me to it.

I glanced to my right. The woman next to me was calmly catching batches of foil plates in her hand then, on reaching the required number, she'd deftly hold the stack on the counter while taking hold of a plastic bag with her free hand, shaking it open and thrusting the open end over the plates before putting them into a cardboard box. She appeared to do all this in one easy, smooth movement and, by the time she'd put the trays in the box, another 10 were waiting for her on the counter. With a sweep of her hand

242

she scooped the plates together and carried on catching a fresh batch. She made the whole process look very easy indeed.

I checked my box and plastic bags were in position and pressed the green button. Flat aluminium plates hurtled down the conveyor belt in front of me. I caught the first three but then the fourth one hit my thumb and flew off to the side, bouncing along the counter. I tried to grab it but two more plates flew down almost immediately and, hands out of position, I missed both of them, one flying off to the left the other to the right. I left the plates where they fell and concentrated on trying to stack the new plates instead which were coming at me with increasing speed. I managed to get about 30 into a stack, but then, as I held it with my left hand the whole stack concertinaed and collapsed around me. Plates took off in all directions and, as I floundered again, the stream continued. In amongst all this I vaguely remember a co-worker leaning across me and pressing the red button, while shouting something unintelligible in my ear. It was the woman at the next station.

"Having trouble?" she shouted and I nodded – what else could I say? She carried on shouting: "Don't worry - you'll get the hang of it. Throw these in the bin and start again and don't bother about any you miss; just keep stacking the ones you catch and the minute you feel yourself panicking - HIT THE BUTTON." She smiled, partly to encourage me and partly because, I'm sure it was very funny seeing the new girl struggle. So I tried again and slowly, very, very slowly, I began to grasp the knack of packing aluminium plates and by the end of the day I was just about keeping up with the machine. As I prepared to leave the factory, the supervisor had a few words to say.

"You seem to have got the hang of it. We'll try you out on a faster machine tomorrow."

'Thanks a lot,' I thought to myself, *'I can't wait'*.

I was tired after my first shift but consoled myself with the thought that the intensity of the packing had made the hours fly by. When I got home I went straight to bed, slept until 10 o'clock the next morning, and then started work on the farm.

After a month or so of this schedule, with just three or four hours sleep a night, exhaustion hit me with all the force of a brick wall. My eyes were permanently tired and my head was muggy. When I got home after each shift I'd feel exhausted but, lying in bed, unable to sleep, I'd go over all the things I had to do before dropping off about half an hour before I was due to get up then I'd stumble out of bed, disorientated and light-headed. I don't know how long I could have kept this up without doing some permanent damage, but after six months I'd managed to save some money and the dry-stone walling work was flooding in, so I left the factory, thankful for the work I had been given but even more thankful to be leaving. The job, I have to say, was instantly forgettable.

Things were taking shape now at the farm. I'd finally got rid of Anthony and Mitchell, sold the cottage and paid off all my debts. I'd replaced the small caravan with a large mobile home, with electric, hot water, toilet and shower and my order book for dry-stone walling work was full to bursting. I'd also been offered a job with a local college, teaching dry-stone walling three days a week at a very good rate of pay. With the money I was earning from this I'd bought eight beef heifers to rear as the basis of a new suckler herd and drawn up plans to convert the farm and the herd to organic production. I'd also obtained a Stewardship Agreement with Defra which would pay me for managing the farm in an environmentally friendly way, bringing in some welcome additional funds.

As I settled down for the night in front of the TV in my cosy new mobile home I felt a calmness wash over me that I hadn't felt in years. I got up to make a cup of tea, forcing myself to stay awake for at least another hour. That way, I would fall asleep as soon as my head hit the pillow. I opened the cupboard to dig out my favourite mug when the list on the back of the door caught my eye and even though I knew it by heart, I recited it out loud like a mantra:

Get out of bed

Feed the dogs

Get washed

Get dressed

Make a cup of tea, eat a slice of toast.

I won't pretend I didn't feel my usual increased heartbeat as I read it out loud because I did, but I also managed to think past my nightmares and made a mental note that 'feed the dogs' was no longer a priority and that's when I realised I missed having a companion and wondered if I should do something about it.

Chapter Thirty-Two

Henry

2000

"Take him home - he's all yours."

I looked down at the small, rather pathetic brown dog tied to the bumper of the car with a length of baling string and considered the offer.

It all began 24 hours earlier. I was working with Edith and Gemma on a dry-stone walling job, high up in the Peak District hills. They'd arrived with Jake, their black and tan Weimeraner, but they'd also brought a terrier called Henry with them; a funny looking thing with broad, heavy shoulders, a long curling tail and short legs. They'd collected Henry just a few weeks ago from a dog's home in Sheffield thinking he would be good company for Jake - but Henry had other ideas.

Henry's life on the streets of Sheffield had obviously taught him to stand up for himself and as soon as he arrived at Edith and Gemma's home he made his move, attacking Jake and forcing him into a corner. Then he collected all Jake's toys and anything edible he could find, put it all in a pile and sat there guarding his treasure like a canine version of King Midas.

Following Edith's introduction I put my hand out to pat Henry's head but the terrier immediately bared his teeth and went for me, his mouth snapping shut an inch from my fingers. Memories of first meeting Bonny, one of the Shires on Round Wood at the age of 12, came flooding back, making me smile.

"We're taking him back to the home tomorrow," said Edith. "Jake's absolutely terrified of him. It's such a shame since he seemed perfectly fine in the kennels."

'*How stupid some people are*' I thought. Henry wasn't a puppy and there was no doubt he'd been through a lot in his short life: abandoned, taken to a dogs' home, farmed out to two women who already owned a dog and then expected him to act as if nothing had happened. I felt sorry for him. I looked at the terrier and wondered what sad tales he could tell if only he could talk but I wasn't interested in his stories because I didn't want a terrier and I certainly didn't want a fat, ugly, middle-aged terrier like Henry.

As I drove home with the fat, ugly, middle-aged terrier

sitting beside me on the passenger seat of my pickup, I wondered just how much I would regret this decision. But I knew I couldn't just sit by and watch the girls take him back to the dog's home. What would Henry be faced with on his return if they did that? More unsuitable, would-be dog owners like them no doubt, who might offer him a home but end up taking him back - possibly worse.

Back at Ball Beard Farm I watched him climb down from the pickup as if he didn't quite trust the farmyard floor then I followed him a few paces behind as he sniffed all the walls and gates, his attention taken by the strange sights and smells all around him. When he'd finished he wandered up the yard towards the cottage, with me just a little way behind.

Ball Beard Cottage had been bought by a couple who'd also recently become owners of a dog; a pampered poodle by the name of Pip. Pip was a delicate-looking creature with a feisty character and as expected, he came out to inspect the new arrival.

"This is Pip, your neigh…" I began, but my introduction was cut short as Henry flew at the poodle, grabbing him by the neck and worrying him to the ground. Cries echoed around the yard as the three of us lunged at Henry. I got there first and grabbed hold of him just in time, hauling him up into my arms where he promptly bit my finger. I clung on, blood dripping onto my jeans, as I apologised to Pip's owners before hurrying away with Henry grumbling and growling in my arms and Pip was rushed off to the vets.

"Well, that was way too much excitement for one day," I said as Henry carried on inspecting his new surroundings. I thought about his behaviour and realised it was no-one's fault but my own. I had done exactly what I'd criticise others for doing: I had brought Henry to a strange place expecting him to know how I wanted him to behave and he'd reacted with panic and fear. No wonder he was such a mess.

I decided to start again and looked out an old collar and lead before taking Henry out into the fields. As he trotted along in front of me I noticed that his tail, which had been permanently clamped to his bottom all day, was now raised up and wagging gently. He had also begun to respond to my voice.

Later that evening, as I sat in front of the television with my meal on my lap and Henry leaning against my legs, I couldn't help but notice that each time I stood up he followed me.

Bedtime approached. I made a bed up for him next to the fire, adding a cuddly toy for company then I waited until the last moment before creeping across to the bedroom. Henry followed. "No, Henry, lie down, good boy, I'll see you tomorrow," I said, before closing the door in his face and climbing into bed.

I lay there listening to Henry's scratching and whining until I couldn't stand it a moment longer. I opened the door ready to give him some more curt instructions but he was one step ahead of me; he shot across the bedroom, leapt onto my bed and curled up on the duvet cover before I had to chance to stop him, then lay there, peering at me anxiously through the wiry hair hanging like a brush over his eyes. Well, what else could I do?

"Okay, okay, just for tonight," I said, with little conviction.

Henry watched me closely as I climbed into bed then, as I put my hand up to switch off the light, he ducked and began to tremble. So that was it, I thought, he'd been beaten. He was clearly expecting it now. I gently caressed the top of his head. "Don't jump lad, I'm not going to hurt you. This is your home now; a place where you'll be safe and where you can run about and have lots of fun. How does that sound?" I switched the light off and heard Henry give one final sigh before curling up against my feet and finally falling asleep.

The next morning he was my shadow, following me everywhere I went, reaching into every corner, every nook and every cranny of Ball Beard Farm. Whenever I turned to look at him, he was there, looking back at me, just as closely.

Henry was a strange but loveable character; he loved to ride in my pickup truck with his hind feet on the passenger seat, front feet on the dashboard, looking out of the windscreen and barking at every passing cyclist and pedestrian along the route. Before long he lost his anxious, aggressive persona and became a happy little extrovert who went everywhere with me; to walling jobs, agricultural shows and even show jumping events. He was my constant companion.

He was also an avid footballer, able to dribble the ball skilfully with his nose while running at full speed. He could jump as high as my shoulder and head the ball if I asked him to, and many a happy hour was spent with Henry when I should have been working; me watching him as he effortlessly dribbled the ball across the farmyard and back, only to have me give it back to him so he could do it all over again. He made me laugh out loud with his antics and he became well known in the area. My walling customers loved him.

Within a month I felt as if Henry had been at my side for years and I found it difficult to imagine that I'd ever told Edith and Gemma that I didn't want him.

In August 2005 I took a walling job in Prestwich, a posh suburb on the outskirts of Manchester. I left Henry in the pickup while I introduced myself to Mrs Jackson, my customer, whose property was a handsome three-storey terrace situated on what was once the original road into Manchester.

Mrs Jackson led me into the garden where I think I might gasped out loud at the view; we'd literally stepped into another world, leaving the noise of the traffic behind and entering a calm oasis overlooking the flood plains of Salford, where you could hear the birds calling and the wind whistling casually through the trees. From the top of the York stone patio the view meandered down a central path, zigzagging through the trees and up to the banks of a small river. It was incredibly picturesque.

The job took me three weeks and initially Henry loved every minute of it. When we arrived each morning he would run down the path, bark at the river and then run back up the hill again, his short legs just about managing to jump the steep steps back onto the patio. Every time he went through the routine I laughed and every time I laughed he did it again – I think he knew that I found his antics funny.

But then at the beginning of the second week he seemed to get bored of this routine and he'd come into the garden and flop down at my feet instead. I don't think it was the warm weather making him lazy or the fact he'd suddenly realised his legs were too short: something was wrong.

There were just two days left on Mrs. Jackson's job and I was on tenterhooks waiting for a phone call from the vet's surgery. Henry's malaise had worsened and he was now suffering bouts of debilitating sickness. The vet had examined him under anaesthetic but she couldn't find anything wrong so she'd taken samples and biopsies and I was waiting for the results. I'd expected the call at the beginning of the week but it was Thursday now and I still hadn't heard a thing. I watched Henry scrabbling at a stone, too big to get in his mouth and I tried not to worry.

When she finally called I could hear the regret in her voice straight away. She told me that Henry had a rare auto-immune disease which, in all the cases she'd come across before, had proved fatal. She began to tell me of treatments we could try but I knew from her voice that Henry's chances of survival were slim. "I wouldn't build your hopes up," she said gently. I stared at the beautiful view stretched out in front of me; I heard the larks up above and I heard the sound of the river flowing gently over stones at the bottom of the garden and my heart felt as heavy as the flags

I'd put in place earlier that week.

Henry didn't improve, in spite of the numerous treatments we tried. He gradually failed and, just under two months later, I had him put to sleep, just four short years after I'd met him. I buried him in one of the fields at Ball Beard Farm alongside one of his favourite toys.

The work I did at Prestwich was the last walling job I ever did. It wasn't the same without Henry. I would open the pickup door and wait for him to leap in and take up his stance on the passenger side and for many weeks after he'd gone I would feel an awful, aching emptiness when I opened that door.

I've had many dogs over the years and currently have five assorted mutts running around wherever I go, but none of them have the same place in my heart as Henry – he was the dog I loved the most, which was ironic, since he was the dog I really didn't want.

Chapter Thirty-Three

12 April 2010 (cont)

I had been thinking about Henry when I arrived for my third session with Dr Belinda Browne-Thomas which could have been why all my memories suddenly came tumbling out in a rush: could all this thinking about the past have dislodged something in my mind? I don't know.

That afternoon I also remember feeling particularly vulnerable as I read the plaque detailing the doctor's achievements on the wall outside her office - all those letters after her name - and I suddenly felt disappointed that I hadn't had a career to be proud of too. I'd made a living, don't get me wrong and I'd had success, up to a point but I also felt I'd had a lot of sadness and today I was feeling it. No more laughing and no more joking to cover the seriousness of a situation, today my heart felt raw and bruised. I felt as if I had a blanket wrapped around me, restricting my movements, binding my limbs to my body like a swaddled baby.

And then, there I was, back at Ball Beard Farm in March 1976 and I'd just sorted out the dead piglets and I'd cleaned out the midden and then I'd gone round to the front to get the hay from the shippon.

The last thing I remember is watching the doctor's hand move back and to in front of my eyes. She was listening to me but I don't remember her saying anything at first. The room I was sitting in seemed to disappear and I was back in the shippon where I could smell the hay and I could feel the harsh rasp of it on my skin. I was at Ball Beard Farm, it was bitterly cold and I still hadn't seen Fred; he wasn't in the yard and he wasn't doing his usual chores. It was Sunday 14 March 1976. I was telling her the story. I was remembering what happened for the first time in 34 years.

"I was pulling the hay out like I usually do when whoosh! – I heard a noise like a great load falling behind me. I jumped, startled, then turned behind me and there was Fred. He'd dropped from the hay in the top of the barn and landed right next to me. I thought he'd slipped and fallen and the idea of it made me laugh out loud; hay was sticking out from his cap, his clothes even more dishevelled than usual and I was asking him, between gasps for breath: "*'Are you alright*?' but as soon as I spoke I realized something was wrong, so I stopped laughing and watched him as he started to come towards me. He stopped right there, his eyes steely and his breath smelling of whiskey and he put his hand on my shoulder and then…and then he pushed me backwards against the hay.

What did he do that for? I lost my balance and then all of a sudden he's trying to kiss me and I'm pushing his face away as hard as I can, saying: '*Stop it, what are you doin'?*' and he's sayin' '*I just want to kiss y' stand still, I just want to kiss y'* and I'm pushing him and pushing him but I can't get him off, he's leaning against me and I'm saying '*Stop it, what you doin'?*' and he can't hold me still enough to kiss me and all the time, he's talking to me as if we're having a normal conversation…

"And then…and then he's got one hand against my throat, pushing me back against the hay and the other hand is on my breast and I'm shouting the whole time: '*What you doing, I said stop it, get away from me*'" but he's talking to me as if we're having a normal conversation and he's saying: "*You know I've been waiting for this for a long time*" and then his hand drops to my jeans and he's pushing his hand inside my jeans and I know what he's going to do…oh God, I know what he's going to do…please no, don't….

"… And I start fighting…and scratching and fighting…and I scratch and punch but he won't stop. I keep fighting and punching, trying to get him off me, I try so hard. I keep fighting him - *but he won't stop*. He puts his hand on my face and then he smashes my head against the wall. I think I'm going to faint; my legs turn to jelly…I can hardly stand; my head hurts. He says '*Stop, or I shall do that again*' and I just feel everything draining out of me. I just stop fighting; I can't fight any more…

"He unzips my trousers and he puts his hand inside and pushes his fingers up me. Everything he's doing is hurting - everything. He's still got his arm across my throat and I think I'm going to pass out and I start begging '*Please stop, please just stop…* ' but I can barely breathe and he's not listening to me, he's not listening to me…he's talking to me like we're having a normal conversation: he's saying: '*You'll love this; you'll really like this, you'll be glad you've waited, I know you've waited for me.* I just stop talking. But he won't stop. He undoes his trousers and gets his penis out and he's pushing that inside and it hurts so much and I tell him '*You're really hurting, please stop, please let me go outside, let's talk, outside. And he pushes against me and he's moaning and moaning and moaning….* "

"And then he sighs and he stops talking and I'm wondering if he's going to kill me; it seems the most obvious thing to do. I'm thinking: perhaps he'll ram my head into the wall like he did before - I want him to do it; I want him to finish me off. And then he starts talking to me again. He's talking rubbish, saying: '*See how much you enjoyed that, we can get married, we could have children…*' But it's rubbish. He's pulling my trousers up, saying he knew I was a virgin, he knew I'd waited for him and he doesn't kill me. He takes my wrist and says: '*Come on, we'll go outside.*' He moves away from me and I smell his BO and the stench of whiskey…and we walk outside – we walk out of the shippon and I think "'*I just want to get home now, I want to get home, please - oh please - just let me go home'.*

"We're walking towards the house, I'm trying to get my wrist away…away from him…and he pulls me with him…and…I realize he hasn't finished; he's only just started. He puts his hand

257

around my neck in a headlock and says: *'Come on.'*

"Janet? Are you ok? Can you hear me? Janet."

I can hear a voice; it's not Fred's and it's not mine. Whose voice is it? It comes again. It's asking me who I am and I realise I don't know. Who am I? I start to panic. Where am I? What's happening? What is Fred doing to me? Why is he doing this to me? Oh God what's happening?

"Janet can you hear me? Janet!"

I can see a woman sitting opposite me but I don't know who she is. Why is she asking me these questions? What was she doing with her hand? It was moving back and to in front of my face and now it's stopped. Where am I?

"There was no cottage back in 1976," I say, seeing the farmyard clearly. "And there was no wall around the house. There was a bath outside the shippon where we would collect water for the animals, and just next to the bath were three pig sties."

Dr Browne- Thomas looks at me warily.

"There is a pig in each, delivering piglets and there's muck in the midden and then there's the little shippon - converted into the cottage now - with four cows, a pig sty at the side and a hen cote.

"There are cobbles all around the stable where the horses are tied. The stable's next to the …house."

I pause, seeing Ball Beard as it was in 1976 is like watching a film; I can see the detail and hear the sounds, but unlike a film, I can smell him too.

"We come out of the shippon….." and although I know I'm whispering Dr Browne-Thomas doesn't seem to have a problem hearing me.

"I think I can get away….he's walking up the yard, towards the house, pulling me, his hand tight around my wrist. He's put his arm around my neck and I want to fight and struggle…but I've no energy left…I know what he's intending to do…I try, but my legs go limp, falling to the ground. He just drags me up and lifts me like a sack of corn and then he stops near the front of the house….puts his hand on my throat and squeezes and I think I'm going to pass out…he's talking all the time as if we're having a normal conversation…He's telling me to stop struggling…he tells me it only hurt the first time because I was struggling and if I stop I'll really enjoy it…and he pulls me through the door and into the kitchen and shuts the door….and then he pushes me against the table and he takes his coat off and he throws it on the flags and he tells me to lie down…."

I am trying hard to control my breathing but it's difficult. I want to tell the doctor what happened; it's important that I tell her.

"And I'm pleading with him; 'Can't we have a cup of tea and talk for a minute?' But he's not listening. He doesn't seem to be listening to anything I say…. He gets me by the throat again and he says: 'Don't make me hit you again; you're just making it worse all the time, just relax and lie down, Janet'…"

"He bends down and he…pulls…my jeans…and pants down…I must keep breathing – keep breathing….

"He's talking…what's he saying? He's talking rubbish, saying he knows I've got lots of boyfriends, he knows I went with one of them yesterday but he says that when he's finished I won't want anyone else."

I can feel the tears on my face but I can't move my hand to wipe them away. I realise I can't move at all.

"He drops his trousers….he's got an erection, I don't want to look at him, I turn my head to the wall, trying to pretend it's not happening, he's pushing my jumper and t-shirt up, he's kneeling down, he's lying on top of me, he's trying to get inside me, he's telling me to open my legs, I won't, he's doing it anyway, the pain…it hurts….it hurts so much…I'm crying…I'm telling him….he's just not…it feels like he's pushing a red hot iron inside of me, he's trying to kiss me….I shake my head side to side, my head hurts, he comes up and starts biting my breast really hard, he's trying to kiss me…but no, he hasn't managed to kiss my lips, not my lips…I don't know why that matters…but it does…and I put my head to one side…to the wall…and there's a spider on the wall…and I'm staring at this spider…wondering how long it'll take to…climb the wall and it's…strange…my brain…my head's floating…perhaps this is what it's like…and all the pain's gone…and I know he's there but…and I watch this spider and I'm…I'm thinking about yesterday with Ann …and laying the trail…she took me a way we hadn't been before…we jumped a wall into a field and there was a big drop on the other side…she's always trying to make me fall off my pony and she stopped before

260

she jumped and I was right behind. She said my face was a picture, I fell off, I landed, she was laughing so much she had to get off her horse, and that started me laughing. We were supposed to keep 20 minutes ahead of the hounds but we were laughing so much we couldn't get back on.

"We went to the pub afterwards...

"We rode home…oh, it was such a good day…oh, I wish I could ride like Ann …she's such …a good rider…It's all going distant….I'm in the kitchen again, lying on the floor and my brain's coming back….STOP…I just want him to stop, I want him to kill me, I want him to strangle me, make him stop…He's moaning and groaning, he collapses on top of me and he's silent. He starts talking again. I want to tear his hand off; I want to hit him and kick him, I can't…I can't…."

And suddenly I'm angry. I shout and I scream. I don't know where my energy is coming from.

"I start to scream at him…I'll make him kill me…I'll make him so angry he'll kill me…I think of all the swear words…everything I can think of…I start to scream. *'You fucking bastard…You fucking bastard…You're not fit to do anything…you worthless fucking bastard…you bastard….*And he kneels up, pulls his trousers up and I look at his face…he's gone really funny, he's looking down at me…his eyes are not seeing me…they're dull, staring….and his face is like stone and he's not speaking….what's he going to do? I'm holding my breath and he just stands up…he just stands up and says: '*You can go if you want.*'

261

"And I laugh inside. What's he saying: *You can go if you want*...I should be laughing and then he just walks off...across the kitchen, into the living room and shuts the door. And I'm lying there. My head's shouting '*Go, quick, go...*' And I sit up, pull my trousers up, there's blood and stuff all over me, all over my legs...I pull them up, I stand up, I'm only two feet from the door, the door that Fred painted last year...he said it would brighten up the room...the red paint he found in the barn...but I can't move...I'm petrified, I can't breathe.

"He's silent; if I move I'll make a noise and he's going to come back through that door and he's going to get hold of me.....I can't move....my brain's screaming: run...run...but I can't....I put my hand out...all I've got to do is lift the latch...just go...just go....take a step forward....I seem to be making so much noise....and he still doesn't move...I put my hand out....I can touch the latch....and I lift it....and it seems to be so loud...and he still doesn't come in...I'm so scared, I'm so scared, I'm in the kitchen and I'm so scared.

"I want to get home, I'm running down the yard, I'm running, I'm running so fast...running down the field, I'm sure he's behind me, so fast, I fall and slide in the mud, I get up and run....run...run down to the stile and I daren't look back, I'm sure he's there behind me....run...run...run...I can't see properly, I'm crying so much, I can't see.

"And then I'm down the path and I fall into the kitchen at home and I slam the door. I'm back.

"I can feel my heart beating in my chest. It slows down slightly. I'm not going to die; he's not going to kill me.

"Mum's upstairs. Dad's been ill again. She's cleaning up; I can hear her upstairs and I don't know what to do. I want a bath; I so want a bath. I shout to Mum I'm home but I can't think of any words. I shout I'm going to have a bath. I run the water and rip all my clothes off and Mum's at the door asking me to pass some clean sheets out of the airing cupboard and I get the sheets. I open the door and she looks at me and says what on earth have you done, you're covered in mud, look at the state of you. I so want to tell her…but the words won't come, I can't think of any words to say so I say I've fallen off Apache and she's telling me off for riding him in the hunt and the times I've fallen off I'm going to end up hurting myself and she's carrying on and I'm getting the sheets and it sounds so good to hear her shouting at me and then she goes into the bedroom. I shut the door and get in the bath. I wash myself with soap, I can't get clean. I get a scrubbing brush and I'm scrubbing myself but *I can't get clean* so I run some more water and make it hotter but it's not working. I get the bleach from under the sink and I tip some bleach into the bath. I think it'll sting but it doesn't – not at first, so I put bleach on the scrubbing brush and scrub myself everywhere he's touched me – everywhere - but it doesn't seem to be working. I give up in the end and dry myself. I let the water out, put some clean pyjamas on…"

I stop for a moment and look at the other woman in the room. Who is she? What is she doing here? She asks me my name and I can't tell her. She hands me a tissue and I blow my nose.

"My mum's on the landing and I just want to open the door and tell her. I can't. I open the door and she's gone back downstairs. I go past the landing to my Dad's bedroom and my Dad's asleep and I sit on the side of the bed. He looks so pale.

"I love my Dad so much. When I was little I'd come running in with a scratch on my leg and he'd give me a hug and he'd say '*Don't worry, I'll make it alright.*' And I wanted to be that little girl again now. I wanted him to wake up and tell me that everything would be alright again now. But he can't make this right. Nobody can make this right. I'm supposed to be an adult now. I'm supposed to know how to not make this happen. I'm supposed to know what to do. What if I told him and he thought I hadn't tried to get away? What if he thought I'd let it happen? He'd be so ashamed. Oh, I couldn't stand that. But he didn't wake up. And I'm glad he didn't. I'm glad he didn't have to deal with it."

I'm crying again now. I wipe the tears away and look up at the other woman in the room. She is crying too, the tears are falling slowly down her cheeks and on to the desk.

"I'm going to be sick," I say and lurch from the room to the tiny loo next door. I retch violently.

It is a while before I come back out again and I see the other woman standing by her desk. She looks agitated and she is pacing up and down. "The ambulance is on its way," she says, staring out of the window. "Don't worry the ambulance will be

264

here soon."

I look around me. Is there someone else in the room, someone who is ill, someone who needs an ambulance? I can't see anyone else.

She sits down opposite me and asks me if I know who she is. I look at her; at her striking eyebrows, kind impassive face and the mass of steel grey hair and I realise that although I feel at ease with her I don't know who she is.

She asks me my name. What a stupid question! I am going to tell her my name, of course I am. I sit quite still with my hands in my lap and then I look up at her.

"Yes of course... my name." But I can't remember my name. Who am I?

She seems uneasy. She never stands up during our sessions. Ah yes, our sessions. I have been coming here to see a doctor to talk about my nightmares. Why have I been having nightmares?

"I should pay you for my session," I say, taking my cheque book out of my handbag. "Is it £120 as usual? £120 an hour..." I look at my watch and frown. It can't be. "How long have I been here?" I ask, suddenly nervous.

She looks away from the window. "The ambulance is here now," she says. "Don't worry, the ambulance is here."

"How long have I been here?" I ask again.

She sits back down at her desk and clasps her hands in front of her. "Five hours," she says. "You have been with me for five hours, Janet. I just need to make sure you are okay before we go any further."

Recent photo of the shippon at Ball Beard Farm showing the doorway into the hay barn

Chapter Thirty-Four

April 2010

The last 34 years have been turned on their head. I don't know who I am anymore. Fred attacked and raped me on Sunday 14 March 1976 and I have buried that knowledge deep inside me – until now. I feel as though it happened only yesterday; my mind brings back to me all the sounds, smells, feelings and pain.

When I finally leave Dr Browne-Thomas' consulting rooms it is 8 o'clock in the evening. She lets me leave only when I have signed the medical release form. I can feel it folded into a flimsy rectangle in my coat pocket and after getting into my pickup truck I pull it out and read it. I recognise my signature but I don't remember writing it and then I read what the paramedics have written next to it:

Crew aided by psychiatrist to assess patient's capacity and see if she would require A & E intervention after a single episode of amnesia post-consultation. Patient refused A & E. Capacity completed, home advice given.

I drive home slowly, staring through the windscreen, saying my name and my dogs' names out loud as I turn up the hill towards Ball Beard Farm. As soon as I get home I take a shower.

I arrange to meet Mary for a coffee in Geo's and I tell her what I have discovered about myself; just the bare bones this time – I'm not able to repeat the detail and she can hardly believe it. While I'm at it, I tell her about my affair with Miles: my twenty-year relationship with a married man; my ex-boss, the man who lost his livelihood because of the crime I committed and Mary looks at me as if she doesn't know who I am. I'm not sure I know who I am either. But she can see the fallout; she sees the blank look in my eyes and she is worried about my sanity. I am worried about my sanity. She advises me not to make any snap decisions; she tells me I need to let the reality sink in before I act on what I have discovered.

"I can understand completely why you blanked it out for 34 years," she says softly. "It was a man you trusted; someone you saw as a father figure or an uncle. How could he do this to you? How could anyone do this to you?"

I stare down at my coffee and stir a sixth spoonful of sugar into my cup. "It wasn't the attack that made me forget," I say slowly, watching the spoon going round and round in ever decreasing circles. I can literally feel Mary's warmth as she leans in closer. "After Fred attacked me I walked around with the knowledge of what he'd done to me burning into my brain. I relived every single moment of what he'd done to me over and over again. I couldn't get it out of my mind."

"Then what..."

"I knew I had to keep going up to the fields because I had

268

to feed my ponies so that's what I did – but I couldn't bring myself to go up to the farm. I couldn't bear the thought of seeing Fred Handford ever again as long as I lived. I ran up to the stable every morning, fed my horses and then ran back down again. I'd made arrangements to move my horses to a neighbouring farm that weekend but on the Thursday - Thursday 18 March - I found the note."

"What note?"

"It was pinned to the stable door. *'Sorry, please look after the animals'* it said. It was in Fred's handwriting. I…I pulled it off the door, I read it and then I threw it on the ground. I didn't know what it meant. What did it mean: *please look after the animals*? Was he asking me to look after the animals because he wasn't going to be there to do it himself? And then it suddenly came into my mind: was Fred going to kill himself? And was he going to kill himself because of me?

"I ran home and all night I couldn't get the words of the note out of my mind. I tossed and turned, tossed and turned in bed. Was he going to kill himself and was it because of me? I didn't know what to do; I honestly didn't know what to do and when I woke up again in the morning everything was gone. My dirty wellingtons were next to my bed and I couldn't remember a thing. I couldn't remember the attack; I couldn't remember the note – nothing."

Mary looks at me long and hard. "It was a suicide note," she says, reaching out and holding my hand and I nod, still stirring the sugar round and round in my cup.

"Yes, I think it was."

On the advice of Dr Browne-Thomas I make an appointment to see my GP.

My doctor advises me to make an appointment with the DRC – the Derbyshire Rape Centre. I can feel a certain coolness in her manner when I tell her I paid privately to see Belinda Browne-Thomas, which is quite interesting as, prior to finding out about what Fred did to me, I don't think I would have been attuned to my GP's feelings at all. The shock is obviously having an effect on me in more ways than one. At home I wander around aimlessly, unable to concentrate on anything. I feel as if I've been hit by a truck – I just didn't see it coming. I stay inside as much as I can. I just didn't see it coming.

I can't get clean: I suddenly feel a need to shower not once, twice or even three times a day but 10, sometimes 15 times a day. After a few days, another compulsion: I feel I have to exercise all the time – cycling, walking, going to the gym, it doesn't matter what I do as long as I keep moving; I have no desire to eat and finally, and most importantly, I have a burning desire to leave Ball Beard Farm as soon as possible – and never, ever come back.

I can't tell Mary the full details of the attack yet, but I know I will eventually. Until that time I try to take positive action in order to move forward but it's difficult and every time I try something happens and I slip back again. Thank goodness for the dogs; without them I don't think I'd bother getting up in the morning. I open the cupboard door in the kitchen and glance at the list. It offers me comfort in a vague sort of way.

Get out of bed

Feed the dogs

Get washed

Get dressed

Make a cup of tea, eat a slice of toast.

Not that it matters anymore. The only thing that matters is that I leave Ball Beard Farm. I'm now living permanently in the caravan. I had to move out of the mobile home as the heating system was too efficient: I was able to take too many showers and the water was scorching my skin. The caravan only has enough water for one three minute shower a day, two if I'm desperate.

I open the caravan door and step outside. I take two large steps to the right and find myself standing in the small shippon. There is no hay stored here at the moment, it's all gone. I look up to the loft above my head. I can see the dusty beams, the cracks in the wood and the pale blue sky beyond. That's where Fred lay in wait for me 34 years ago; that's where he hid and watched me walk in, get the hay for the cows, then turn to leave. That's where he slid down from the loft to my feet and pushed me back against the beam, that's where he banged my head – once, twice – that's where he attacked me, that's where he raped me. That's where he changed my life forever.

I turn away and look back at the caravan. I have lived in the Peak District all my life; a place of rugged beauty and natural, unspoilt countryside but today all I can see are ugly vistas in every direction, stretching way, way into the distance. There's no beauty here now. How could I have stood on the top of Round Wood and declared that I wanted nothing more than this in my life? How could I have made that childish promise to myself that one day I was going to own this land and I was going to farm it just as generations of people had done before me? I laugh at my naivety. That girl isn't me anymore and I no longer feel a scrap of affection for the land on which I stand. The sale of Ball Beard Farm will go through and I will set off with the caravan and my five dogs and I will go to Scotland and I will never come back. Dr Belinda Browne-Thomas asked me to choose a 'safe place' and I chose Ball Beard Farm but I'd chosen a place that my mind had warned me against; a place my subconscious had protected me from for 34 years. No wonder the fallout had been spectacular and no wonder Dr Browne-Thomas had to call an ambulance: while I was running from the horror of Fred's attack I had been running towards my safe place. It was like that clichéd scene in every horror film; the heroine bolts the door, locks the windows and thinks she's secure while, all the time, she's locking her attacker in with her. The thought of it makes the nausea rise in my throat. I run out of the chippon and retch yet again. I feel my stomach muscles clench and relax, clench and relax, expelling what little food is left inside and then I smell the whiskey and the BO and he is right there, next to me – just as he was 34 years ago.

I find the DRC difficult to get hold of and when I do

manage to arrange an appointment I get the impression they are struggling for finance: it's obvious they have to share their premises with other organisations. Not that I'm criticising the volunteers who run the place because I'm not. I go for my first meeting but the rented room they use is a dreadful place and while I'm sitting in a sort of 'holding area' I realise the woman next to me is attending an interview concerning her benefits payments - and I can't help but overhear the whole thing. My first meeting is for an assessment rather than for a counselling session; the counsellor doesn't have a vacancy until July and I know I can't wait until July. As soon as I get home I call Dr Belinda Browne-Thomas and arrange for a series of follow-up sessions.

"The brain is capable of allowing you to forget and deny that something has happened," she says at one point and I nod as her soothing voice washes over me. There are a lot of tears in my first session but I don't care and Dr Browne-Thomas doesn't seem to mind. She apologizes for calling the ambulance but says that my reaction precipitated it as I became extremely distressed during the treatment. I tell her that she has nothing to apologise for.

"You've admitted that the attack happened and that's important. It's essential, in fact, in learning to live with it successfully."

I'm not sure about 'successfully' but I know I have to learn to live with it. I tell her that I've already told Mary what Fred did to me and that I feel guilty about this. She tells me it's entirely up to me who I tell. She says that this is also a good sign. All the time she's speaking I can tell she's not judging me; she's simply listening and encouraging. Her face is expressionless. I am coming to think of her as safety net, ready to catch me should my brain decide to do something unpredictable for a second time.

"In the last week I've had two panic attacks," I say. "I was walking up the lane near the farm on Wednesday, pushing my bike up a steep bit, when a man came up behind me. I knew in a flash that if he came any closer I wouldn't be able to get away from him so I climbed up the bank at the side of the road and I held the bike in front of me, ready to throw it at him if he so much as took one step in my direction. My whole body was shaking and I could hardly breathe; my hands were wobbling so much I could barely hold the bike steady but it was the only weapon I had and so I stood there, shielding my body with this, this bloody bike…"

"And what happened?" asks the doctor.

"Nothing," I say. "He walked past; I doubt he even noticed me."

Dr Belinda tells me it's the primeval part of my brain telling me: '*that's the enemy*' and it's true. I feel as if every man is a threat to me now; every man I come across might attack me just as Fred attacked me. She says the trauma is worse because I trusted him, that he was a man I'd thought I'd known. And then of course I feel guilty again: should I have seen the signs? I'd known Fred for 14 years. Should I have seen evidence of inappropriate behaviour and kept my distance? Should I have fought harder to get away? Why was I paralysed and unable to move? Was it somehow my fault? Was it my fault he committed suicide? I've never had any reason to doubt myself or feel threatened in the past - but all that's changed now.

"I feel like a stranger in my own life," I say.

Dr Browne-Thomas puts her head to one side. "It is possible to deal with your reactions so that it doesn't affect your day-to-day life," she says. "Remember Janet: you have a choice."

Chapter Thirty-Five

4 May 2010

Today is my second follow-up session with Dr Browne-Thomas. I feel as if she is delving into my brain and in the process ordering my thoughts for me. She keeps telling me I have a choice. I keep reminding myself of that fact when I'm not with her, focusing on her down-to-earth, common sense approach. I used to be like Dr Browne-Thomas: pragmatic, sensible, rational. I'm not sure I'm like that any more.

There are fewer tears in the consulting room this time but I know I'm only coping because I'm refusing to think about the detail. "I don't want to go down that route because I feel guilty," I say. "I don't want to think about Fred killing himself because of what he did to me; I don't want to think of him throwing himself down that mine shaft. Do you think I should talk about the detail?"

"Do you want to?"

"Not at the moment, no."

"Then there's your answer."

"I am scared there might be a rerun of last month if I talk about it too much. I'm not sure if I'll be able to pull back from the brink the next time." She is silent for a moment, her dark eyes watchful. "It is all about control," she says softly.

I tell her that I feel as if I am grieving; some days are good, some are bad. "My brain seems to be taking a tour of the insanity factory; one minute I'm feeling one emotion, next minute it's another."

"That's perfectly normal and we will shortly begin to examine techniques that will give you the ability to cope."

I want to believe her; I don't want to be a victim, held hostage by what Fred did to me 34 years ago but I'm not sure I have the strength to do as she advises. But then I remind myself I've never been a victim before so there's no reason why I should start now.

"I've always had a terrible temper," I say suddenly. "My reactions have often been out of proportion to what's been happening around me. I've never really understood why the anger has always been so close to the surface." I tell her about an incident in work when I threw a desk across the room simply because I couldn't find a particular document and then the time I was with Mary and I nearly swung for that driver who'd cut me up on the high street. "But the anger's all gone now; I feel totally different. Mary said I might feel angry at the realisation of what Fred did to me, but strangely I don't, it's the opposite."

Dr Browne-Thomas mulls over what I've just said. "After Fred attacked you there was a lot of anger there but no-one to direct it at. The brain couldn't do anything with it, so on a secondary level it was simmering away in the background all the time." I tell her that this makes sense to me. "And how do you feel about Fred now?"

"I hate him – but then he went on to kill himself, so it's balanced. I know there's no point feeling guilty, I understand that, but I do ask myself: should I have seen the signs? Should I have stopped going to the farm."

"Those are destructive feelings, Janet. There is no answer to that question."

"You feel dirty. You feel as if it's your fault. You can't explain it. It sounds so simple: Tell someone the truth. Even Mary said to me: *why didn't you tell your Mum* but she doesn't understand: how could I tell my Mum when it's taken 34 years to admit it to myself?" I look up at her, willing her to say something else but she doesn't; she just waits for me to go on. "I keep thinking about the note," I say quietly. "*Sorry, please look after the animals.* But was he sorry? Was he really sorry?"

I think back to Kate Barton and her strange conversation with Miles the day we were choosing a goose for his Christmas dinner. Kate must have had some sort of insight into what happened when Fred disappeared. I certainly hadn't told anyone there had been a suicide note because I hadn't remembered there was one. I'd blanked that knowledge from my mind, just as I'd subsequently blanked all the details of Fred's attack from my mind. The one was linked to the other and I just wasn't capable of dealing with any of it.

"If you want to discuss the note we can, Janet."

278

I thought about refusing but, after a moment or two's silence, I felt capable of telling her what I could remember.

"I had to go up to the stables every day to feed my ponies. So I forced myself up to the fields above my house, about half way to the farm, each day after the Sunday when Fred attacked me. At this stage I know what he's done to me which is why I don't go up to the farm – I keep away but I can't keep away from my horses. Every day I feel his eyes on me, watching me, waiting for me and every day I feel the horror that he'll get me and rape me again. I've arranged to move my ponies to another farmer's field at the weekend but until then I have to dash up and back as quickly as I can.

"It's during these four days – on the Wednesday - that I chase the escaped heifer up the field and Ernie sees me. But in chasing the animal I end up closer to the farm than is safe and I see Fred, I see him coming down the cow lane, I see the top of his head and he's calling to me: he's saying, "*Janet, I just want to talk*" but my heart's beating like mad and I run off, petrified. I think he's going to attack me again – I don't know if he is – but I'm not going to give myself the opportunity to find out.

"Then on the Thursday I see the note and that night, in bed, I can't stop thinking of what he's written: *'I'm sorry, please look after the animals'* and I toss and turn, thoughts of Fred killing himself going round and round my brain. It's my fault; it's my fault he's killed himself and then the next morning - nothing; it's all gone. And then I wake on Friday and I see the muddy boots next to my bed and I can't remember a thing and I go up to the farm with this terrible feeling of fear and foreboding but I don't know why and as I get closer to the farm, the feeling gets stronger and stronger."

I take a couple of deep breaths. I've got a choice; I know I have. I just have to make sure I make the right one.

"There are some other things that now make sense to me."

"What do you mean?"

"I didn't mention it initially as it's so - personal, but I had some terribly painful blisters. I thought I must have injured myself when I fell off Apache after riding in the drag hunt with Ann but I realise now that it was after I'd been scrubbing myself with the bleach. It chafed when I walked." I look up, embarrassed, but the doctor's expression is completely neutral.

"I know that I'm looking back at my past through different eyes so I'm not sure I'm remembering things as I saw them at the time but it's the guilt. I had every reason to trust him..."

"You cannot see things now as you saw them then," says Dr Browne-Thomas firmly and I nod to say I know she's right, but it's so … difficult.

"Knowing what I know now, I'm convinced that Fred committed suicide but…having gone through everything I've gone through in the last couple of weeks I feel as if I *would* have the strength to kill him. I know the gossip in the village says I killed him so I could inherit the farm - but that's so stupid I can't even discuss it. I was so petrified I couldn't have done it; I was

280

incapable." I look straight at the doctor. "But I could do it now, oh yes, I could do it now."

Chapter Thirty-Six

17 May 2010

I'm talking to Mary over a coffee in Geo's. I'm having a good day today. Molly, Mary's chocolate Labrador, is sitting at our feet.

"All the men in my life have been bastards," I say, with a grimace. "Apart from my Dad of course, he was a one-off. No-one could have asked for a lovelier Dad." I've been thinking of Dad a lot lately, wishing he was still alive but I also know I could never have told him about what Fred did to me: it would have destroyed him.

Mary looks at me over her cup of cappuccino. "It's not your fault," she says sharply. "You're better off without them if you ask me. Anyway, we're not here to talk about men, we're here to talk about Mags and the booklet she wrote about her life."

"Did you track down the copy?"

"Yes I did. Don't ask me how. All I can say is it cost me a fortune in lattes and lemon Madeira cake. The secretary of the Local History Society is a sucker for afternoon tea. She didn't stand a chance."

I laugh with her. "What happened to the 10 copies that

Mags was supposed to have bequeathed to the nation?"

"No idea. If you believe Sue at the History Society this is the only copy in existence and I have to give it back tomorrow."

"Well, pass it over then." I hold out a hand.

"Now, hold on a minute." Mary spreads her hands on the table, palm down. "Not so quick…"

"But this is Mags' elusive life story, the one that gives us her view of Fred's disappearance. I'd like to read what she has to say about the matter."

"I'm not sure you do."

I lean in closer. "You've read it then?"

"Yes."

"And now you're censoring it?"

"Yes, I might do; I mean, it might be a good idea if I do."

"Mary, I don't want to have to chase you round Geo's; for one thing the other customers might think it's a bit odd if I go running after my friend in a confined space and, for another, Molly might get upset."

Mary shifts in her seat. "Well, it doesn't shed any light on Fred's disappearance as far as I can make out. She has no more idea than you about what happened to him and I don't see how reading it can help."

"Don't you think I should be the judge of that?" I was puzzled now. "Oh, I see what all this is about: you think that after my sessions with Dr Browne-Thomas I've become – unstable, is that it?"

"No-o, well, yes-ish".

"Look. I don't really care what Mags has to say; I'm just curious. I know about all the gossip in New Mills but whatever Mags wrote eight years ago can't make gossip the truth, now can it?"

"No, I suppose not; but Mags was your friend. Reading it in black and white might make it worse somehow."

I almost laugh. "My friend! You do know don't you that because of me Mags' granddaughter had to defend herself in court?"

"Yes, you told me that."

"I know what Mags thinks of me and I can assure you, she doesn't think of me as a friend."

Mary considers this at some length while I take my chance. I reach out and snatch her rucksack, the one she always carries with her, convinced that the booklet is in there - and I'm not wrong.

"I'm just warning you," she says sternly. "When the local History Society was given the copies it had to hold a special meeting: the members were pretty shocked at the contents."

I look up, but only for a moment. Mary has marked the pages with yellow post-it notes. I turn to the middle and as soon as I start reading I feel every bit of Mags' anger, recrimination and accusation come pouring forth from the badly written pages. As Dr Browne-Thomas might say in one of her farmyard analogies: it's as if someone's poured a bucket full of muck over my head.

284

Ten minutes later I put the booklet down on the table in front of me. In some ways it is not as bad as I imagined it to be. A lot of Mags' anger appears to be focused on the fact I sold the farmhouse to 'outsiders' rather than anything else. I wonder if the reason the History Society tried to censor the booklet was as much to do with the mention of my affair with Miles as it was with Fred's disappearance. Miles is still a prominent figure in the area and, as far as I know, well respected.

"Well?" Mary looks at me expectantly.

"Awful," I say shaking my head.

"I know. If someone had written those things about me I doubt I'd want to show my face in New Mills again. I think we should give it back to the History Society and ask them to burn it."

"Awful," I say again.

"I told you I shouldn't have shown it to you." Mary is visibly upset now.

"The grammar's terrible, some of the facts are wrong and she has the cheek to say she'd always had her doubts about me – or her *reservations* as she puts it - which is patently not true. She only changed her tune after I went to prison and that was nothing at all to do with Fred's disappearance."

Mary glances across at me. "But what about the rest of it? She's also saying that you'll *come round in your own good time*. What does she mean by that?"

"I think I'd take it to mean what the rest of the village is taking it to mean."

285

"That you, you know…?"

"Yes, that I killed him."

Mary breathes in deeply. When she speaks again her voice is so soft I have to lean towards her across the table to hear what she's saying. "Did you? Did you kill him, Janet?"

"No," I say firmly. "I did not; in spite of what Mags and the rest of the town of New Mills thinks, I did not kill Fred Handford."

Chapter Thirty-Seven

18 May 2010

Today I have my third follow up session with Dr Browne-Thomas. Initially I'd set the end of June as the date for leaving Ball Beard Farm but Mary is determined that I should hang around for her 50th birthday party and so I tell her I'll postpone setting off for Scotland until 19 July. It's not such a bad idea; at least it gives me more time to adjust to what I now know happened 34 years ago: I'm not coping particularly well with the knowledge at the moment; I'm showering too often, running and cycling too much and tormenting myself with the idea that all men are rapists. I can't bear it if a man, any man, comes near me. I've stopped drinking since the smell of alcohol – particularly whiskey - brings it all rushing back and I've lost more than two stone in weight. There are new rumours going around the village that I've got terminal cancer which, if it wasn't so disrespectful to those who've got the disease, would be funny. The only good thing to come out of all this is the fact that, at long last, the nightmares have stopped. I go to bed now and I sleep. It's only been a month and I'm not taking anything for granted, but it's wonderful.

The sale of the land at the farm is going through – albeit slowly and I've now told the buyer that I don't want first refusal anymore if he should decide to sell it on. I can't wait to get away from this bloody place and I've got no intention of ever coming back and that's what I tell the doctor as we begin our next session.

"The obsessive activities you describe; the cycling, the showering are all normal reactions to what you have just experienced. Remember, although the attack took place many years ago, for you it has just happened," she says and I go on to explain that even when Alan Gunning, my neighbour who lives with his wife and family in the farmhouse, a man who I know wouldn't hurt a fly, approaches me for a chat or to ask how I'm going on, I just want to run away, shut him out of my vision completely for fear of what he might do to me.

"And yet I must know deep down that he's not going to do anything to me; my mind's just playing tricks."

Dr Browne-Thomas gives me one of her nods and acknowledges that my distress is very much bound up with Ball Beard Farm. "Alan is still living in the farmhouse where it happened," she says calmly.

"And I won't be giving any of it a backward glance."

"But you must try to separate the man from the farm and the man from the animals because it is only *one* man who did this to you."

And although I know this is the truth it's very difficult to believe. "It's only my dogs keeping me sane," I tell her.

"Are you attempting to put some of those coping mechanisms we discussed into practice, Janet?"

288

I tell her I'm trying my best; I'm living in the caravan and I'm restricting my showers to one a day but then I suddenly feel an urge to explain further, to force her to understand. "You feel dirty and you assume that others think the same which is ironic given that before I started coming to see you I was always mucky; I'd have dirt in my finger nails, oil from the tractors all over my hands, muck from the silage, cows, farmyard, you name it, I was covered in it, and it never bothered me."

"I would advise you to talk yourself out of this urge to shower," she says firmly.

"That's just the sort of thing I'd scoff at in the past – but I'm not laughing now, I can tell you. You're right and so I try to tell myself: *this is all in your head Janet, you're clean.* I try to tell myself that something that happened to me 34 years ago can't contaminate me now."

Dr Browne-Thomas tips her head to one side in her customary way. "Then by the time you have completed this thinking the hope is that the urge will have passed."

"But I just turn up the temperature. I want the water to *scald* me clean." She says nothing. "It's just that the process is so difficult; I'm sorry, but it is."

"There is no need to apologise, Janet. I understand. You are doing very well; you have made excellent progress. "

I shake my head. "It's the guilt," I say again. "Should I have seen the change in him? Was it my fault he killed himself? And why then, after 14 years?"

"No-one can answer those questions for you. You must try not to go down that road; you must do other things to distract yourself: pick up a book, take the dogs for a walk."

"But how? Sometimes I'm watching telly and I realise I've been thinking about Fred Handford for the last 10 or 15 minutes and it's too late to say: *Don't go down that road* because I'm already down it." I look into the distance over Dr Browne-Thomas's shoulder. Deep down I know that things are improving, I know they are. Apart from the nightmares, the anger has gone. I still suffer bursts of emotion, that's true, but I know now what it's directed at; it doesn't take me completely by surprise any more.

The hour is over and as usual, I feel exhausted.

"Do you think that's helped you today?" Dr Browne-Thomas asks and I tell her that it has, then she gives me that half smile, the one that says she is pleased that her patient is doing so well.

Chapter Thirty-Eight

3 June 2010

An old school friend pops into the farm to say hello. We have a good chat; catch up on old times and then she asks the question that almost makes me choke on my cup of tea.

"So Janet, how're you getting on with your biography? I'll bet it's full of funny stories, isn't it - an absolute hoot. I hope you're putting it all in?"

I tell her I don't know what she means by *putting it all in*.

"I was only thinking the other day about that time when your bullock escaped – the one you were taking to the abattoir. I nearly died when I heard it on the news! There it was running down Glossop High Street with you and all those policemen in tow. Didn't they have to bring a police marksman over from Ripley in the end by helicopter?"

"Yes, they did," I say, relieved that by *putting it all in* she isn't referring to my recent counselling sessions. I remember only too clearly the drama of the escaped bullock and the chaos it caused. I remember the sound of the shots ringing out from the roof of one of Glossop's factories and the look of horror on the faces of all the workers as they watched the drama unfold from inside the locked building. Police officers had captured the animal in the car park and the poor creature didn't stand a chance. All this because the bullock had spooked at the sound of a passing vehicle when I'd been taking him for slaughter and instead of ambling obediently into the abattoir like all the others, he'd shot off in the other direction, jumping out of my trailer and leaping over the backyard walls of Glossop's terraced houses like a steeplechaser with no jockey. The abattoir staff could only look on in horror. It was a miracle no-one was injured.

"I might just put it in," I say, although bearing in mind what I've just discovered about my life I'm not sure if I want to write my biography at all now. My friends have been telling me for years that they wanted to read about my funny stories but now, well, I've found that a lot of the humour has disappeared.

On Saturday morning, while out walking the hills of High Peak, I tell Mary about my visitor. She looks serious for a moment. "That's the problem," she says, shaking her head.

"What is?"

"Well, the story you wanted to write at the beginning is not the story you'd write now is it? I mean, when you considered writing a biography it was because we all told you your life was full of 'amusing anecdotes' but that's not the case now, is it? Not even you can make this story funny.

"And there's one other thing," she adds, her eyes as round as yo-yos, "You do realise that with the revelation of what Fred's done to you – you now have a motive for…" She stops mid-sentence as another walker goes by in the opposite direction. "A motive for…"

"For killing him?" I say. "Yes, that fact has occurred to me, you'll be pleased to know."

"So you can't put it into the book," she says, her voice rising in alarm.

"Not unless I want people to know the full truth."

Mary looks at me aghast. "But are you sure people will believe you?"

"Do you believe me?"

"Of course I do. I saw your reaction when you told me what happened. No-one could look like that if they weren't telling the truth. I know Fred raped you as clearly as if I saw him do it myself." She stared at me in horror. "Oh Janet…I, I'm so sorry, I didn't mean..." She looks mortified but I tell her not to worry. It's all water under the bridge now, which I'm hoping it will be - sometime in the future. Unfortunately I'm some way off feeling that at the moment. Even after another follow-up session with Dr Browne-Thomas the fallout is still causing me serious difficulties; the coping mechanisms don't always work and I think I know why this is: I honestly feel as if I've been plunged back 34 years. The sights and sounds associated with what Fred did to me are clearer now than they've ever been. Just as Dr Belinda had warned, '*the feelings you recall will probably stay with you for the rest of your life…*"

"I…I can't wait to get away, Mary," I say. "That's all."

She nods. "I know. It won't be long now and I see now that it'll be for the best but how will you do for money?"

I tell her that I'm selling the land for £260,000 but that I have mortgages of £200,000. I also have other debts of £15,000 and of course, there are solicitors' fees to consider. I tell Mary I have a state pension that will kick in from February 2011 and a tiny private pension paying £600 every March plus about £18,000 in savings. "But I'm not worried because I know I'll be able to live cheaply where I'm going," I say, by which, I mean travelling to the west coast of Scotland. Something in Mary's expression makes me think she believes I'm referring to something else.

"I'm not going to do anything stupid," I reassure her. "I'm not that daft. I might be traumatised by what I've found out in the last few weeks but I'm not about to punish myself any more for what Fred did to me." She nods, placated. My words sound plausible, even to my own ears and I wonder if I say them often enough I might believe them too.

I've got two more follow-up sessions with Dr Belinda and Mary's 50th birthday party to attend and then I'm off. I'm looking forward to leaving Ball Beard Farm almost more than I can say.

Chapter Thirty-Nine

18 July 2010

Mary, Claire and Carol are meeting me at the White Horse for a farewell supper and an early 60th birthday celebration combined. When I arrive I see that Mary has tied helium balloons to my chair. She'll have done this to embarrass me and she's succeeded so I react in the only way I know how – I make a joke of it.

"Right, all change," I say, forcing the three of them to stand up. "I have to sit by the door in case you all start singing happy birthday: I might need to make a swift getaway." They groan but miraculously, they do as I ask.

If only they knew the truth. I can hear the sound of men's voices behind me and I want to make sure I can see what they're doing as well as hear them. Just the idea of a man lurking somewhere out of sight is enough to make my heart race – and I don't mean that in a good way.

Claire and Carol haven't seen me for a couple of weeks and I can tell they're shocked at my appearance. "You've lost so much weight," they say in unison.

"It suits you," says Mary, softly.

"Thanks, I've cut down on the alcohol." I nod at my glass of cordial but omit a description of all the exercise I've been taking which probably has more to do with this new, slimmer me than the lack of liquids.

"When are you actually leaving Ball Beard Farm?"

"Monday," I say at the same time as Mary. We look at each other but neither of us can bring ourselves to smile. "Monday evening."

"We'll call round after work to give you a proper send-off, shall we?" asks Claire.

"You mean you'll call round to make sure I do what I say I'm going to do," I counter with a grin. "I can tell you don't believe I'm actually going."

A silence falls again. I've hit a nerve.

"Well, it's all so strange," says Carol, shaking her head. "I never thought I'd see the day when Janet Holt leaves Ball Beard Farm – not unless she's in a wooden box and can't fight the eviction."

I want to say that if I don't leave sooner rather than later I probably *will* be leaving in a box, sent mad by the realisation of what happened to me in a place I'd once loved with all my heart.

"Time for a change," I say instead and Mary says nothing; she just slides a small rectangular parcel towards me across the table.

"What's this, a going-away present?"

"Yes," she says. "But you have to open it now and you have to figure out how to use it before tomorrow evening or else you're not going." I rip off the paper. It's a Blackberry phone.

"I want to make sure you're contactable," she says. "And I want to give you the option of taking photos of all the lovely places you're going to visit because I want you to have some happy memories of your holiday to look back on in the future."

I look up at her. I can hear the serious school teacher and the worried friend talking to me at the same time. "Thank you; it's a great idea. I'll read the instructions when I get home, I promise."

She nods. "And then when you're settled, let me know where you are and I'm going to come up for a week's holiday. I've always wanted to visit Scotland."

"So have I," says Claire.

"Me too," adds Carol.

"Well, there's an irony; I'm the only one who's never bothered about a holiday and here I am about to set off for goodness knows how long. There must be a word for that."

"Difficult."

"Awkward."

"Contrary," says Mary, with feeling.

I look from Mary, to Claire and Carol then back to Mary again. Three friends I've known for a sum total of almost 90 years and yet here I am wondering if they've ever got to know the real me. We met after 1976, which means they only know the woman I've become.

We spend the evening laughing and joking about old times, the three of them promising to continue to meet up once a week as they've always done and letting me join in via my new Blackberry. "You'll have to set up a conference call to the White Horse Inn so you can keep us up to speed on the wonders of a life with no responsibilities and not a care in the world," says Claire.

"I'm jealous already," says Carol.

Mary says nothing. I can tell just by looking at her that she's thinking something completely different. She's worrying about how I'll cope in Scotland with just my dogs for company; she's worried that with the rigours of a farming life stripped away I might prove unpredictable; put simply, I can tell she's worried about my sanity.

Forty-eight years. That's how long it's been since I first walked into the yard at Ball Beard Farm as a 14-year-old girl. In all that time one thing has remained steadfast and that's my love for a way of life that I dreamed of in 1964, a way of life that I have constantly and vigorously fought to retain. So it seems very strange that, on 19 July 2010 as I drive out of the farmyard for the very last time, I have no feelings about leaving: there is no sadness, tears, anger or regret; I don't even look back. I'm leaving behind the events and the revelations of the past six months as well as 35 years of nightmares and that can only be a good thing I suppose.

I drive down Laneside Road for the last time pulling my caravan behind me, my five dogs barking their farewells as my friends stand in the farmyard waving their goodbyes. Mary's tears are in stark contrast to my dry eyes.

When I started writing my story I don't think I believed that there was any 'truth' to uncover – what I thought I was doing was finding a way to reduce or stop my nightmares; I firmly believed I couldn't make them any worse. The first draft took me a long time; I had to keep stopping as the feelings I was unearthing were so overwhelming but once I'd put my first nightmare down on paper it began to get easier. In the past I'd never considered seeking professional help because I was cynical about the ability of hypnotherapists and psychotherapists to do anything other than take my money. I now accept that this was short-sighted of me. Without Dr Belinda Browne-Thomas I would never have come to understand why my nightmares were so severe or why they continued to haunt me for so long and, ultimately, why I lost four days of my life.

I'm still not sure why I decided to sell the farm when I did. I made the decision in 2009 when I had been working on my book for six months and within four weeks I'd sold the cattle and much of the farm deadstock and placed the property in the hands of agents. In the past I think it's fair to say that, with high mortgage repayments I was continually struggling to keep up with commitments and always had a stack of bills waiting to be paid but this was nothing new, it had been the situation for years and in the past I'd always fought and come out on top. My biggest commitments, my mortgage repayments, were due to reduce from

£850 a month to £290 early in 2011 but, for some reason, this doesn't seem to matter to me any more. Dr Belinda tells me it's quite possible that in writing about the nightmares I'd stirred something in my subconscious even though I wasn't aware of it and this could well have played a part in my decision to go.

As I set off on my 400 mile journey north the dogs are still wide awake in the back. I gave them their medication an hour ago before nipping into the farmhouse with Judith and Alan for a final brew but it doesn't seem to have had any effect and I fear for my sanity based on the noise levels alone! Carol and Claire wish me well; Mary and I hug and I hear her whisper in my ear. She asks if I have any hopes for the future.

"Yes," I say, "Wouldn't it be wonderful if, one day, I could say that I had finally become the person I always should have been."

Chapter Forty

Three of my dogs enjoying the West of Scotland

August 2010

I'm sitting at the side of the river, watching the dogs sniff their way along the riverbank, their tails wagging with the excitement of it all. The sky is a vivid, royal blue dotted here and there with clumps of pale, wispy clouds that seem too fragile for the wild landscape all around me. The hills are steeper and more rugged than the Peak District peaks but still, they remind me of home in that I feel insignificant but protected, as if the remoteness will somehow shelter me from harm. I've set up camp at my first destination while I decide what to do next and my life has taken on a simple, serene routine of walking and cycling and generally taking life at a much slower pace. The sale of the land has finally gone through and I am relieved to report that I no longer have any links to Ball Beard Farm.

I watch a farmer in the distance as he drives his tractor over the field, carrying a large bale of silage in the back. I'm smiling to myself as his cows come across to meet him, their heavy heads lolling awkwardly with the effort as they try to pick up speed. The scene pulls at my heart. This time last year that was me. I ask myself if I would still like to be farming and the answer is yes, I would. Would I like to be back at Ball Beard Farm? No, never.

I cannot find the words to describe the last six months; in fact, I think I'm still recovering from the shock of it all. I also don't think I'm in a fit state to make any decisions about my future. As I said to Dr Browne-Thomas I feel like a stranger in my own life and for the moment I feel content just to take it one day at a time. I haven't had a nightmare for over four months now: I go to bed at night and I sleep. I'm still concerned with cleanliness but I don't think I'm as obsessed as I was and besides, it's a small price to pay for feeling almost normal again. I don't see many people up here and I'm happy with that. I'm keeping in touch with Mary via the internet and I exchange the occasional text message with Claire and Carol and that will do just fine for now. I still get days when I feel as if I've been hit by a truck but I deal with them the only way

I know how; I leave the caravan and go for a bike ride or I take the dogs for a five mile hike because then I know I won't have to think too much, I concentrate instead on putting one foot in front of the other. I haven't been introspective for 34 years and it wouldn't suit me to start now.

Chapter Forty-One

Chico at River Cannich, Scotland

December 2010

The snow is a foot deep up here in Cannich but the dogs are keeping me warm. In fact, I'm too hot at night because they sleep on top of me like five living, breathing duvets. I've moved the caravan to a small inland site for the winter intending to drive back towards the coast when spring comes around again; it makes sense to shelter from the worst of the weather and I've no desire to get blown into the sea, thank you very much.

I've had news from Mary that Judith and Alan have sold the farmhouse at Ball Beard and are intent on moving to Cumbria as soon as possible and I'm relieved to hear it. I like the idea of them making a fresh start. I've no intention of ever meeting the new owners and it feels like another chapter in my life has finally come to a close.

I'm still not making any plans for the future but taking it one day at a time; walking, cycling, tramping through the snow. There are few other caravans this far north at this time of the year – surprise, surprise – so I've got the place almost to myself. The only problem is, it's almost half a day's journey to the nearest petrol station so when the gauge is low I combine filling the pickup with fuel with a game of badminton at the nearest sports centre. I've managed to find a group of middle-aged players who don't mind another one in their midst every now and again; they don't feel the need to ask me any questions, or else they're too polite, and I don't volunteer any information but it is nice to have a conversation using words rather than dog whistles once in a while.

Up here in the Highlands I'm surrounded by mountains, and one rather spectacular waterfall. Unfortunately, I've got no signal for my phone, telly, radio or internet so if I want to speak to Mary I have to set off on a three mile hike with the dogs right up to the top of 'Jelly Falls' where, on a clear day and with the wind blowing in the right direction, I can get just enough signal to enjoy a brief conversation, assuming I've got any breath left of course. It was during one of these walks last week that I realised something was wrong; it wasn't just the huffing and puffing that was bothering me, it was an uncharacteristic dizziness so, the next time I went to fill the pickup with petrol, I made an appointment to see a doctor.

Doctor Bell asked me about my background and for the first time ever I actually said the word 'retired' out loud, in that I supposed if I was used to working 16 hours a day but was now doing practically nothing so I must be *retired*.

"Well, you couldn't have picked a more relaxing spot to do it in," he said in a lovely Scottish brogue. The music in his voice made every word sound like poetry. He suggested taking my pulse and I was prompted to ask what was normal.

"Adult pulse rate should be between 60 to 100 beats a minute; well toned athletes of the Olympic persuasion: 40 to 60 beats a minute."

I nodded and waited for the prognosis. "And I assume, Janet, that you are not yourself in training for any particular discipline?"

"No, nothing specific; a few cross country walks and the occasional bike ride," I said, playing down my activities a little.

"Well, your pulse rate is 38 beats a minute and I think only Sob Coo's was lower than that at his peak. Something definitely not right here, my dear." He checked my heart and pronounced it healthy and then asked me if I was on any medication.

"Blood pressure tablets," I replied. "I've been on them for more than 15 years but thinking about it, my stress levels have

306

dropped quite a lot since I started taking them." I thought of the difficulties of running the farm, working as a legal executive and trying to come to terms with my nightmares all at the same time. None of these things were in my life now.

"I think we can safely wean you off the pills over the next couple of weeks," he said, looking at me closely. "I'm sure you'll find that your blood pressure will be quite normal without the drugs, Janet. Your lifestyle is obviously conducive to relaxed living. Carry on doing what you're doing; taking walks with your dogs, riding your bike, eating well and I'm sure the dizzy spells will stop."

I did as Dr Bell suggested and for the first time in my life I began to feel completely and utterly normal. My weight stabilised at about seven and a half stone (about right for someone an inch or so shy of five foot, I'd say), my skin was clear and my headaches and nightmares non-existent. I wasn't ready to think back over all the details of my life yet but all I had to do was keep reminding myself of Dr Browne-Thomas' coping mechanisms and I knew things would be fine. I'd also begun to think about the future and the possibility of staying in Scotland for the long term. I'd grown to love the silence and the huge great open vistas of the Highlands; I liked the idea of renting a half derelict croft and converting it into a home then moving in with the dogs and possibly creating a small holding and becoming self sufficient in the process. It wasn't an impossible dream and it was one I began to think of more and more as the winter progressed and, let's be honest, if I could survive a winter in a caravan in the Highlands I could survive pretty well anything.

Well, actually, not quite anything.

Chapter Forty-Two

Two of my dogs at Strathconan Forest, Western Scotland

April 2011

The spring of 2011 is a spectacular one in the Highlands. We have better weather in one brief season than we've had for the rest of the year put together; the winter was bitterly cold, the summer is all set to be a wash out but, by some miracle, April is absolutely gorgeous. With amazing prescience Mary has told David she's going to come up in the school's Easter holidays to see me and it turns out to be a week that neither of us will ever forget.

On one of the hottest days of the year Mary and I stand perched at the top of the cliff looking down on the stunning crescent-shaped beach below. Jelly leans against my leg with all the resistance of a rag doll while the other four lean over the edge and bark with fevered excitement.

"We're not going down there are we?" Mary looks at me as if I'm mad.

"I don't think we've any choice," I laugh. "The dogs are going anyway by the looks of things, at least four of them are, I might have to carry Jelly in my rucksack but if we stick to the path we should be okay and besides, you can't go back to Derbyshire and say you've missed out on a beach like that."

"What path?"

I point at what looks like a route down to the golden sand and the blue-green sea below but given the brightness of the sun, I can't be sure. "You can follow me and then if you slip I'll catch you."

"Oh no, I don't think so. If I fall we both go down and then we crack our heads open on those rocks at the bottom."

I look to where she is pointing. "Don't be daft, Mary; you've got your walking boots on haven't you? We'll be fine." I set off before Mary can come up with any more objections, half sitting, half sliding down the first hundred yards or so and by the sounds of distress behind me, my friend has decided to follow suit.

It is a good 40 minutes before we get to the bottom, by which time my jeans are covered in muck and Mary is puce from the effort needed to keep from tumbling into me. The dogs have been down on the beach a good 20 minutes already and even Jelly is haring up and down the deserted sands like a demented thing, barking at the oyster-catchers, her short legs splashing through the clear water with as much joy as a child. I'm not usually one to anthropomorphise my pets, but sometimes it's such an obvious comparison even I have to make it: my dogs can - and often do - act like kids.

Mary and I stand there, puffing and panting, staring at the iridescent water as if we've never seen the sea before.

"It's beautiful."

"I know." I shield my eyes from the sun, my heart ebbing and flowing with the rise and fall of the waves. It is such a different scene to the one I'm used to in Derbyshire but it is equally as powerful, possibly more so. This view doesn't just alter with the seasons; it alters day by day, hour by hour. I have been here many times since moving to this part of Scotland and every time I come it offers me something different. Today the turquoise sea, yellow sand and vivid blue sky reminds me of a Hockney painting, last week I'd looked down from the cliffs through driving rain and a roaring wind and I'd felt as insignificant as a grain of sand. Nature seems to have this power: to heal if she wants to but also to wound if she feels so disposed. Today, feeling the sun on my face and the peace all around me, I feel as if I am finally on my way to being healed.

We drop our rucksacks on the sand, then flop down next to

311

each other, relieved to see that there is no-one else sharing this little bit of heaven: we are completely alone, surrounded by the cliffs on three sides and the sea out in front. There are only the guillemots and razorbills to keep us company, and the sound of an occasional kittiwake ringing out over the noise of the waves.

"It's like the Caribbean without the palm trees," says Mary.

"Or the jet lag."

"Or the balmy evenings."

"Oh, Mary, were you cold last night? You should have said; I would have made you up a hot water bottle."

Mary laughs. "I'll borrow Jelly tonight, shall I? She can lie on me and do her canine blanket impression."

I look over to where my five faithful companions are now digging in the sand, their attention distracted occasionally by the birds overhead and I wonder if I'd be sitting here now if I hadn't had them to keep me company these last 12 months. Without Jelly and Co I wouldn't have had to get up in the mornings; without my five ugly mutts I could have turned over and gone back to sleep each morning and no-one would have cared. Well, that's not strictly true; I'd like to think that Mary might have missed me just a little. *"Sorry, please look after the animals."*

"What did you say?"

"Nothing."

"Yes, you did, you said something. What did you say? Something about the animals."

"I said, sorry, please look after the animals." I stare at her, trying to understand.

"Why, where are you going? Why do I need to look after your animals?"

"You don't. I do."

Mary looks worried. "Janet, what are you talking about?" She looks around her as if someone on the beach can help her understand but there isn't a soul out there; just the sea, the sand and those magnificent towering cliffs behind us.

"That's what the note said: *Please look after the animals*."

"Yes, I remember. You told me."

"Fred's note."

"Yes."

"It was pinned to the stable door. The stable where I kept my ponies; the one in the fields above my house, about half way up to the farm. I was so traumatised at the idea of what it meant - the idea of Fred committing suicide – that I blanked it out and then I blanked out the memory of the attack with it - but even though I'd put it out of my mind I knew something terrible had happened, I just didn't know what it was. And then I went up to Ball Beard on Friday, for the first time in five days, feeling this awful panic, I didn't know *why* I was feeling panicked."

I feel Mary's hand on my arm. "I think we can take it that he felt terrible at what he had done to you and couldn't think of any other way to make amends."

My brain is working overtime. "No, that's not it Mary. I don't think that's what he meant at all."

She looks at me but I don't look back. I am staring out to sea and watching the foam-flecked waves as they roll in, the whiteness at the tips a stunning contrast to the vivid green underneath. I can feel my heart beating in my chest but I am calmed and soothed by the sights and sounds all around me; I feel the coping mechanisms I've learnt coming into play. I am in control now. Finally, I feel as if I have a choice.

"On the Friday I remember rushing through the fields, hurrying along as if someone was coming up behind me, chasing me. I went past the stables and then stopped briefly to chat to Ernie, which was when he told me he'd seen me chase the heifer a few days before and I didn't know what he was talking about. I remember slowing down once I'd reached the farmyard, my heart beating like mad, petrified that someone was somewhere nearby, watching me, stalking me – just waiting for me to come back to Ball Beard. I couldn't remember why I was petrified – but I had to look after the animals because that's what I always did so I couldn't stay away; there was no way on this earth I could stay away from the farm."

"What had you done with the note?"

"I don't know; I'd stamped on it, trampled on it. I panicked but ..." I screw my eyes up. I'm not panicking now. I am putting another piece in the jigsaw and I am doing it on my own terms.

"When you read that note did you know that he'd raped you?"

"Yes. But, Mary, I'm telling you now he wasn't the sort of

314

man to kill himself; that's what Mags told the police and that's what I believe too. "

"So, you threw the note on the ground and then what did you do?"

"I ran home. I didn't want to think about it for a moment longer than I had to. I went to bed and when I woke up in the morning it was all gone."

Mary takes her hand away and sighs. "It's as if your brain was protecting you. The trauma was too much. You didn't want to think of Fred committing suicide and you didn't want to think of what he'd done to you, so you blanked it."

"I'm not sure…"

"Well, I'm no psychologist so I'm only surmising, of course – but… don't you think that explanation could be feasible?"

"No, because I know, deep down, that the note wasn't a suicide note."

"What? Then what was it?"

"It was Fred's way of getting me back into the farmhouse. That's why he wrote the note, Mary: to get me back there."

"What are you saying, Janet?"

"I'm saying it was a ruse; he wasn't sorry about what he'd done to me at all."

"But if that's the case and it wasn't a suicide note then presumably… presumably he wasn't dead when you were reading it?"

I shake my head. The pieces aren't all in their proper place

315

yet but they are getting there. I am amazed at how calm I am feeling.

"Then where is he; where did he go?"

I shake my head again. "I don't know; I don't think he'd gone anywhere at this point. He could have been in the farmhouse waiting for me for all I know. I can't remember; I think there's more to come."

I can tell that Mary believes me. She wants to know more and so do I; unfortunately my brain isn't quite ready yet to tell me. But as I keep telling myself: I've waited 34 years for the truth to reveal itself so one more month isn't going to make much difference, is it?

Chapter Forty-Three

June 2011

The balminess of April gives way to two months of fairly non-descript late spring weather that is still wonderful as far as I'm concerned – just not particularly warm.

My life continues to progress in a calm and measured way: I remain on the campsite near the coast, I take long, relaxing walks, I go for bike rides, I cook on my tiny cooker in my miniscule kitchen and I read and watch telly. Once a week, sometimes more, I email Mary on my Blackberry, or I speak to her. She tells me that she and David are about to celebrate their 25th wedding anniversary and she asks if I will consider driving back down to Derbyshire for the party. I surprise myself when I tell her I might just do that.

"As long as I can find a kennels up here in the Highlands daft enough to take my five dogs, I'd love to come," I say.

There is a pause at the other end of the line. I know what she wants to ask me but she's wary. I've discovered recently that Mary doesn't like to talk to me about anything too personal unless she can see my face. She says I'm too adept at hiding my real feelings on the phone.

"No more pieces in the jigsaw if that's what you're wondering, so you don't have to tie yourself in knots by wanting to ask and not daring to."

"I don't know what you mean."

"Perhaps I'll never know for sure."

She stops pretending then. "No, I suppose not. You're all right then?"

"Yes, I'm fine. Why wouldn't I be?"

"I wouldn't like to think of you….finding out something when you're up there on your own. It has occurred to me that…"

"What?"

"That you might have seen him – you know."

"No, I don't know."

"You might have seen him – seen Fred – kill himself and that's why it's too awful to…"

I consider for a moment what Mary has just said. Could that be it? Could I have seen Fred kill himself? But then, in a moment of complete clarity I suddenly realise that's not it at all. The note he'd written was not a suicide note; I'm convinced of that now. It was his way of getting me back into the farmhouse - and I'd fallen for it.

"I've got to go," I say suddenly. "Jolly's pestering me for a walk. I'll call you later."

"Promise?"

"Yes, I promise."

"Where are you going?"

"To the beach."

"The same one…"

"Yes."

"Janet?"

"Yes?"

"Take a photo for me. Email it to me when you get back."

"When I get back?"

"Yes – when you get back."

I gesture to Jelly to follow me. "I've got to go, Mary. I'll be losing signal soon. I'll be in touch." And I hang up.

I whistle for the other four and they come running in an instant. I grab my rucksack, a packet of biscuits and my bottle filled with water. There are one or two other caravans parked near me now and I nod to the owners of one of them before setting off. Barney and his wife, Joyce are a lovely couple but even so, it might be time to move on; I imagine summer in this particular part of the Highlands will bring too many other visitors in their wake.

I reach the path within 20 minutes and begin my 500 metre slip-slide down onto the beach. The sea looks darker than last time but it still soothes me. There are no white-flecked waves today, just an opaque glassiness, like a sheet of solid black ice. I breathe in the scent of the air and feel my lungs expand. I feel calmer than I've ever felt in my life.

I'm not ready to sit down on the sand so I pick up a stone and throw it into the sea. Four of the dogs chase after it while Jelly stands on the edge debating whether to compete. Chicco emerges victorious and rushes up and drops the stone at my feet. I repeat the process and he gets it again. I throw it one more time and watch as it sails through the air just at the moment when the sun emerges from behind a cloud, shining a yellow shaft of light down onto the water. Like a low wattage bulb the rays struggle to illuminate the darkness but the water is too deep and it does nothing more than cast a glow. Nothing is revealed. The stone falls with a splash. I sit down on the sand. The sun will shine more strongly in a moment. I can wait.

Once again there is no-one on the beach with me. I close my eyes. I can feel myself relaxing. I haven't had a nightmare in over a year. This is how it should be; calm and rational, the demons of the night banished for ever. Jelly comes panting up from the water's edge and lies next to me, her wet muzzle resting on my knee. I stroke her head and think of all the dogs I've had over the years, from Ned to Henry and all the others, to Jelly and her four companions and I find myself feeling nostalgic for the past; I think of all the horses I've ridden and the horses I've bred. I wonder where they all are now. I think of the pigs I've mucked out and the cows I've milked; I think of the fields I've ploughed and the walls I've built.

Please look after the animals.

The sun comes out again and I feel a subtle warmth on my skin. Jelly sighs as I feel her head grow heavy. I open my eyes again and screw them up against the glare, staring at the horizon and, although I can't see much out there, I begin to see something.

I wonder if this is the last piece of the jigsaw falling into place. Fred didn't commit suicide, I shot him. And I buried his body.

The beach, West Coast of Scotland

Chapter Forty-Four

June 2011

When Mary asked me if I'd killed Fred Handford I honestly believed I hadn't. That was the truth when she asked me the question. How could I kill him? It was too ridiculous for words

But the truth has changed. I know now that I did kill him and this is what happened.

I went up to the stables in the fields half way to the farm every day after Fred raped me: I had to feed the ponies but I had to avoid Fred; I couldn't bear to see him, let alone speak to him. Not only did I hate him, I feared him too. I was frightened he would try to rape me again and I was frightened that, for whatever reason, he wasn't the Fred Handford I had come to know since the first time I'd arrived at Ball Beard Farm. The Fred Handford who'd raped me was a completely different animal altogether.

Ernie saw me on Wednesday when I'd chased the heifer back up the field and on Thursday I'd found the note pinned to the stable door. I threw it on the floor and then I dashed home, the words of the note going round and round in my head. My brain wouldn't let me think of Fred killing himself because if it did I would have to think of *why* he'd killed himself and I didn't want to do that: the guilt was simply too awful for words.

And so when I woke up on Friday 19 March my memories had gone and I'd forgotten everything: the note, the rape – everything. I went back up to Ball Beard Farm and I searched the farmhouse. On the way up there I felt as if someone was following me, watching me. The weight of something terrible was forcing me to run so fast I could barely breathe. I was terrified - but of what I had no idea. I searched downstairs and then I went upstairs in the farmhouse but he wasn't in the bedroom and so I came back down again and that's when the truth changes.

When I come back down the stairs Fred is in the kitchen, waiting, and when I look at him it all begins to come back to me. He starts talking to me about how he loves me and how we're going to get married. He's lost his mind – but listening to him and watching him standing there in the farmhouse with the red door to the farmyard behind him, I can tell that he believes he's making sense. He keeps talking about us making love. We didn't make love; I realise in that one moment that he raped me. I'm petrified, absolutely and completely petrified. Fear is the only thing I can remember; complete, and utter fear. He is standing in the doorway and I realise I've just put myself right back in the place I was in four days ago. He's making plans for our future. He's asking me if I've told my parents what he's done and I think if I lie I'll be able to get away and so I say *'Yes, Dad's down at the police station*

323

right now telling them everything.' And just as I say that the rape comes back to me in all its horrific detail. I remember the sensation of what he's done and I start shaking. *'The police are going to be here at any minute'* and he starts to smile at me.

"No they're not. You wouldn't be 'ere now if that were the case." He takes a step closer. "We'll have a cup of tea, shall we?"

Something in his manner makes me think he is going to do it again; he's going to rape me again. I say, yes, I'll have a cup of tea and then he moves away from the door and I step forward. I catch sight of his gun in the corner of the kitchen, where it always is, leaning against the wall like an umbrella. I stare at it, the panic like a noose around my neck: one tiny move and I could be dead. Then, taking the smallest of steps, he turns behind him and he puts the latch on the door. He's locking me into the farmhouse. I'm trapped in here with him. There's nothing I can do; my heart is beating uncontrollably in my chest, the sound reverberating in my ears. He must be able to hear it; he must. My legs turn to liquid. I sit down again. He gets the kettle and he starts filling it. I know it's going to take at least a minute because the water comes in slowly from the hosepipe outside. I've got a minute to do something. He's standing there filling the kettle with his back to me. I look at the gun and I look at him and suddenly all the emotions switch off in my head; I stop shaking. I reach out and take hold of it. I've never used a gun in my life. He is still filling the kettle. I pick it up, turn around and then I point the gun at him: I point it and I try to pull the trigger but it doesn't work; the gun hasn't fired. I look down at it. I push the safety catch back and I try again. This time it fires. I shoot him. He drops to the floor. The kettle clatters on the flagstones. Then I put the gun back and I go outside into the yard and I stand there. I stand there for half an hour. I don't think, I don't feel, I just stand there. It's like I'm going in and out of...I know what's happened and yet I don't know what's happened and I keep telling Ned to go and find him but I know all along where he is. It's like there are two sides to my brain: one side that knows what's happened and one side that doesn't. And then I go into the large shippon and I milk Marjorie, all the time knowing what's happened and yet believing he's missing – and then I go back into the farmhouse and I look at his body. I know I have to do something but I don't know what.

I walk back out into the farmyard and I fetch the wheelbarrow. And then it fades away again; I can't remember what I did. I know I won't have taken him far but I'm not sure where. I remember fetching a spade from the bottom of the farmyard - near the barn. I can remember going down to the bottom of the barn and the spade is there, sticking out of the mud and I'm struggling to get it out. I don't remember feeling panicked; I don't remember feeling anything and yet this was in the middle of the day and anyone could have seen me.

I've put the gun back against the wall. It's covered in my finger prints; the shell is still in it. It's all very, very real. I know I'm not mistaken. There's no emotion now but I think that's because there was no emotion then. As I say, it's like someone's flicked a switch.

I've pushed myself too hard for so many years and now I've suddenly stopped. Dr Browne-Thomas said there was a possibility that some of my forgotten memories would return even without my EMDR sessions but I'm glad that I had those sessions because now I can deal with it. It makes me wonder if relaxing was the key. But there's just one more piece of the jigsaw: Where did I put his body?

Since coming up to Scotland, my memory has been trickling through steadily, bit by bit and I'm sure the last bit of detail will come through in its own good time and then I'll go to the police. Fred's daughter and his sister have a right to know. I think of the booklet Mags wrote and distributed and realise, she was right: I *did* kill her brother. But I didn't kill him for the reason she believes. I didn't kill him for the farm; I killed him because I believed he was going to attack me and if he'd raped me again I believe he would have killed me.

I'm sure Mags will say '*I told you so*' but that's irrelevant, isn't it? I can't get around the fact that it's morally right for her to know what happened to her brother. She's entitled to know and so is Katrina.

The police will ask me when I picked up the gun did I know what I was doing and I'll say: '*Yes I did. I pulled the trigger intentionally and then I buried him*'. I don't think the police will be interested in what's gone before.

I remember getting him into the wheelbarrow with a corn

hook. I couldn't touch him. I remember going down the yard, over the flagstones and having the spade with me…I think over the next month I'll remember where he is. I have no emotion about it at all. It's weird but it's the truth. I could make it easier for myself and lie to the police; tell them I shot him just after he attacked me but there's no point because if I'm going to tell the truth, I'm going to tell the truth - and that's the only way to do it.

I know the outcome won't be good. I know I said at the beginning that there was no way I could have done something like this but I'm certain now; I'm absolutely certain. I killed Fred Handford.

I also know it will be a minimum of five years in prison.

Chapter Forty-Five

September 2011

Last year, when I remembered what Fred did to me, it was as if it had just happened; each one of my senses was acutely alive to the detail of his attack and to a great extent those feelings are with me now. I feel as if Fred attacked me last week not 35 years ago.

But this memory isn't like that. When I came back down the stairs into the kitchen at Ball Beard Farm and I saw him standing there my body began to shake with more emotion than I could physically handle. He was going to rape me again; I knew that as clearly as if he'd spoken the words out loud and that thought was utterly terrifying but once I'd sat down at the table and I saw the shotgun leaning against the wall it was as if somebody had flicked a switch in my brain and turned my emotions off.

I can't believe I pulled that trigger. I find the idea ludicrous. Part of me believes it wasn't me; I mean, I know it *was* me but the idea that I could actually kill someone is totally and utterly ridiculous. I can't say I knew what would happen when I pulled that trigger; I just pointed it and pulled. I don't remember hearing the sound of gunfire. He dropped the kettle and then he crumpled. I walked out. I didn't feel anything then - and I don't feel anything now.

If there weren't any surviving relatives then perhaps I wouldn't be doing what I'm about to do but he's got a 94-year-old sister and a daughter my own age. If I'd tipped him down a mine shaft and there was no body to recover perhaps I'd also think twice, but he's up there at the farm and I can't think of an alternative.

I'm going back to Derbyshire soon for Mary's party and I intend to turn myself in to the police just as soon as I get things in order. I've got five dogs to find a home for and then I'll be going to Buxton police station to tell them what happened 35 years ago.

Please look after the animals

Fred left his 'suicide note' deliberately. He'd written it because he wanted me to go back to the farmhouse. He'd laughed at me when I was in the kitchen, knowing that I couldn't escape. He was talking gibberish about how we were going to get married and how he loved me: I'm sure he'd lost his marbles.

'*But you left a note,*' I said.

'*I thought that'd get you back. I know you; you can't leave these animals wantin'.*'

But on 19 March 1976 I don't remember this. All I remember is waking up in bed with my dirty wellies next to me. It was like one minute I knew and the next minute I didn't. When I told Mum he'd disappeared I believed that. I honestly believed that.

I can't even bear to write his name now.

I dig out a box of old photographs and rummage through them, trying not to get emotional but there are some lovely memories here of Mum and Dad; I particularly like the one of both of them at my brother, Pete's wedding looking elegant. Mum always looked smart; she must have wondered what had hit her when she had me! Dad looks so handsome. I pick out a black and white image of me dressed as an Indian brave sitting astride a bareback Apache and another with Ann, on our horses in Chinley High Street eating ice-creams. I've got quite a few pictures of Ball Beard Farm; grainy images of the '50s and '60s through to faded Polaroids of the '70s and later. I've even got a few of Fred, but they're not very clear and at least one of them is water damaged. I'm tempted to burn them now. I pull out the picture of me and Fred haymaking on a glorious September day sometime in the early 70s and I try to remember who took it. It couldn't have been Miles; he didn't start coming to Ball Beard Farm until 1977, although I remember he used to like that time of year, it was always his favourite - as long as he didn't have to get his hands dirty. I stare at the battered and creased image, screwing up my eyes until the faded yellow of the hay blurs into the misty blue of the sky and I don't know where the field ends and the sky begins and then I feel my heart begin to pound. It's not the sight of Hero pulling the flat cart that makes me nervous or Ned in the foreground running towards the camera, it's the field we're in. I recognise it for many reasons; it's not far from the farmyard and it's a field I've crossed many times on the way up to Round Wood. I look from the picture in my hand to the view outside the caravan window. The sun is still shining. I feel the last piece of the jigsaw falling finally into place. I'm sure now; this is the field where I buried Fred; this is the field I dug with the spade then tipped him in, all the time convincing myself that I was burying a sack of corn and not a body.

I'm standing in the yard, doing nothing and thinking of nothing. I stand there for half an hour. I know Fred is on the farmhouse floor because I've just shot him and yet I go around the farm looking for him with Ned by my side; I run into the shippon and the barn; I check the stables, the hen house and the pig sties, but I can't find him anywhere. I milk Marjorie and I ask Ned: *'Where's Fred; find Fred.'* My brain has split into two; half belongs to me, half to someone else.

I fetch a wheelbarrow and I wheel it into the kitchen. I take a farm implement off the shelf, the one Fred uses to drag sacks of corn around the yard and I use it now to haul him into the barrow. I don't want to touch him. Then I wheel him out into the yard and towards the field. I imagine I have a sack full of bad corn in the barrow and I have to dispose of it. I know you don't bury bags of corn, bad or otherwise, but I push that thought to the back of my mind and then I dig a hole in broad daylight, in full view of any walkers there might be up on Round Wood and I tip him in. I fill the hole and then I go back to the farmhouse. Everything goes blank again. I don't know where Fred is. Where's Fred? I feel as if

331

I'm losing my mind. I start running. Dad will know what to do; Dad will know exactly what to do.

But that was 35 years ago. My Dad is dead and I have no-one else in my life whose advice I can ask. I look out of the caravan to the sky outside, watching as the colour darkens from pale grey to dark pewter and I make a decision. I will arrange one last appointment with Dr Belinda Browne-Thomas before I turn myself in. I realise I have to tell her the full story.

Chapter Forty-Six

September 2011

I discover fairly quickly that a psychologist's rule of confidentiality towards a patient ends when violence towards another person is involved. When I tell Dr Belinda about my revelations she advises me to go to the police and I assure her that I will – just as soon as I've organised homes for the dogs. I imagine walking into the police station, confessing my crime and not being allowed home again. Jelly is nervous enough without me springing this on her – hence her name – but the doctor isn't keen to wait. It's a case of if I don't go to the police immediately then she will.

I'm back in England now. I drove down with the dogs as soon as I could after speaking to an old friend, Diane, who confirmed I could park my caravan on her arable farm in Staffordshire and stay for a while. I accepted her offer, grateful for the chance to take a few deep breaths before I turn myself in. Dr Browne-Thomas is due to set off in a day or two for a three-week trip to New Zealand and she is keen to see a conclusion as quickly as possible. She also tells me that I must be prepared for the worst.

"What do you mean?" I ask as I sit perched on the chair in

her consulting room.

"You have to accept that there is a chance that the police will not be able to find a body, Janet. It was a long time ago. You also have to be prepared for this to be a false memory and you have to be strong; you have to call on your coping mechanisms, just as we discussed, do you remember?"

"Yes," I say, nodding and frowning at the same time. "But I know I did it; I know I killed Fred Handford and I remember burying his body at Ball Beard Farm. There is no doubt in my mind that this is not a false memory." I'm not sure she believes me but something about her expression makes me wonder. "But if they don't find a body, what then?"

"I'm not sure; I'm a psychologist, Janet, not a lawyer. I don't know if one can be charged with murder if there is no body." She speaks so gently, as if she really is concerned for my well being and yet I want to tell her not to worry; I feel a detachment I can't explain other than to say that I don't feel any emotion now simply because I didn't feel any emotion then.

I don't have time to call Mary. By the time she gets round to phoning me the following day I'm in a police car on the way to the station. The desk sergeant had insisted that the police come to me rather than the other way round. So, now they know where I've parked the caravan and I have ten minutes in which to explain to my friend that in 1976 I killed a man. She can't take it in.

"I'm sorry," I say, "I didn't want to have to tell you this, but I've got no choice." And she looks at me, speechless and bemused. We haven't seen each other for two years and now, here I am, giving her this barely believable news.

"Don't worry about the dogs," she says, focusing on something tangible as I'm led out of her kitchen. "They'll be fine; I'll look after them." And with that comforting thought in my head I climb into the back of the police car and sit, silently, staring out of the window.

My Blackberry rings. It's Mary. "I can't speak," I say.

"What's wrong, Janet? Where are you?"

"I'm in a car on the way to Buxton," I say, leaving out the fact that it's a police car. There's a silence at the end of the line. I pretend she's still speaking to me and offer some vague chit chat. "Yes, I know; no, of course not, I see." And she realises straight away that it's serious.

"Just contact me when you can," she says. "Let me know if you need anything." And I tell her not to worry, I will, just as soon as I've sorted out an urgent matter I tell her I'll be in touch.

What follows next is neither a blow-by-blow account of what happened nor a subjective view of events where I leave out everything that makes me look bad. This is a record of what I can remember in the order I remember it happening. I imagined telling the police what I'd done and I imagined them believing me and then I imagined going to prison. That's about all I had in my mind when I confessed to killing Fred Handford; I hadn't thought about it in any more detail than that but, as ever with my life, things don't go according to plan.

Of course, the police question me and, at first, I answer their questions one by one.

"Yes," I say, "I killed Fred Handford and I buried his body." I have a duty solicitor, John Bunting sitting with me and he's fidgeting in his chair. The poor man is totally confused by the concept of having a client who insists on being found guilty rather than one desperate to prove their innocence and I can see him becoming more and more uncomfortable as the questioning goes on.

They keep me in a cell but carry on with their questioning at midnight. They ask me over and over again, until four in the morning, to tell them what happened 35 years ago.

"Why did you kill him?" they ask and I tell them; I give the reason but none of the detail. I make it very clear that I am not prepared to discuss the rape other than to say that Fred attacked me. I can't repeat the experience because I know I won't be able to cope. If I relive what Fred did to me on 14 March 1976 I know I won't be strong enough to pull myself back from the brink a second time. I was able to tell Dr Browne-Thomas about the rape but I won't be able to tell the police – I know that as surely as if the doctor has warned me herself. She has given me coping mechanisms for dealing with the fallout - but not for reliving it.

Unfortunately my answers aren't proving satisfactory enough for the police to believe me and I begin to wonder about the direction the questions are taking. It's subtle at first, but it isn't long before I get the gist of what they think my motive is for turning myself in.

"So, you're writing a book about your experiences are you?" I nod to indicate that, yes, that's exactly what I'm doing. I've put the details down in writing, partly so I don't have to speak of it ever again.

"And how much money are you hoping to make from this book, then Janet?"

I stare at the detective, not understanding. "I'm sorry…"

"Come on. How much money were you hoping to make from this piece of fiction? One million, two million? Admit it; you've made the whole thing up."

I'm not quite sure how to answer him. Does he honestly think I've fabricated this whole sorry mess and then waited half a lifetime before 'admitting' to it? I'd have to be a bloody good actor if that was the case; an Oscar-winning one to be precise. And why would I wait 35 years before cashing in? I'm hoping that Dr Belinda Browne-Thomas' notes will be produced eventually as evidence to show that this isn't a figment of my imagination but a long buried experience that's taken expert coaxing by a qualified professional before I've been able to reveal the truth – not just to the police but to myself but I answer his question as best as I can.

"I've had a look at the possibility of self-publishing on the internet and if you take into account the publishing company's commission, the cost of producing the book and the likelihood of selling any copies I think I might clear ten quid if I'm lucky."

He looks at me, half angry, half disappointed. My solicitor,

John objects to the turn the questioning has taken and advises me not to answer any more in this vein. I take his advice and go quiet. In the manner of the famous quiz show I am allowed to phone a friend and I call Mary to ask if she's able to bring me a change of clothes.

"You're where?" she asks, incredulous. "Why?" And I try to give her a potted version of what I've been doing for the last day and a half. Something in her response makes me nervous.

"Oh Janet, is there no end to this?" She sounds weary, disappointed. I feel the sting of tears for the first time in 48 hours.

"I'm hoping this will be the end," I say with feeling. "I had to tell the truth Mary, I hope you can see that. I had to tell the police what happened. Mags and Katrina have a right to know."

There is a long pause at the end of the line. "But are you sure, Janet?" she asks eventually. "Are you really sure?"

I remember the answer I gave to that same question when we were sitting in Geo's coffee shop last year. This time my answer is completely different. "Yes, Mary, I'm absolutely sure; I killed Fred Handford and I buried his body up at Ball Beard Farm."

Can things get worse than your best friend doubting you? Well, yes they can. The detective who speaks to me the following morning is less than half my age and appears to have been given the task of asking me questions in the hope, I suppose, that woman-to-woman I might reveal more than I did to her male colleague.

"How old are you, Janet?" she asks.

"Sixty," I say, looking at her steadily.

"And have you ever been married?"

"No," I say, "I haven't." I am tempted to ask what business is it of hers but honestly, I can't be bothered.

She leans in a bit closer and tucks her hair behind her ear before she speaks - to make sure I can lip read, I suppose: well, I am 60 years old so she probably assumes I'm deaf. "Do you really know what rape means, Janet?" she asks, enunciating each syllable very carefully.

I stare at her, not quite sure the words have come from her mouth, but yes, she is actually waiting for a response to the question: *'Do I really know what rape means'* and I have to stop myself from laughing out loud. She'll probably think I'm mad if I do that; sent round the twist by a husband-less life and only my animals to keep me company. I remember being questioned by the police in 1976 with their abrupt, sexist attitude and their accusations that Fred and I were having a *relationship* and I wonder if anything's changed in 2011. Well, yes, something obviously has: female detectives can do it just as well as their male counterparts now - neither of them takes rape seriously.

It's up to the victim to do that, I suppose.

Chapter Forty-Seven

September 2011

I am allowed out on bail provided I report to my local police station at 4pm each day. This is a situation that will be ongoing until the middle of December when the police tell me they will be making a decision as to whether or not they intend to bring charges. I realise I could be in prison by Christmas and if that's the case, I doubt very much I'll be free again in my lifetime since what else can they charge me with but murder?

I assume the police will be speaking to everyone I've texted, phoned or emailed in the last 12 months as they've confiscated both my Blackberry and my computer. Goodness knows what they must be thinking after reading the texts from Carol and Claire: details of quiz nights at the pub, information on the badminton league and possibly the latest jokes on *Have I Got News for You*. Or maybe detectives think I've invented a sophisticated secret messaging service and that I'm communicating more sinister information? I'm sure they'll be interested in the number of times Mary and I have contacted each other over the last year which leads me to believe she'll be questioned by officers too – and I'm not wrong, before the week is out they request an interview at Mary's home, which means, of course, that she will have to explain to her husband David why the police are knocking on their door in the middle of the afternoon and I suddenly realise that I've unleashed a terrible chain of events.

The police warn me that they are going to take me to Ball Beard Farm so I can point out to them where Fred's body is buried. They have already started digging but, as yet, they've found nothing. I feel my blood pressure begin to rise at the thought of going back there. I try to imagine the scenery in the Scottish Highlands, walking with my dogs on the beach and watching the rise and fall of the waves but suddenly those images are no longer in my head. I haven't been to Ball Beard in over a year and I begin to panic. I try so hard to recall the coping mechanisms that Dr Belinda Browne-Thomas spent time describing to me but suddenly it becomes difficult to remember these too. I hear my breathing becoming louder and louder in my head until the detective's voice is just another noise in the background. I have to go back to the farm, I have no choice, but I ask them to consider a few provisos.

"Please make sure the gate to the farmyard is open so we can drive straight in and past the farmhouse and please, please don't ask me anything about what Fred Handford did to me when he attacked me."

The detective nods but I can tell she's not listening and the experience is much worse than I could ever imagine; it's just as Dr Belinda Browne-Thomas warned me it would be and I relive it all - it's 1976 all over again. I feel as if I'm suffocating. We drive up the lane, my heart beating so loudly in my chest it drowns out any

341

other sounds. I can see the gate to the farmyard in front of me and the farmhouse on the right. The police car slows. From the back seat I peer through the windscreen. The gate is locked. I can see the padlock securely fastened and I feel an awful dread dragging through my limbs like a slow moving weight. The car has to stop: it can't drive through. Someone has to find a key. We pull up in front of the house and I force myself to stare straight ahead. *'Don't look at the house; don't go back there.'* I mutter, but it's no good. I twist my head to the right and stare at the door. New owners have painted over the peeling red paint but I can still hear the sound of the latch as it closes behind me. I scrabble for the car's door handle. I'm locked in; I can't get out. My heart pumps faster; my head feels as if it is about to explode. *"Please, let me out!"* Pins and needles shoot up my arm. I can't deal with the emotion. The coping mechanisms aren't working. The WPC stares at me as if I'm a child having a tantrum and puts a hand on my shoulder. I can't hear what she's saying but it would be meaningless even if I could. The door opens and I fall out of the car. I force myself upright and try to control my breathing. My heart is beating out an angry rhythm. The pins and needles continue their prickly attack. There are four detectives surrounding me and one of them is filming me on a hand-held camera, gauging my reaction, watching me like a bird of prey, assessing my weaknesses. I don't have any weaknesses other than my memory. My memory is too strong. It all comes back to me. I look across the farmyard towards the covered reservoir and the field where I know he is buried. They are

342

digging where I've instructed them to dig but they have made a terrible error.

The camera follows me as I walk towards the freshly dug ground. They tell me an archaeologist has declared that this field could not possibly have been disturbed in 1976 or at any time since then. He says this with such authority the police assume I must be lying when I tell them that this simply isn't true. I killed Fred Handford and I buried his body right here. How can the archaeologist make such a statement when I know that in 1976 I dug the very ground we're standing on now? I point to the spot but they look at me blankly. They have excavated an area as large as a football pitch and have found nothing - and the reason? They haven't dug down deep enough.

How can this expert possibly say that the ground hasn't been disturbed when, in 1982 United Utilities laid a pipeline right under our feet? This was the pipeline that brought an improved water supply to the High Peak area; I was paid £2,000 in compensation for allowing access across my land. The police say United Utilities didn't dig up the ground in 1982 but I have a photograph of one of the bright yellow diggers brought over from Ireland especially for the purpose. My horses can be seen clearly in the foreground. Perhaps the problem is they simply don't *want* to believe me? It's obvious I am inconveniencing them and perhaps they feel as if I'm wasting their time but if I was Fred Handford's sister or Fred Handford's daughter I'd want to know what had happened to my relative. I'd want closure. And that's why I went to the police: Mags and Katrina have a moral right to know the truth and no matter what happens to me, I can't escape that fact. Those United Utility diggers were capable of shifting five tonnes of soil in one go. For all I know, his body could have been moved in the process.

I am eventually taken back to Buxton Police Station and I ask to see a doctor. My pins and needles won't go away; my heart is still racing. I believe I've suffered a panic attack and I can feel Dr Belinda Browne-Thomas' sound advice receding further and further into the distance.

When the doctor arrives a couple of hours later she confirms my suspicions. She also tells me that I have dangerously high blood pressure. The realisation that I have come full circle is a thoroughly depressing thought and seven months later, when a medic at Macclesfield General Hospital tells me there is a strong possibility that I've suffered a heart attack in the last year, I realise this must have been the day that it happened.

My solicitor is a calm voice of reason. Once he has grasped the concept that, unlike most of his clients I am not trying to prove my innocence but, rather, attempting to provide the answer to the question that everyone has been asking for 35 years: *Did Janet Holt kill Fred Handford* he is extremely professional. The fact the police are unable to find a body to prove my guilt doesn't appear to be hampering his support.

At the end of the day I am allowed to return to my temporary home – the caravan, which is still parked on my friend

Diane's land. When I get back it's obvious I've had visitors. The police have confiscated all my notes for the book along with anything else they believe might be useful to them and the caravan is looking a little dishevelled, to say the least. I close all cupboard doors, shut all drawers and concentrate on returning everything to its proper place and, as I restore order, my heart begins to slow. *'Nothing's so broken it can't be fixed'* as my mother used to say and then I turn to the barn on the opposite side of the yard preparing to unlock the door and release Jelly and co. who, by now, are feverishly barking their disapproval at having to wait so long for their tea. They follow me back to the caravan where I reach for the dog biscuits and immediately catch sight of the list:

Get out of bed

Feed the dogs

Get washed

Get dressed

Make a cup of tea, eat a slice of toast.

My heart slows down further. I tip the biscuits into the bowl and place it on the floor outside the caravan door then I step back in, pick up the kettle and fill it with water ready for a cup of tea. It's still light outside. I realise I've got time for a bike ride. Ten miles should do it – maybe 15 – and after that I'll take a shower; a hot, scalding shower before falling into bed. I know the police think I'm a strong, difficult woman but, as Mum also used to say to me: *Appearances can be deceptive, Janet* and bearing in mind the day I've had, I'm more than inclined to agree with her.

345

Chapter Forty-Eight

March 2012

I expect the police to charge me but they don't; instead they extend bail until the end of March. The Crown Prosecution Service has requested two more lines of enquiry. I have no idea what they are but I wonder how long it will take.

The hatred I felt towards Fred Handford seems to have completely disappeared and I've come to accept that if I go back to prison then so be it. I find it difficult to understand why I'm feeling so calm – but I do. I feel as if it's finally over.

I wonder if anyone really understands why I turned myself in. Mary hasn't contacted me since that fateful day when I spoke to her from the back of the police car on the way to Buxton police station which, if I think about it now, is almost too painful to put into words - but I can understand her decision. As a friend I know I've put Mary through a lot and I don't think she was able to cope with the drama any longer. Meanwhile the police seem to believe I confessed to a crime I may or may not have committed in order to make a fortune from a book but, as I've already told them, I'm not that calculating – or organised. Letting Fred Handford's sister and daughter know what happened is part of the reason I wanted to tell the truth but, just as important is the fact that I don't want to live the rest of my life keeping secrets. I've spent 40 years doing that: not telling anyone what Fred Handford did to me immediately after he attacked me or what happened in the days that followed; not telling anyone about the nightmares or my loss of memory and, of course, not telling anyone about my 20-year affair with Miles Ingleby. Contrary to what Dr Browne-Thomas may say: I have no choice this time because if I don't tell the truth then I automatically make everyone else complicit in hiding it.

My day-to-day life at the moment is not dissimilar to the life I had when I was farming. I have my caravan parked on my friend, Diane's land and in return I am cutting logs for her, erecting fences, mowing lawns, planting conifers and generally making a nuisance of myself with the JCB. The dogs are happy, so I'm happy. I'm also able to keep my horse, Chloe at livery in Diane's stable. Chloe is the last in a long line of horses I've bred and raised over the years but she's 24 now and not in the best of health. On a good day I feel a quiet contentment that she could be living out her final days in a place like this with me by her side.

The police have now told me that I don't have to report to the station every day as a condition of bail, which means I'm free to carry on working after 3.30pm if I want to. I've also found a group of badminton players who've said I'm welcome to join them for a game once a week. If I bike it to the sports centre and back it's a 60-mile round trip but the nights are getting lighter now so that's not a problem. All in all I believe I'm coping with the waiting quite well – most of the time - but what I don't want to wait for any longer is a decision about my phone and laptop so I decide it's about time I bought replacements. Carol and Claire might have found out from Mary why I haven't been in touch for a few months, but no-one else will know the reason and I haven't heard from a soul in months. I've no idea if the police have been responding to any calls or emails I've been receiving but I doubt they will have been as helpful as to give out my forwarding address.

On 30 March the police extend bail once more – this time to the end of May.

It is while I'm choosing a new phone that I realise I have a headache. At first I think it's simply the strain of dealing with new technology but by the time I leave the shop I can barely think straight and by the time I park the pickup in the yard the pain is so severe I feel sick. I knock on Diane's door to ask if she has a couple of painkillers but there's no answer and I'm just about to turn away when I feel a hand on my shoulder. I spin round, my head pounding even more with the movement. It's Don, Diane's husband. What the hell's he doing creeping up on me like this? I mutter something unintelligible and hurry away, my breathing suddenly erratic and my heart banging against my ribcage almost as loudly as the noise in my head. *"Janet, did you want something?"* Are the last words I hear as I dash into Chloe's stable, slamming the door behind me. I lean against her warm flank and close my eyes.

"Breathe, you idiot, it's only Don." I run a hand along Chloe's back but the headache persists.

By teatime I've managed to find some out-of-date pills at the back of one of the caravan drawers but the headache won't shift. I wince when Diane knocks on the door.

"Are you okay?" she says, coming to sit next to me. Diane knows all about my past now but, to be honest, she's still a little shell-shocked. Having not seen me for two years I casually pop by and ask if I can park my caravan on her land and then tell her that I've killed a man. When she relayed the story to Don he'd responded in a way that only a man can.

"So – she's decided to come out then," he'd said, nodding sagely.

"She's what?"

"Come out – as a lesbian. Explains why she's so upset doesn't it?"

"She was raped, you idiot," said Diane. "She has a right to be upset."

But Don had looked at his wife as if to say: *'But it's only sex'* because I've come to realise that that's what men think. *It's only sex so why can't she get over it?* But rape isn't about sex. It's about violence, force, intimidation and control and it takes away a part of you which you can never get back.

On Friday 13 April I ring to make an appointment to see the doctor. I describe my symptoms and the fact I can't shake off this bloody headache.

"I'd like you to come in to see me straight away," he says and I do as he asks. After my appointment, his words 'possibility of a slow bleed' stay with me long after I've driven to the hospital.

I have needles stuck into me; I nod when appropriate and flinch when prodded. I answer question after question but I admit I'm a little vague when asked if I have been taking part in any excessive physical activity lately. It's becoming harder and harder to focus on Dr Belinda's advice and the benefits of my follow-up sessions with her are receding further and further into the distance. I am asked to come back on Monday for a scan and as I drive away from the hospital I feel temporarily calm again. If this is the way I'm going to die then that's fine by me: if I drop dead while mucking out Chloe's stable then I can't think of a better way to go.

Turns out, I've got a classic 'tension headache' and the registrar asks me if there is anything specific causing me anxiety or worry. I look at him and smile: I don't know where to start.

The results of the scan come back. Apparently I've had a small heart attack or stroke sometime in the last year and I think back to September when the police took me to Ball Beard Farm and filmed the whole thing in the process. I'm in no doubt that's when it happened. I'm given some strong painkillers and a couple of words of caution - my blood pressure is too spikey, high one day and low the next so he prescribes Ramipril. I look at the bottle and sigh; I've come full circle. All I can think of now is: roll on the end of May.

350

Chapter Forty-Nine

April 2012

As time passes I begin to feel that the fact that the police haven't unearthed any remains, or the pending possibility of any charges against me and the possibility of going back to prison, matters any more. Instead, I feel an increasing calmness because I feel that finally, it's all over – it's all in the past and I can put it where it belongs, back in 1976. I am certain, beyond any doubt, that I shot Fred Handford and buried his body but I also believe that there are perfectly logical reasons why the police haven't found his remains. Those remains lie where I buried them and I am sure that one day in the future they will be discovered. I mull this over quietly to myself as I finish planting a new hedgerow and then at 5pm I take the dogs for a two hour walk. The weather is cold and damp but it doesn't affect my mood one way or the other.

I still haven't heard a word from Mary and this is the only thing bothering me at the moment. I know it'll cause more harm than good if I contact her so I don't. This is one occasion where I know it's better to let sleeping dogs lie.

The police still have my laptop and phone in their possession and so I console myself with the thought that perhaps

Carol and Claire have been trying to contact me and are simply bemused by my silence. I wonder if Judith and Alan Gunning, my old neighbours at Ball Beard, now living in Cumbria, have tried too and, even if they haven't, thinking about them offers some comfort. No-one wants to feel totally alone in this world and the sight of just one or two emails in my inbox would have helped dispel the niggling thought in my mind that maybe I am alone.

I'm mowing Diane and Don's huge front lawn when I suddenly remember I have some of my friends' email addresses listed in my diary. I leap off the mower and run to the caravan. After a 15 minute search I find it at the back of the cutlery drawer and flick quickly to the notes pages where I find, not just Carol and Claire's addresses, but Judith and Alan, Mags, Debra, Trevor (he of the flying dairy herd in Cheshire), a couple of old school friends and some dry-stone walling clients. I sit down at my laptop and fire off an innocuous '*How are you? Thought you might like to know I now have a new email address and would love to hear your news*' and send it to everyone on my list apart from Mags. Then feeling slightly more optimistic I go back to my mowing before taking the dogs for another six mile walk.

On Friday I discover that Chloe is lame. This isn't surprising given her age but when I speak to the local vet, Lydia Cohen, she suggests box rest and promises that she'll pop by this evening to give her a quick once-over. In the meantime, I crack on with sawing more logs and at teatime I check my emails. Not one reply.

Lydia examines Chloe and by some miracle – or is it contrariness? – declares her completely sound again. She suggests Bryonia, a homeopathic remedy recommended for arthritis and I make a note of the name. Chloe meanwhile seems to like the attention she's getting and shows me up with her friskiness.

"She twenty-four, you say?" asks Lydia with some amazement and I can only nod, equally amazed.

On Saturday the sun shines for the first time in weeks and I find I'm on my own more or less all day. Don and Diana are attending a show jumping event on the other side of the county so I keep myself busy by laying a new floor in the barn. The dogs help by getting in the way.

On Monday I try a Tai Chi class for the first time. The class I've chosen is a bit of a journey; a round trip of 30 miles in fact, which now takes my weekly bike riding to over 100 miles which is exactly the same as the mileage I was doing in Scotland.

On Tuesday I decide to spring clean the caravan and make a valiant attempt to vacuum up the dog hair. I'm not sure I manage to get rid of it all but at least it keeps me busy while the rain bounces off the caravan roof.

On Wednesday part of my carefully constructed muck heap collapses under the constant barrage of rain so I pull on my oldest jeans and attempt to rebuild it. I realise, as I'm standing knee deep in muck that this is quite a rare and important skill; I make a mental note to put it on my CV next time I go job hunting.

That evening I log on to my email account and find it's still empty so, I make the decision that I'm going to have to close this chapter of my life once and for all. I realise I've been thinking about little else over last few weeks and I simply can't figure out why there is a blanket silence. Even an abusive contact would be preferable. I focus instead on the fact I'm still on bail and wonder if I can ask my solicitor to put pressure on the police to make a decision about my future. I can't shake this feeling that my life is in limbo – because it is - and I realise only a decision one way or the other will solve the problem.

I sign up for yoga classes. I was intending to choose between Tai Chi and yoga but I don't see a problem with doing both since I've obviously got the time. I've also discovered the delights of tracing your family tree and since this appears to be the wettest April since Noah launched his ark I've taken to doing this when my chores are rained off. It's an addictive and extremely interesting pastime but before long I find I lose track of time and on more than one occasion I've found that I'm still logged on at two in the morning after sitting down and promising myself I'll only be 'an hour or so'.

I garden - between rain showers - and then on 24 April I phone John Bunting and ask for his advice. I realise the police are perfectly within their rights to keep extending bail as long as they wish but I'm sure they've stopped searching for Fred Handford's body now and are just waiting in the hope I'll do something definitive – like have a heart attack perhaps.

"I think now's the time to kick up a fuss," says John, in his

354

carefully moderated tones.

I ask him to elaborate.

"If you're rebailed on 23 May I'll be asking for specific reasons for the police's actions but, in doing so, we may force their hand; they will either release you without charge or, since they are entitled to keep you in custody for up to four days before charging you officially, they may do that and not allow you home again."

As I put down the phone I realise there is no other option. I make a note to call John again in the morning to finalise my Will and then I promise myself I'll try to make contingency plans for the dogs. I check my email account one more time. There are no replies.

Chapter Fifty

23 May 2012

So – just one final loose end to sort out: am I going to be released without charge or am I going to be imprisoned for murder? I try not to think about it either way as I get into the pickup and prepare to set off for the drive from Diane and Don's Staffordshire farm to Buxton police station. I think about other loose ends that I've managed to sort out: I've rewritten my Will, I've had a chat with Diane about my dogs and I've taken one last look at my emails. The inbox remains resolutely empty.

I think back. Are there any other loose ends? I think of the calendar at the farmhouse: the Shire horse pulling the plough across the field, never quite reaching the other side, the date forever stuck on Sunday 14 March and I realise that this was the day that my life changed for ever. Fred Handford used to turn those diary pages over religiously every day and then he stopped. Was that indicative of his state of mind? All I can say is I believe his 'normal' world came to a halt on 14 March 1976 – as did mine.

I drive slowly down the lane towards the motorway, thinking of what it has cost me to find out the truth but I know I can't allow myself the luxury of regret; it wouldn't make any sense. The truth is what it is and yes, I know some people will judge me because of that – Mags and Katrina to name just two - while there are other people who won't believe it at all. I wonder about Mary and as I'm thinking of her, my phone rings. I pull over onto the grass verge.

It's Diane. She tells me that my solicitor, John, is trying to contact me. I call him straight away. He's already at the police station in Buxton. I look at my watch, wondering if I'm late, but no, I've left Diane's with plenty of time to spare.

"There's no need to come in," he says straight away in his calm, unruffled manner. "The police have decided to release you without charge." When I don't say anything in reply he repeats the sentence. "You are free to go," he says again. "You're a free woman, Janet. Go home. It's over."

I sit quite still for a moment or two so the words can sink in. I can't decide what I feel; I can't decide whether to laugh or cry – literally. So I do nothing and stare out of the car window, watching as a cow stares back at me from the field next to the lane. Her eyes are as brown as the soil she's standing on and I'm close enough to see that her eyelashes are as long and silky as a spider's legs. I watch as her huge pink tongue comes out and rolls out up to her nostril; once, twice, three times and on the final lick I find myself smiling to myself. "I'm a free woman," I say out loud and then the tongue comes out again, licking sideways as if slurping on an ice-cream. "I can go home." I am just about to turn the key in the ignition when the phone rings again. I don't recognise the number but I pick it up anyway and hold it to my ear.

"Is that Janet?"

"Yes, Janet speaking." It's a man's voice but I can't quite place whose it is.

"It's Alan; Alan Gunning, your old neighbour from Ball Beard Farm."

I don't know what to say. On the one hand I'm overjoyed that one of my friends has finally decided to contact me but at the same time I'm worried as to why now, after months of silence.

"Alan! How are you?"

"I'm fine; I'm more concerned with how you are. Judith and I haven't heard from you in ages and we were wondering what you were up to – especially after the police came to dig up the kitchen floor in the farmhouse…"

I splutter into the phone. "They did what?"

"Or so we heard on the New Mills grapevine…"

"Where everyone knows everyone else's business," I say, finishing his sentence for him.

"The new owners of Ball Beard bumped into our eldest daughter a couple of months ago when she was back in the area visiting friends and gave her a blow-by-blow account of squad cars and helicopters surrounding the area and officers bursting into the farm like a scene from The Sweeney announcing that…well, I think you know the rest?"

I assure him that I know most of it but obviously not this bit. "They won't have found anything," I say.

"No, we gathered that," says Alan and I realise by his tone of voice that he knows why. With a sigh of relief I also realise that the Alan talking to me now is exactly the same Alan I knew when we were neighbours: charming, easy-going and with a healthy but jaundiced view of the world and all its failings. I rub my eyes with the back of my hand.

"How's Judith?" I ask.

"Very well. She asked me to pass on her regards and to let you know we'd be delighted if you'd come up to see us in Cumbria sometime...if you're free."

I tell him I am - although I don't mention that I've been free for only a matter of minutes - and then he tells me why they haven't contacted me since my last email communication.

"We didn't read it properly. We've been sending emails to your old address. Did you get them?"

I think of the police, still in possession of my old Blackberry and my laptop and say that I didn't - but others might very well have done.

Alan is full of sympathy. "Oh Janet, what a nightmare!"

A nightmare indeed. Suddenly, I feel exhausted.

"If only you knew the truth, Alan" I say softly. "Oh, if only you knew the truth."

And then it goes through my mind that perhaps I ought to tell him the truth: perhaps I should tell him the full story? It all started with an attempt to sort out the nightmares I'd suffered since March 1976. When I think back now to how those nightmares made me feel I realise just how much better my life is without them. Whether I'm free or in prison, living in a house or a caravan, on a farm or travelling round the country, the end of those nightmares is the one thing that makes everything okay.

Because the truth is: my life is now very good indeed.

The End

Author's Note

Helen Parker

As a result of agreeing to help Janet write this book I have been questioned by the police in great detail. I have had my notes taken in evidence (and not returned) and I have been asked the question outright *"Do you think Janet Holt killed Fred Handford?"*

Janet contacted me in January 2010 with a request that I help her write a book about the 40 years she spent working as a farmer in New Mills, in the Peak District of Derbyshire. She described her life as a rewarding one, full of 'funny stories and amusing anecdotes' but when I read her original manuscript it was the nightmares, the lost four days and the disappearance of her business partner, Fred Handford, that really gripped me and, as a journalist, I guessed that this was the part of her life that would grip others too. But in January 2010 she had no explanation for Fred Handford's suspected suicide: she wrote of her business relationship with him and the nightmares were described in terrible detail, but no reason for these nightmares was ever suggested.

I kept a note of all our conversations. I made a note too of my first impressions. In amongst the first 1,000 words I have written that perhaps Fred Handford did not commit suicide at all and perhaps Janet had killed him – just as the police and most of the locals in the village appeared to suspect.

But when I met Janet and I asked her the question outright, the strength of her assertion that she had not killed her business partner convinced me that she was telling the truth. There was no apparent motive, there was no body, and, far from making Janet's life easier, the disappearance of Fred Handford had made Janet's life very difficult indeed.

Having read the book, I hope you will believe me when I say that every word is true, in fact I have no doubt at all that everything Janet has told me is the truth. But in researching this book and realising the criminal file was still open, it appeared to me that the police did not believe Janet in 1976 and, I fear, they still do not believe her now.

In July 2012 Janet was asked to report to Buxton Police Station yet again, where she was arrested once more - for wasting police time. Their next question: "*Is Helen Parker still assisting you with your story?*" convinced me they were worried, not just about Janet's motive but about my motives too.

Janet's solicitor explained the law to her. The Magistrates Courts Act made clear that the time for the police to bring proceedings had now expired. There was nothing to worry about. But Janet was still questioned for two hours during which time her solicitor advised her not to utter a single word. She had already told them everything she knew; there was nothing else to add. It wasn't easy, but she managed it. The police brought in two female detectives, one of whom was an acknowledged expert in getting suspects to talk. Still, she said nothing.

As part of the process she was told that an expert had advised the police that EMDR therapy is suitable only for those who have suffered trauma as children. But I have spoken to other experienced therapists who do not agree with this assertion. The 'expert' engaged by Derbyshire Police went on to say that there could not have been further revelations when Janet was in Scotland as she had effectively been removed from the triggers that would have prompted the return of memory. But, on reading the book, I hope you will believe, as I do, that it's fairly obvious it was the fact that Janet was able to relax for the first time in 34 years that brought a lot of her memory back. The therapy was simply the catalyst.

In January 2010, Janet Holt contacted me and asked me to help her to write her story. It has taken almost three years to uncover the truth. It has been an incredible three years during which time I have spoken to Fred Handford's family members, including his sister and daughter, as well as to the police and, it's clear to me, they all suspected foul play. I also spoke to experienced psychologists who have explained to me the manner in which EMDR therapy can work.

In writing this book with Janet, my intention has been to describe Janet's life through her own eyes and not through mine but I realise now, on coming to the end, that I believe her story as if I have lived it myself. I have come to know the person who existed before 1976 and who still exists today. That person is intelligent, moral, hard working and tenacious, all qualities that have helped her get to the truth.

Helen Parker November 2012

Acknowledgements

To Mum and Dad, who gave me the best childhood anyone could want. And to Mary, whose help and support has been incomparable and whose friendship I've pushed to the limit.

3772698R00201

Printed in Great Britain
by Amazon.co.uk, Ltd.,
Marston Gate.